The City of Gold and Blue
Marquette Basketball, Milwaukee Identity, and the Afterlife of Al McGuire

The City of Gold and Blue

Marquette Basketball, Milwaukee Identity, and the Afterlife of Al McGuire

Bill Johns

Peninsula Network Security, LLC
2025

DEDICATION

To the people who kept faith in a city that has always carried its hope with a certain stubborn grace. To the players who learned their craft on cold Milwaukee streets, to the families and teachers who pushed them toward the gold-and-blue, and to the coaches who believed that discipline, imagination, and a sense of place could build something lasting on Wisconsin Avenue.

To the workers who poured out of factories and shops to fill the old MECCA, to the students who carried the noise of youth into every winter night, and to the Jesuit communities who taught that character is shaped in the tensions between grit and mercy. Your devotion made Marquette basketball more than a program; you made it a language the city could speak even when divided by work, weather, or the long distances of life.

And to the legacy of Al McGuire, whose restless vision still lingers in the corners of Milwaukee's gyms and in the imagination of anyone who understands that basketball, at its best, is a kind of urban prayer. Your spirit built the ground this story stands on.

TABLE OF CONTENTS

The City of Gold and Blue
Marquette Basketball, Milwaukee Identity, and the Afterlife of Al McGuire

PREFACE — WINTER LIGHT ON WISCONSIN AVENUE

"Sometimes the gym is the only place that tells you who you are."
— Al McGuire

Winter settles differently along Wisconsin Avenue. It does not arrive with a single storm or a theatrical drop in temperature, but with a gradual tightening of the air, the way the wind begins to curl around buildings built in the era when Milwaukee believed steel, brick, and discipline could order the world. The sidewalks gleam faintly after dusk, and the streetlamps cast long, pale cones of light that make the pavement look older than the city itself. When the cold grows deep enough, sound travels farther than it should. A ball bouncing inside a gym half a block away gains the clarity of a struck bell, and the low, rising murmur of a crowd preparing for tipoff seems to hover above the street like a temperature inversion, a cloud of expectation suspended between campus and the city's industrial spine.

This is the landscape in which Marquette basketball took root, and it remains the atmosphere through which its memory travels. Even now, if someone stands near the old Gymnasium on Sixteenth Street, long after it ceased to serve as the program's competitive heart, there is the uncanny sense that the building is not entirely empty. The walls seem to remember the era before the MECCA and the Bradley Center, before the Big East banners and the national television broadcasts, before the cultural magnetism that transformed

Marquette from a regional name into a national presence. In those early years, when practices ran hot and tight and the air smelled of varnish and sweat, the gym belonged to a college trying to find itself in a city that rewarded intensity more than pedigree. Coaches came and went; freshmen hardened under the fluorescent glare; and Milwaukee, with its patchwork of immigrant neighborhoods and factories humming through the night, shaped a program that would eventually learn to mirror its own metropolis.

On some evenings, especially in the late 1960s, the winter wind would hit the windows just as the team was running its final drills, rattling the glass with a percussion that somehow made the interior feel warmer. Players who would later become legends moved across a floor that had no illusions about glamour: quick cuts, long passes that threaded the half court, the sharp squeal of sneakers stopping at the edge of a charge. The game had not yet been touched by the bright modernities of broadcast spectacle, but the rhythm already carried the stubbornness that Milwaukee recognized as its own. Even Al McGuire, not yet the mystic of the sidelines he would become, understood that something in the city's temperament was shaping him as much as he was shaping the program. His players often said he could read them before they spoke, as if he could feel the emotional humidity of a room. What they rarely mentioned was how much that instinct came from learning to coach in a place where identity is formed not through smoothness but friction.

Walking outside after those practices, especially near exam season, students felt a change in the city's pulse whenever the team approached another milestone. The tension had little to do with conference standings or national rankings. It was a deeper recognition, the sense that the men on the court carried the symbolic weight of a city often underestimated by the rest of the country. Milwaukee was never granted the effortless prestige of Chicago nor the collegiate polish of Madison. It was a working city, a layered city, a city whose pride expressed itself through craft more than flair. Marquette's teams, even in the years before greatness, had begun to function as emissaries of that civic character. Their victories felt earned rather than arranged. Their losses read less as failures than as interruptions in a larger accumulation of will.

To understand this atmosphere is to understand why the program's eventual rise felt not like an anomaly but like a culmination. For those who walked the campus at night, with the lake wind cutting a line up Michigan Street and the city's grain elevators silhouetted against the low sky, Marquette basketball did not represent a diversion from academic life or urban life; it was part of the same movement, driven by the same blend of ambition and grit. In the bars along State Street, people discussed shooting percentages in the same tone they used to discuss factory shifts or neighborhood politics. The details mattered—dates, names, sequences of plays not because they were trivia but because they formed a narrative spine that helped the community recognize itself.

There are nights in the city when the snow begins falling earlier than expected, and the light grows dim before the doors open at the arena. Students line up outside, shoulders tucked into coats, stamping their feet for warmth, the anticipation rising through their chests like breath fogging a window. The glow of the MECCA in the McGuire years, especially during the long run toward the 1977 championship, was something spiritual without being sentimental. The old yellow floor—its bold shapes curling and intersecting like an abstracted map of the city—seemed to pulse under the lights. Those who entered felt as if they were crossing a threshold into a space where Milwaukee's layered identities could briefly align. Croatian, Polish, Irish, African American, German, Italian, Puerto Rican —none of these communities surrendered their histories at the door. Instead, their stories blended into a shared roar that rose whenever a steal at midcourt turned into a break, or a defensive stand held longer than physics should allow.

The sound in that building was not the reverberant thunder of a massive dome; it was narrower, denser, shaped by the intimacy between the crowd and the floor. When Maurice Lucas played there, long before he became one of the fiercest presences in professional basketball, the noise sharpened around him like a blade honing itself. When Dean Meminger drove to the rim, the crowd leaned with him, a collective gesture that felt less like fandom and more like participation. And when McGuire paced the sideline, at times muttering to himself, at times conducting the game with a flourish that would have seemed theatrical in any other city, he became the embodiment of something Milwaukee prized: a man who could turn instinct into art without losing the hardness required to survive.

The cadence of winter deepened during that championship season. People remember the 1977 title game because of its outcome, of course, but those who lived through it remember something else: the sensation of watching a city made whole, if only for forty minutes at a time. McGuire's tears in the final seconds became part of Marquette's collective memory not because they represented victory, but because they revealed the cost of sustaining belief. He had built a program on the tension between improvisation and discipline, between intuition and strategy, between the beauty of the game and the brutality it demands. When he wept, the city saw itself reflected back—a place that understood how triumph is braided with exhaustion.

Yet the power of Marquette basketball lies not only in those historic peaks, but in the continuity that runs beneath them. Long after McGuire's voice faded from the tunnel and the Bradley Center became the new stage, the winter walk to the arena still carried the same emotional gravity. Generations of students learned to orient themselves by the schedule taped to their dorm walls. And the names—Raymonds, Hank

Egan, Kevin O'Neill, Mike Deane, Tom Crean, Buzz Williams, Wojciechowski—entered the city's vocabulary not as passing authorities but as chapters in a larger civic narrative. Marquette was never a program that could be understood without its dates and events; they functioned as markers in a chronicle that helped the city trace its own evolution.

In those later arenas, with their vaulted ceilings and amplified lighting, the sound changed but the feeling did not. A three-pointer from the corner elicited the same rising note of expectation that once filled the old Gym. A defensive rotation snapping into place carried the same collective satisfaction that the MECCA crowds had felt decades earlier. Even the losses had continuity: a recognition that struggle is part of belonging, that effort in defeat can bind a community as tightly as a championship run.

For many who grew up in Milwaukee or came to the university from distant cities, the first real understanding of Marquette's place in the world arrived through the experience of attending a game on a bitter night. Snow drifting across the plaza, the arena lights glowing against the low, cloud-thick sky, the hum of the crowd layered with the throb of heaters behind the entrances. Inside, the brightness of the court felt almost shocking after the dim blue-gray streets. Players warming up seemed to move faster than the eye could follow, as if the game existed at a different speed from ordinary life. The first time one witnesses this transition—from the frozen dark to the golden interior—it feels like entering a narrative that has been unfolding long before one's arrival, waiting only for the latest witness to take their seat.

The sensory world surrounding the program creates its own quiet insistence, shaping understanding long before any chronology asserts itself. The cold Milwaukee air forces jackets higher on the shoulders; the brick of the older campus buildings seems to hold faint echoes of voices that once surged from gym doors; the warmth that escapes each time those doors open carries the mingled scents of popcorn, sweat, and anticipation. Atmosphere becomes the first teacher. Place becomes the first archive. Dates and names only take on meaning once they are felt inside this environment, where the city's winters harden the edges of experience and soften the interior spaces where people gather to watch a game.

What remains afterward is the slow, reflective walk away from the arena. The crowd dissolves into side streets, and the lights behind the doors dim to a low glow. Steam rises through iron grates. Conversations drift across intersections with a clarity the daytime never grants. The final possession of the night replays itself without prompting, stitched to the cadence of footsteps on frozen pavement. The lake wind threads its way between buildings, never hurrying, never absent. In that passage from noise to quiet, from heat to cold, the meaning of Marquette basketball reveals itself not in spectacle but in continuity. It reflects a city shaped by labor and migration, by the steadiness of faith and the endurance of ordinary people, by the resilience that has long defined Milwaukee's sense of itself.

The recognition forms slowly, carried home in the breath of winter.

Milwaukee's history leaves its imprint on the program with a steadiness that rarely announces itself. The city's early decades were shaped by immigrant blocks pressed against one another—Polish South Side parishes marked by their tall brick steeples, German craft neighborhoods where breweries sent their scent into the winter air, African American communities along Walnut Street building their own civic institutions during an era of restricted movement. Each cluster carried its own rhythms and loyalties, its own understanding of what strength should look like. When these communities found themselves drawn toward Marquette basketball, the pull came from recognition rather than novelty. The way the team pressed the floor or absorbed contact along the lane seemed to echo the way the city confronted its circumstances. Grit was not a posture; it was the learned endurance of a place accustomed to cold mornings, shift work, and the unglamorous satisfaction of meeting expectations no one outside the region understood.

By the time Marquette stepped into national prominence under Al McGuire, the city had already undergone decades of industrial consolidation and political recalibration. McGuire's rise did not shape the city as much as it illuminated qualities already present. His reputation for intuition, his sideline wanderings, his talent for sensing the emotional direction of a game—all of it meshed with Milwaukee's preference for authenticity over ornament. His teams did not play like visitors in their own gym. They moved with the confidence of people who knew the geography of pressure, the tricky angles of a hard life that demanded both resilience and improvisation. When the Warriors won the 1970 NIT, and when the 1977 NCAA tournament run carried the program into the highest tier of the sport, Milwaukee felt those triumphs not in abstract pride but in the concrete sense that the city's values had been made visible to the rest of the country.

Historic names began to build the program's lineage in ways that still feel immediate. Dean Meminger slicing through a defense with a first step that opponents could predict but rarely contain. Jim Chones anchoring the middle with a presence that suggested the court had been carved to his dimensions. Bo Ellis moving with the grace of someone who understood that style and durability were not opposites. Maurice Lucas, fierce and controlled, extending the reach of the university far beyond campus boundaries. These players became part of Milwaukee's cultural vocabulary. People discussed them in diners and corner bars, at factory gates and after church services, as if their performances belonged to the city's collective labor.

When Marquette moved from the intimate intensity of the old Gymnasium to the larger stage of the MECCA Arena, the shift reflected Milwaukee's own trajectory. The city was entering years of deindustrialization, adjusting to tightened budgets, changing demographics, and the slow erosion of certain economic certainties. The bold, colorful floor designed by Robert Indiana captured this tension—an audacious expression of identity during a period when many cities of similar size were retreating from civic ambition. People still speak about that floor in tones that mix affection and disbelief, as if the sheer visual daring announced that a Midwest city could claim its own aesthetic authority. Marquette's play during those years harnessed that energy. The team thrived in the tension between hard-nosed defense and the creative spontaneity McGuire allowed, reflecting Milwaukee's insistence that survival meant more than durability; it required imagination.

As the decades progressed, coaching transitions shaped the contours of the program's identity. Hank Raymonds brought order without diminishing the competitive edge that McGuire had cultivated. Rick Majerus emerged as a young assistant with a tactical mind sharpened by his upbringing in the city, learning the early habits that later defined his own storied coaching life. Kevin O'Neill entered with the fire of someone who understood the emotional torque required to carry a program through uneven years. Mike Deane provided steadiness, restoring balance at a moment when the program needed recalibration. Tom Crean reinvigorated Marquette at the turn of the century, guiding the team to the 2003 Final Four behind the brilliance of Dwyane Wade, whose performance against Kentucky remains one of the most complete tournament displays ever delivered by a Big East outsider. Wade's rise from overlooked recruit to generational player fit seamlessly into the city's cultural narrative: excellence blossoming in a landscape where many outsiders see only limits.

The shift into the Big East era introduced a new layer of identity. Milwaukee, long familiar with blue-collar grit and regional loyalties, suddenly found itself connected to an eastern basketball corridor with its own dynasties, expectations, and traditions. Games at the Bradley Center and later at Fiserv Forum became gatherings of a different scale, but the underlying emotion remained familiar. The city embraced the notion that Marquette was no longer a local emblem alone; it had become a national competitor without abandoning its old habits of effort and precision. Buzz Williams pushed this tension further, drawing on the city's ethic of labor to forge teams that outworked opponents through sheer relentlessness. He often spoke of the responsibility he felt coaching in a place where people tied their identity to commitment. That sentiment was not rhetoric; it reflected a deeply rooted civic value, one that had shaped Marquette basketball from its earliest decades.

Names and dates form the backbone of this history, yet the story carries a moral dimension that extends beyond the record book. Each generation confronted its own pressures— shifts in conferences, economic swings in the city, the rise of televised spectacle, the challenges of recruiting against national powers. What remained constant was the sense that Marquette basketball was not simply an athletic enterprise but a civic expression, a venue in which Milwaukee could reconcile its contradictions: its pride and its humility, its toughness and its vulnerability, its desire to be seen and its instinct to guard the core of its identity. The program served as a meeting point where the city's varied communities could find a shared pulse, at least for the length of a game.

Those who grew up with the program learned to chart their memories according to rosters and seasons. Mention 1977, and people recall not only the championship but the winter storms that preceded it, the heavy coats piled in the lobby of the MECCA, the stories of strangers celebrating together on cold streets. Mention 2003, and conversations turn to Wade's agility, the shock on a Kentucky defender's face as the game slipped away, the sense that a small Jesuit university in a northern city had captured the national imagination. These memories reveal the power of dates and names when lived in context; they mark the intersection of personal experience and civic identity.

In a city that never relied on glamor to tell its story, the program's history continues to serve as a testament to the way sport can become a vessel for something larger than competition. The arenas have changed, the conferences have shifted, the uniforms have evolved, yet the emotional core remains steady. People still file into games during blizzards, shaking snow from their shoulders as they find their seats. Conversations still stretch across generations as grandparents describe McGuire's sideline presence or Lucas's ferocity to children seeing the court for the first time. The city continues to measure itself against the resilience displayed on the floor.

Through these decades, Milwaukee and Marquette remain intertwined. The city's industrial past, its immigrant character, its cultural fusions, and its winter severity form the constant background against which the program's story unfolds. The team moves through eras of triumph and struggle, but the grounding force is always the same: a community that recognizes itself in the way the players defend a possession, fight for a rebound, chase a loose ball that seems destined to skitter out of bounds. The details—names, dates, scores—carry weight because they reflect lived experience. They speak to a city that measures achievement not by ease but by effort.

The layers of this history settle into the consciousness of anyone who watches closely. The court becomes a map of Milwaukee's longstanding virtues: persistence, creativity, and the ability to endure change without abandoning the pride of place that sits quietly beneath the surface. Even in seasons when victories are scarce, the program never feels rootless. It carries too much of the city's memory to slip into irrelevance. The continuity is not a matter of nostalgia; it is the natural consequence of decades in which basketball offered Milwaukee a way to express its collective temperament.

Across generations, the program's legacy becomes braided with the city's evolving identity. Each new era adds texture without erasing what came before. New coaches build on old foundations. New players draw applause from fans who still recall the movements of Meminger, the footwork of Ellis, the poise of Wade. The city absorbs these transitions with the same resilience it has shown in facing industrial decline, cultural reinvention, and the challenges of modern urban life. Marquette basketball remains one of the few arenas—literal and symbolic—where Milwaukee sees its past and present held in the same frame.

This relationship, forged over decades, continues to deepen with time. The program's history holds a mirror to the city's shifting self-understanding. The lessons drawn from both triumph and hardship linger in the rhythms of daily life, echoing in the spaces between games. The story's power does not diminish as generations pass; it expands, gathering meaning from the persistence of memory itself.

Memory enters quietly, often long before anyone realizes it has begun to take shape. For some, it forms in the modest apartments clustered near campus, where radios once carried the sound of Marquette games through winter nights. A child might sit cross-legged on the carpet, hearing names like Meminger, Chones, and Lucas spoken with the same familiarity as family members. The announcer's voice would rise and fall with the urgency of each possession, and even without seeing the court, the listener could feel the texture of the game: the crisp snap of a pass, the thud of a hard foul absorbed without complaint, the sudden shift in tempo when

McGuire sensed that chaos might tilt the balance. These early experiences did not instruct; they imprinted. They taught that a basketball program could carry meaning that extended beyond the boundaries of competition, that it could function as a civic memory system capable of absorbing the emotions of a city and returning them in distilled form.

In later years, the first live game often delivered a sensation that felt surprisingly familiar, as if the arena simply revealed what the radio had already suggested. The light on the hardwood shimmered in a way that contrasted with the gray Milwaukee sky glimpsed through the concourse windows. The crowd's sound rose not in a wave but in a series of pulses, synchronized yet composed of distinct voices. The players emerged from the tunnel with a focus that belonged entirely to the moment, but also to decades of expectation. For those standing in the upper rows, looking down at the play unfolding beneath a canopy of rafters heavy with history, the experience had the quality of stepping into a narrative already in progress. No instruction was needed to understand its significance. It was enough to feel how the crowd leaned together during free throws or how the silence before a crucial inbound pass carried a weight the city knew well from its own periods of uncertainty.

There is a particular kind of recognition that occurs when a college program becomes interwoven with the emotional life of its community. For Milwaukee, Marquette basketball became one of the central threads linking generations who otherwise lived in different versions of the city. The parents who remembered McGuire's championship run spoke of it not as an isolated achievement but as part of an era when the city's working-class pride rose into national view. Their children, raised during the Crean years or the intensity of Buzz Williams's tenure, associated the program with a different set of emotions—restlessness, effort, the sense that belief required endurance more than glamour. Grandparents could still recall the sound inside the MECCA on a night when the roof seemed barely able to contain the noise; grandchildren learned to read the new arenas not as replacements but as continuations of an atmosphere their elders insisted could not be replicated. What held these memories together was not agreement on a single defining moment, but the shared conviction that the program revealed something essential about the city's character.

For many, the deepest understanding came not during triumphant seasons but in years marked by transition. Coaching changes, conference realignments, disappointing finishes—these periods revealed how firmly the program had anchored itself in Milwaukee's sense of identity. Even when the national spotlight drifted elsewhere, the community's commitment did not loosen. Fans still braved the lake wind to attend games. Conversations in diners still circled back to the same questions: Who would step into the leadership role? How would the team adapt? Which players felt ready to carry the weight of expectation? These questions were never posed with detachment. They carried the seriousness of people who understood that the program had become part of their own biography, shaped by the same forces that shaped the city.

As memory accumulates, it becomes easier to see how a program's history does not reside solely in its victories. It resides in the landscapes surrounding those victories—the neighborhoods where fans gathered to celebrate, the bars where debates lasted into the night, the sidewalks where children dribbled basketballs that echoed against brick walls softened by decades of winter. It resides in the quiet gestures after a loss, when players walked off the court with their heads held in the particular posture that Milwaukee respects: disappointment tempered by determination. The city recognized this look. It was the same expression worn by generations of workers leaving factory gates after long shifts, the same expression that marked immigrant parents who crossed oceans with more hope than certainty, the same expression that defined a community acquainted with resilience as a daily practice. When Marquette players carried themselves this way, the city did not merely approve; it identified.

There is also the matter of arrival, a feeling that defies chronology. Some encounter the program as newcomers—students from distant states or countries, unfamiliar with the city's industrial past. Their first winter on campus often functions as an initiation. They learn the rhythm of the wind off Lake Michigan, the way the cold can sharpen concentration, the way the walk to the arena builds anticipation step by step. By the time they attend their second or third game, something subtle has shifted. The program no longer feels like part of the university alone; it feels connected to the city beyond it. Even those who have never heard of Al McGuire or Dean Meminger begin to sense that the court has absorbed decades of emotion, that it carries a gravity shaped by thousands of people who invested fragments of their own stories into this team.

Others come to the program through a single unforgettable moment. It may be Wade rising for a block that seemed physically impossible, or a last-minute three-pointer that sent the arena into a tremor, or a defensive stand that lasted long enough to make time feel suspended. These moments often become the entry points through which people begin exploring the program's past. A spectacular play sparks a question, and the question leads to a memory someone else is eager to share. The stories expand outward—McGuire's sideline wanderings, the bold floor of the MECCA, the tears that marked a championship farewell, the nights when the crowd's noise carried through the city blocks. Each memory layers itself over the others until the individual experience becomes part of a collective one.

Through this accumulation, the significance of dates and names deepens rather than diminishes. They are no longer markers in a timeline but expressions of continuity. Mention 1977, and one hears a tone in the speaker's voice that contains more than historical fact. Mention the 2003 Final Four run, and the room shifts slightly, as if everyone present understands that a single season can reshape a university's place in the larger landscape of the sport. Mention the Big East battles of the past decade, and the conversation often turns to the contrast between Milwaukee's grounded ethos and the high-profile arenas of its conference rivals. These references, shared and repeated, form a map of belonging.

Over time, the connection between the program and the city grows so deeply rooted that it becomes difficult to separate the two. Milwaukee's fluctuations—its industrial changes, its demographic shifts, its cycles of challenge and renewal—echo in the fortunes of the team. The program's moments of clarity often correspond to periods when the city feels poised for reinvention. Its setbacks feel tempered by the knowledge that resilience is the region's most enduring inheritance. People learn to see these patterns not through analysis but through experience: the walk to the arena, the noise swelling at the right moment, the sharp quiet afterward when the night regains its hold on the streets.

Memory then becomes more than recollection; it becomes a lens through which the present is interpreted. Those who return to Milwaukee after years away often find that attending a Marquette game functions as a kind of recalibration. The arena may be new, the players unfamiliar, yet the sensation remains intact. The court still emits a particular brightness. The crowd still shifts its weight in unison during pivotal moments. The city's winter air still grips the doorway as one steps outside, causing breath to rise in thin white strands that dissipate toward the lake. These constants reveal why the program endures in the imagination long after individual seasons fade.

In the quiet after the game, when people drift back toward

their neighborhoods or dormitories, something unspoken passes among them. It is not triumph or disappointment, though both may be present. It is recognition. A shared understanding that this program, across all its eras, expresses something essential about the way Milwaukee moves through the world. The details—the names, the dates, the unforgettable plays—carry weight because they articulate the values the city holds closest: effort, dignity, loyalty, and the refusal to surrender identity in the face of shifting circumstances.

That recognition settles slowly, deepening with each return to the arena, with each winter walk home through the streets where the cold has a way of sharpening the memory of what matters.

The city grows quiet again once the last voices fade into the winter dark. A thin veil of cold settles over Wisconsin Avenue, and the steam rising from the manhole grates drifts upward like a slow exhalation. The arena doors close with a soft clang that echoes briefly before being absorbed by the surrounding buildings. In that stillness, the impressions of the evening begin to reorganize themselves. The bright court, the layered noise, the sudden shifts in tempo, the faces turned upward in collective anticipation—all of it thins into memory without losing its texture. Milwaukee has always carried its histories this way, not as polished narratives but as sensations that linger after the event has ended.

There is a moment on the walk home when the weight of the night settles differently. The cold sharpens the awareness of what has just unfolded—the effort, the strain, the flashes of clarity, the small collisions that shaped the game's rhythm. These details do not resolve into moral lessons or predictions. They drift into the broader field of experience that gives the city its character. A passerby brushing snow from their coat, a distant horn from a bus heading toward the lakefront, a set of footprints crossing and recrossing the sidewalk: each becomes part of the same quiet recognition that the evening

THE CITY OF GOLD AND BLUE

held something more than entertainment.

For decades, Marquette basketball has lived in this space between noise and silence, where the energy of competition gives way to the reflective calm of a city reacquainting itself with night. Generations have stepped out of bright arenas into this same winter air, carrying with them the residue of games played long before and those still to come. The continuity does not depend on winning streaks or banners. It rests on the steady knowledge that the program has become one of the city's ways of understanding itself—a repository of its resilience, its grit, its flashes of grace.

The streets stretch out ahead, coated in a thin sheen of frost that glows under the lamps. A car passes, leaving a muted trail of tire marks. A few students laugh softly as they turn the corner toward campus. The rest of the city moves in its measured rhythm, as it always has. The clues that link the present to the past are subtle—the echo of a dribble remembered from childhood, the shape of an arena seen from afar, the familiar warmth that lingers in the chest after watching players push themselves through a demanding night.

In that lingering warmth, the program's meaning gathers and holds. It does not announce itself; it waits in the quiet, steady spaces between moments. Milwaukee breathes through those spaces. Marquette basketball endures in them.

INTRODUCTION —
THE URBAN CATHOLIC
IMAGINATION

"Life is about the people you meet along the way."
— Al McGuire

The first impression of Marquette, at least for those who did not grow up within sight of the spires, is rarely the architecture. It is the sense of movement—the students weaving across Wisconsin Avenue, the buses gliding past the old brick buildings, the slow pulse of traffic that seems to carry the weight of a century's worth of immigrant footsteps. At certain hours the city's noise softens just enough that the campus feels like a small enclave set inside a larger organism. Yet it takes only a moment to understand that Marquette never separated itself from Milwaukee. The university grew by absorbing the cadence of the neighborhoods around it, neighborhoods shaped by Catholic devotion, industrial endurance, and the thick moral texture of urban life. The basketball program that eventually emerged from this landscape was not an auxiliary pastime; it was an expression of the city's self-understanding.

Catholic institutions in American cities often begin with a simple premise: that faith is not primarily an argument but a posture toward the world. Marquette inherited that posture early. Its Jesuit founders built a place where thought and struggle were not opposites, and where education meant entering the world more deeply rather than distancing oneself

THE CITY OF GOLD AND BLUE

from it. The spires of Gesu Church did more than mark the campus boundary; they offered an implicit reminder that human excellence, whether spiritual or physical, demands patience with contradiction. A university framed by such sensibilities was destined to approach sport not as spectacle but as a practice of character. Long before the Warriors gained national attention, the Catholic imagination that animated the campus shaped how the game would be played—and more importantly, why it mattered.

Walking west from the lakefront, the city changes texture in small, subtle increments. The polished corporate facades yield to older storefronts, low brick buildings, and the shadows cast by factories that once hummed through the night. For decades, this was the world that fed Marquette's student body. Children of Polish, Irish, German, Croatian, and Italian families encountered education as a bridge between labor and aspiration, between the demands of the day and the hope that tomorrow might hold something different. Milwaukee, like many industrial cities, asked its residents to carry a double consciousness: pride in work that left the body exhausted, and pride in the faith that gave that work meaning. Basketball arrived in this environment as a kind of secular liturgy. It offered a space where effort became visible, where limits were tested, and where a city's yearning for recognition could briefly take form.

By the time Al McGuire walked the campus in the mid-1960s, the foundations for this identity had already been laid. What he brought was the instinct to name it. McGuire understood the Catholic imagination intuitively, though he rarely spoke of it in doctrinal terms. He saw in the streets around the university a mixture of toughness and tenderness that resembled the contradictions he admired in his players. He believed that the gym could become a kind of chapel, not one of silence but of revelation. A place where truth was not spoken but enacted, often in the quickness of a cut, the resilience of a rebound, or the willingness to recognize a teammate's need before one's own. Such sensibilities were not created by McGuire, but he articulated them more clearly than anyone before him. His remark about life being defined by the people one meets was not a throwaway line; it was the philosophy that shaped recruiting, coaching, and the rhythm of the program itself.

To understand the early decades of Marquette basketball is to understand Milwaukee's own moral architecture. The city's Catholic neighborhoods, strong and insular in their loyalties, taught their children that excellence does not erase humility and that success is always communal. The parish gymnasiums of the mid-twentieth century—dimly lit, crowded, echoing with the sound of worn wooden floors—served as unofficial training grounds for generations of players who learned that the court was a place where identity could be sharpened. Coaches in those spaces were part instructor, part moral guide. They insisted that effort mattered more than polish, that defense was a form of discipline, and that losing with dignity required as much courage as winning with flair. These lessons migrated naturally to Marquette, where the university's Jesuit ethos folded them into a broader educational mission.

The origins of the program trace back to the 1910s, when basketball was still a rough, fast game played with minimal structure. The early teams wore uniforms that hung loosely from their frames, and the gyms in which they played were often small enough that the crowd's breath mingled with the sweat of the athletes. Photographs from those decades show faces that seem older than their years—young men shaped by a city that demanded adulthood early. Their commitment to the team did not come from dreams of national acclaim; it came from a desire to represent a school that stood for something in a rapidly shifting urban landscape. As industry expanded and Milwaukee's population swelled with new waves of immigrants, Marquette's sense of mission deepened.

The basketball program became a kind of cultural shorthand, a visible emblem of a university learning to balance tradition with ambition.

There is a particular path one takes across campus that reveals this evolution. Start near the western edge, where the city's hum feels constant, and walk east toward Gesu. The noise thins as the church rises into view, its limestone façade bearing the marks of decades of weather. Continue past it and the city reasserts itself: the rush of buses, the shimmer of traffic on Wisconsin Avenue, the students crossing between classes with hurried determination. The geography itself enacts the core tension of Marquette's identity —the movement between sanctuary and struggle, between reflection and action. The basketball program grew in that same tension. It learned to inhabit both worlds, borrowing discipline from the Jesuits and audacity from the streets surrounding the campus.

McGuire recognized that audacity instantly. His recruiting decisions often baffled outsiders, yet they revealed a profound understanding of urban Catholic culture. He believed that players shaped by hardship possessed an instinctive empathy and resilience that could not be taught. He saw promise in gym rats who had never been invited to elite camps, in youths whose confidence seemed mismatched to their circumstances, in athletes who carried both swagger and uncertainty. To McGuire, these contradictions were gifts. They made the players human, and humanity—unguarded and unpredictable —was his preferred material. He coached with the conviction that basketball should mirror life rather than escape it. The game was its own moral education, and the victories it produced were inseparable from the formation it demanded.

This intuition resonated because it matched the city's own rhythm. Milwaukee, by the mid-century, had begun to understand itself as a place caught between past and future. The factories still roared, but demographic changes, suburban expansion, and political tensions were reshaping its identity. Catholic parishes remained anchors of stability, yet their populations were shifting, their schools merging or shrinking, their influence loosening even as their memories deepened. In such an environment, the basketball program offered continuity. It provided the city with an emblem of shared purpose, a place where ethnic boundaries dissolved into collective cheering, and where the court became a symbolic neighborhood large enough to hold the city's varied loyalties.

To describe this atmosphere is not to romanticize it. Milwaukee's Catholic imagination was never simple. It held within it the struggles of working families, the limitations placed on certain communities, the unresolved tensions of segregation and economic inequality. Yet it also held the belief that human dignity could be defended through small acts of loyalty, courage, and craft. Marquette basketball became one of the city's ways of practicing that belief. Even in years when victories were scarce, the program carried the city's stubborn hope forward.

What is striking, looking back at the early decades, is how naturally the team's identity mirrored the city's. Marquette played with a kind of purposeful turbulence—intense, fast, occasionally chaotic but always grounded in effort. The discipline came later, shaped by McGuire's successors and by the demands of national competition. But the essence was present from the beginning: a willingness to outwork opponents, to embrace the physicality of the game, and to find beauty in the interplay between precision and improvisation.

Standing at the edge of campus on a winter evening, one can almost sense the layers of this history in the air. The cold carries the same bite it did in the 1920s. The streetlights cast the same amber glow on the sidewalks that students have walked for more than a century. The sound of a bouncing ball escaping from an open gym door echoes with a familiarity that transcends time. These details, small and persistent, reveal how the program has remained rooted in place even as the city around it has evolved.

The urban Catholic imagination that shaped Marquette's basketball program is not a doctrine but a way of perceiving the world. It insists that struggle is meaningful, that community is essential, and that beauty can emerge from tension rather than ease. It recognizes that a game played in the heart of a Midwest city can carry the emotional burdens of generations. It understands that excellence requires humility, that pressure can refine character, and that the people one meets along the way matter more than the trophies collected.

McGuire knew this instinctively, which is why his influence lingers long after his voice faded from the sideline. His presence remains woven through the stories told in corner bars, through the memories of alumni who recall his sideline wanderings, through the murals and photographs that still hang in the athletic facilities. He embodied the city's contradictions and its aspirations, and in doing so, he gave Marquette a vocabulary for its identity.

The story lives inside this imagination, carried by a city formed through faith and labor, a university shaped by Jesuit patience and scrutiny, and a program built on the conviction that basketball can disclose the truth of a person's character. The court reflects more than movement; it answers the moods of the city around it. The crowd becomes something like a communal voice, layered with memory, tension, and hope. Milwaukee itself behaves as an archive, not bound by shelves or dates but by the persistence of its own spirit. Out of this mingling of place, belief, and shared devotion, the program takes on a meaning that exceeds the measurements of sport. It becomes a way of apprehending the world, a manner of seeing shaped by resilience, grace, and the human ties that hold a community together.

Catholicism in an American city rarely unfolds in abstractions.

It takes shape in the streets, in the parish basements where fish fries once stretched into crowded evenings, in the small rituals that helped immigrants feel anchored in a place that did not yet resemble home. Milwaukee carried these textures into the twentieth century with a seriousness that came not from rigidity but from repetition. Faith became a rhythm, a way of marking time, an organizing force for communities that had crossed oceans only to find themselves in tight neighborhoods shaped by work, weather, and wary hope. The Jesuits at Marquette recognized these conditions from the beginning. Their vocation required engaging the world rather than retreating from it, and the school they built reflected that mandate. The campus grew not as an enclave but as a bridge —between ethnic groups, between economic classes, between the traditions of the Old World and the industrial drive of the New.

The basketball program grew in this soil long before it gained its signature style. Its earliest decades coincided with enormous demographic shifts, waves of Polish and German Catholics settling near the factories on the Menomonee Valley's edge, new arrivals carving out identities in a city that demanded stamina. The game became a natural extension of this temperament. It rewarded quickness of mind, improvisation, and the kind of physical assertiveness that came easily to youths who worked after school or on weekends. In parish leagues scattered across the South Side and along the riverbanks, boys who had only recently learned English found that the court offered its own vocabulary. A pass, a cut, a loose ball wrestled from an opponent—each gesture carried its own meaning, intelligible to anyone who shared the floor. When a few of these young men reached Marquette, they carried that grammar with them, folding it into a program still learning how to speak.

Inside the neighborhoods that fed the university, Catholic life forged habits of attention that later appeared in the program's play. There was the instinct to gather, first around the altar and later at the arena; the habit of watching authority with a mix of wariness and trust; the understanding that struggle was neither aberration nor failure but a natural part of the daily round. The parish schools, many run by nuns whose sternness held a strange form of tenderness, taught discipline through repetition: handwriting that required precision, catechism lessons committed to memory, chores completed without complaint. These expectations produced young adults who recognized the value of order, even if they did not always embrace it. A coach at Marquette could draw on these instincts without spelling them out. Players accustomed to the strictures of Catholic upbringing carried an internal sense of structure that could be shaped, softened, or hardened as needed.

At the same time, Milwaukee's Catholic imagination never drifted entirely into piety. It carried an irreverent streak, a sense that holiness and humor need not be opposed. Street corners near the university hosted arguments about politics, baseball, unions, and theology; taverns filled with voices that shifted easily from devotion to complaint to laughter. The city learned to live with contradiction, understanding that grace often shared space with bruises. This sensibility prepared it well for the arrival of men like Al McGuire, who recognized the difference between rule-breaking and life-embracing mischief. He saw in Milwaukee a familiarity—immigrant wit, working-class intelligence, a resistance to pretension—and the city saw in him a man who refused to behave as though the sideline were a pulpit. His great gift lay in elevating the ordinary without sanctifying it, finding meaning in the stray detail, the overlooked player, the unguarded moment.

This cultural disposition shaped the program's earliest identity. Marquette did not seek to emulate the Catholic behemoths of the East Coast; it forged a style suitable to a Midwestern city whose loyalties were split between factories

31

and parishes. Its early coaches understood that the team represented more than the university alone. On winter nights, families from the Third Ward and Merrill Park crowded into gyms that smelled of varnish and wool coats, hoping to see young men who resembled their sons and nephews hold their own against opponents whose reputations outstripped their resources. The cheers that erupted from these gatherings did not carry the polish of big-market programs; they carried the grain of Milwaukee's sociological makeup, an unfiltered mixture of pride, skepticism, and weary optimism.

Even before McGuire's arrival, the team performed an unspoken civic function. It offered Milwaukee a glimpse of itself as it wished to be seen—tough, creative, capable of rising above its regional circumstances. The city had long lived in the shadow of Chicago, enduring comparisons that often overlooked its complexity. Basketball allowed Milwaukee to assert its own narrative. A well-fought game refracted the city's energies back toward the stands, reminding spectators that their own histories were visible in each contested rebound or patient defensive stand. The court became a symbolic street corner where differences collapsed into a single rhythm of collective focus.

By the middle of the twentieth century, the interplay between Catholic identity and urban life had grown increasingly intricate. Milwaukee's neighborhoods were shifting as families moved outward, yet the older parishes retained enough gravity to hold memories in place. Weddings, funerals, and festivals continued to bind communities into recognizable shapes, even as the pressures of modernity began to blur boundaries. Marquette, positioned at the center of this changing city, absorbed these transformations. Its student body reflected the frictions and aspirations of its surroundings. The basketball program, even in its less celebrated years, carried that reflection forward with an honesty that people recognized instinctively.

Players who came to Marquette during this era often found themselves navigating two currents simultaneously. One came from the university's Jesuit heritage, which emphasized intellectual rigor, moral reflection, and an education that engaged the world rather than fled from it. The other came from Milwaukee itself, whose lessons were learned on sidewalks, in shops, and on factory floors. These young men straddled both terrains with varying degrees of comfort. Some struggled with the university's demands; others thrived under its structure. All felt the pull of the city beyond the classroom, the sense that learning occurred in countless forms, not all sanctioned by syllabi or advisers. Their basketball careers became an extension of this dual formation, merging the clarity of Jesuit pedagogy with the improvisational intelligence of urban life.

The Jesuits have long maintained that formation occurs through encounter—meeting people where they are, treating every setting as a site for contemplative action. This ethos resonated with the city's own rhythms. Milwaukee offered constant encounters: ethnic groups negotiating space and identity, workers confronting the realities of changing industries, parishes adapting to new social configurations. Marquette's basketball players lived at the intersection of these forces. Those who stayed for four years often emerged with a sense that basketball had expanded, rather than confined, their understanding of human experience. They learned to read a crowd's mood as carefully as they read an opponent's rotation, to sense when a teammate needed encouragement or when a city needed hope. These habits of perception became part of the program's unwritten curriculum.

In this environment, the idea of the "urban Catholic imagination" becomes more than a thematic phrase. It becomes a description of how meaning forms in a place where sacred and secular concerns overlap. The imagination takes shape in the way a city listens to itself after a loss, or how it celebrates when victory seems improbable. It appears in the rituals surrounding game days—the families arriving early, the alumni drifting back into familiar seats, the murmur of recognition when an old name from the McGuire era appears on the video screen. It lives in the small gestures: a player crossing himself before a free throw, an usher greeting patrons as though welcoming them back to a parish pew, a coach pacing the sideline with the inward concentration of someone preparing a homily.

One can sense this imagination most acutely in the periods between triumphs. When seasons falter, when the city's confidence wanes, the underlying faith becomes more visible. People return to the arena not for spectacle but for continuity. The familiar blue and gold, the acoustics of the crowd rising during a defensive stand, the patient hope carried in each possession—these elements create a sense of belonging that resists the fickleness of outcomes. Milwaukee understands that success is cyclical; what endures is the shared commitment to the program's character. This recognition does not require articulation. It is felt in the chest, carried home in the cold, and preserved in memory.

Thinking about the program in these terms allows its earliest decades to come into sharper focus. The modest records of the 1920s, the uneven seasons of the 1930s, the flashes of promise that circulated through the 1940s and 1950s—all of these years reveal a program learning to inhabit its city and its faith simultaneously. The players who donned the uniform during those periods might not have spoken in philosophical terms, yet their presence on the court mirrored the conditions that shaped them: determination under pressure, resilience without complaint, and a willingness to find beauty in the jagged edges of competition.

As the city moved toward the threshold of the McGuire years, these foundations remained intact. The Catholic imagination that sustained Milwaukee's neighborhoods still pulsed beneath the university's daily life. The industrial landscape continued to influence the way people measured effort and evaluated courage. The confluence of these forces —not yet crystallized, but unmistakable—prepared Marquette for a transformation that would later feel inevitable.

The conditions were already present: a city that believed in labor and loyalty, a university grounded in Jesuit inquiry, and a basketball program that carried the emotional residue of both. Out of this terrain, the next era began to gather force, not as an abrupt shift but as the natural expression of a place that had long understood the interplay between grace and struggle.

The character of Marquette basketball did not form solely through victories or the brilliance of a single era. It grew through the slow accumulation of encounters—between city streets and campus corridors, between the Jesuit inclination toward reflection and the urban demand for action, between the weight of Catholic ritual and the improvisational instincts of young men raised in neighborhoods where certainty was never guaranteed. These encounters shaped players long before they took the floor, preparing them to carry not just a uniform but a history. What emerged was a way of understanding competition that treated the game as a human study, a reading of temperament as much as talent.

Long before national broadcasts turned college basketball into a spectacle, Marquette's early teams learned to play in conditions that revealed character. The gyms were small and crowded, sometimes so tight that a deflected ball could ricochet off a wall and return to the court before a whistle sounded. Crowds stood shoulder to shoulder, their reactions immediate and unfiltered. Students watched from makeshift bleachers, stamping their feet when the cold crept through drafty windows. The city's working-class residents stood alongside them, their presence carrying the authority of people who understood endurance better than most athletes ever would. In those settings, players learned that attention could not waver and fatigue could not be indulged. The court functioned as a testing ground for the qualities Milwaukee valued: tenacity, awareness, humility, and the ability to perform under pressure without ornament.

The Jesuit influence on the university added another layer to this formation. For generations, Jesuit schools have approached athletics with a sensibility distinct from that of other institutions. The game is not merely recreational or competitive; it is a site of discernment, a place where one's inner habits reveal themselves under the strain of effort. Coaches at Marquette did not need to articulate this explicitly. The culture itself carried the expectation. Players were encouraged to consider what sustained them, what distracted them, and how they responded to adversity. The Jesuit tradition does not promise comfort. It promises clarity through challenge. As a result, the Marquette program developed an instinct for noticing details—the subtle mistake in defensive rotation, the shift in posture that signaled a teammate's hesitation, the opponent's brief lapse of concentration that opened an opportunity. This attentiveness, cultivated in the classroom and refined in the gym, became a signature of the program's emerging identity.

Yet the school's Catholic imagination did more than sharpen awareness; it shaped the emotional register of the program. Catholic life in Milwaukee was thick with ritual—the cycle of seasons, the sacraments marking stages of belonging, the gestures that conveyed meaning without words. A trace of that ritual found its way into basketball, not in formal symbolism but in pattern and presence. The pregame warmups, the gathering in the locker room, the moment of silence before stepping onto the court: each carried the faint echo of liturgical rhythm. Players might not have framed their actions in religious terms, but the atmosphere of repetition and reverence lent the game a depth that remained even when emotions ran high. The Jesuit emphasis on intention—doing nothing thoughtlessly, understanding the purpose behind action—permeated practices and film sessions as much as it permeated retreats and homilies.

Urban life added its own counterweight to this formation. Milwaukee was not a city that encouraged abstraction. It demanded practicality, demanded that one react quickly to shifting conditions, demanded humor in the face of hardship. Young men who arrived on campus from the surrounding neighborhoods brought with them a sensitivity to the city's rhythm—the mixture of caution and confidence required to navigate streets that could alternate between friendliness and unpredictability. Those who came from farther away learned these instincts through immersion. The city taught them to sense proximity, to feel the weight of eyes in a crowded room, to interpret tone as readily as words. Basketball became an extension of this apprenticeship. The court asked players to read bodies, intentions, and spaces with the same alertness needed to read a changing street corner.

This interplay between Jesuit thoughtfulness and urban immediacy created a distinctive dialect for understanding the game. Players learned to operate in tension, holding discipline and freedom together without collapsing one into the other. They practiced plays that required precision but learned to improvise when circumstances demanded it. They respected hierarchy—coach, captain, seniority—but understood that in moments of crisis, leadership could emerge from any position. The Catholic imagination thrives on paradox, and so did Marquette basketball. The program found its equilibrium not by smoothing contradictions but by inhabiting them fully.

Such contradictions were present in daily life as well. Students who attended morning classes on philosophy or literature walked past the same storefronts and taverns frequented by factory workers finishing overnight shifts. The city and the university shared sidewalks, buses, and diners. The proximity gave the athletic program a sense of porousness: it belonged to the campus but also to the larger Milwaukee identity. Newspaper stories about the team appeared alongside reports on labor negotiations and neighborhood events. Victories generated a civic mood that extended far beyond the student body. Losses worked their way into bar conversations, carrying the tone of both frustration and recognition. In this environment, players came to understand that they represented more than themselves or their classmates; they represented a city negotiating its own transformations.

The physical environment reinforced these lessons. Milwaukee winters have a way of teaching persistence through their sheer indifference to human intention. Practices held in the early dark, games played while snow drifted against arena walls— these conditions shaped the psychological fiber of the team. Cold sharpened focus. The long walk across campus required preparation, foresight, and the acceptance that discomfort was not an obstacle but a constant companion. This climate produced athletes whose bodies learned resilience and whose minds learned patience. The winter streets functioned as silent instructors, reminding players that difficulty was not to be feared but expected.

Inside the gym, difficulty assumed a different form. Drills designed to build endurance pushed players toward thresholds they did not know existed. Coaches demanded attention to details that seemed invisible to outsiders: foot placement on a screen, the angle of a closeout, the timing of a help rotation. These demands were part of a larger ethos that valued internal strength over external flair. A Marquette player was expected to persevere without showmanship, to compete without complaint, and to carry himself in a way that reflected both the school's Jesuit foundation and the city's working-class pride. The strongest players were not always the most talented; they were the ones who understood that character could become an advantage as decisive as athleticism.

The program's moral vocabulary deepened as generations

passed through it. Alumni spoke of their years on the team not simply in terms of wins and losses but in terms of formation—how they learned to observe, to empathize, to lead, and to endure. These reflections echoed themes found in Jesuit education, where the measure of growth lies not in accolades but in the refinement of the self. The players who excelled at Marquette often carried with them an instinct for responsibility, shaped by coaches who saw the team as a community rather than a hierarchy. This instinct traveled with them into adult life, influencing careers, families, and the ways they interpreted success.

The urban Catholic imagination thus extended beyond campus, embedding itself in the wider Milwaukee story. It lived in the architecture of the city, in the stained-glass windows of churches near the university, in the brick facades of aging factories, and in the social clubs where generations of families gathered. When Marquette basketball thrived, it felt as though these spaces brightened; when it faltered, they absorbed the disappointment with the same stoic acceptance that marked the city's response to economic downturns or political upheavals. The team became a vessel for collective memory, a way for the city to narrate its own resilience.

As modernity arrived—television broadcasts, national recruiting, conference realignments—the deeper imagination that had shaped the program did not disappear. It adapted. The same instincts that once guided anonymous parish players now informed athletes navigating national attention. The same Jesuit sensibilities that shaped early coaches found new expression in film rooms equipped with advanced analytics. The same city streets that taught earlier generations how to hold themselves in uncertainty continued to impart their lessons to newcomers. Through all these changes, the core remained: a belief that basketball carried meaning because the community around it carried meaning.

This belief gave Marquette the ability to navigate eras marked by triumph and turbulence alike. The program's identity, rooted in the city's Catholic imagination, did not depend on maintaining perfect continuity. It depended on recognizing that continuity was already present—in the values passed down, in the rituals repeated, in the memories that resurfaced each time the team stepped onto the court. The imagination that shaped the program did not require articulation; it revealed itself through action, through presence, through the quiet certainty that the game expressed something essential about the people who played it and the place that claimed it.

The city's shifting fortunes and the university's evolving mission continued to leave their marks, but the imagination binding them remained strong. It moved in the space between noise and stillness, between faith and effort, between the demands of the present and the heritage of the past. Through these tensions, the Marquette program learned to see its own reflection—not as an isolated institution, but as a living part of Milwaukee's moral landscape.

There are moments in a city's life when the familiar distance between sacred and secular seems to dissolve, not through spectacle but through the quiet convergence of intention. At Marquette, this convergence is most palpable in the hours before a home game, when the campus holds its breath between routine and anticipation. Students cross the grounds with the subdued excitement of a community gathering itself. The lights in the athletic facilities burn a little brighter, reflecting off snow or rain-slick pavement. Inside the Al McGuire Center, sneakers chirp lightly against the practice floor as final preparations unfold. Across the street, the church doors remain open, offering a silence that carries its own weight. This coexistence—chapel stillness and gymnasium energy—reveals something essential about the university's inner life. It is not a contrast but a harmony, the shared recognition that effort and contemplation draw from the same human reservoir.

On certain evenings, a small group of players might slip into the chapel before the pregame routine begins. They take their seats without ceremony, neither rehearsing piety nor constructing ritual. Their presence feels more like instinct, the expression of an unspoken need for composure. The chapel air is cool and dense, scented with old wood and candle wax that seems to have seeped into the walls across decades. One might hear the faint hum of traffic beyond the stained-glass windows, but inside, the world narrows. These players do not come seeking revelation; they seek steadiness, a moment to settle their minds before the demands of the night unfold. There is no prescribed prayer for athletes, no specific devotion meant to stiffen the spine or sharpen the senses. Yet the space itself encourages a sort of inward quiet, a listening that does not require words.

The Jesuit tradition has always understood contemplation not as escape but as preparation for action. In this setting, the players' stillness becomes its own form of readiness. They breathe more deliberately, shoulders easing, the day's noise receding to a distant corner of memory. Some sit with hands folded, others lean forward as though watching something unseen. They are not asking for victory. They are asking for clarity, for courage, for the ability to meet the moment with a steadiness worthy of the jersey they wear. For a few minutes, the competitive stakes of the evening lose their sharp edges. What remains is a sense of vocation, a recognition that the game ahead will require not just skill but restraint, generosity, and an understanding of one another that goes deeper than play diagrams.

Outside, the rhythms of preparation build as tipoff approaches. Buses deliver fans wrapped in blue and gold, their breath rising in small clouds beneath the arena lights. Families shepherd children through the turnstiles, passing down the tradition with the same matter-of-fact tenderness that once accompanied Sunday Mass. Alumni greet each other with the warmth of recognition, exchanging stories that turn games from decades past into moments preserved in amber. The arena becomes a gathering place for a city that has always measured itself through shared labor and shared joy. The Jesuit imagination may frame the university's intellectual life, but the urban imagination shapes the emotional stakes of a game night. Milwaukee brings its whole history with it, stepping through the doors as though returning to a familiar pew.

Inside the locker room, the players reassemble. The chapel's quiet lingers, but now it mixes with the flickering nerves of competition. Jerseys hang in orderly rows. Coaches move with deliberate purpose, their words measured, their voices calibrated to steady the pulse rather than inflame it. There is an almost liturgical structure to the routine—the taping of ankles, the tightening of laces, the low thrum of music that anchors the atmosphere. Even players who did not grow up within Catholic traditions sense the ritual quality of the moment. Pre-game preparation becomes a choreography of intention, each action contributing to the collective focus that will carry the team onto the court.

When the players finally walk the tunnel toward the light of the arena, something subtle happens. The noise swells gradually, a wave rising before it crests. The court emerges in full brightness, its polished surface reflecting the overhead lamps in sharp gleams. The crowd's anticipation is palpable, an almost physical warmth that meets the players as they take their first steps onto the floor. This is where the urban and Catholic imaginations merge most clearly—in the way the city gathers around its team, offering not only admiration but recognition. The fans see themselves in the players' effort and discipline, in their willingness to compete with resilience rather than bravado. The players, in turn, sense the weight of that recognition. They know they stand at the intersection of tradition and present moment, carrying a responsibility that exceeds individual ambition.

In these opening minutes before tipoff, the gym becomes a living crossroad. The banners hanging above recall the triumphs and trials of those who came before, their presence reminding everyone that excellence is not a temporary achievement but a covenant. The coaches stand poised, balancing strategy with intuition. The players exchange glances that communicate trust built through countless hours of labor. The crowd shifts forward, ready to invest emotion into every possession. No one names the deeper structure shaping the atmosphere, yet it vibrates through the space: the Jesuit insistence on presence, the city's belief in hard-earned dignity, and the enduring sense that basketball at Marquette has always been more than a game.

When the ball finally leaves the referee's hand, the chapel's silence and the arena's roar fuse into a single current of meaning. Every cut, every rebound, every contested shot becomes part of a conversation between the players and the city that claims them. The Catholic imagination, with its emphasis on humility, discipline, and grace under pressure, threads itself through the night's unfolding. The urban imagination, with its appetite for resilience and improvisation, brings vitality to each sequence of play. The two forces do not alternate; they interlock, shaping choices made in fractions of a second.

As the game progresses, the deepest truths reveal themselves not in the scoreboard but in the responses to adversity. A missed assignment draws quick correction without resentment. A teammate's stumble prompts immediate support. A moment of brilliance elicits a spark of joy that ripples outward through the arena. These gestures echo the values the program has carried across generations. They turn the court into a site of moral expression, where the questions asked are not about fame or dominance but about solidarity, courage, and the fidelity required to honor a collective inheritance.

When the final buzzer sounds—win or lose—the gym exhales. The crowd withdraws into the night, its energy dispersing through the streets. Players return to the locker room not as conquerors or failures but as participants in a longstanding conversation about what it means to represent a city and a school shaped by faith and effort. The chapel remains open, its stillness waiting like a harbor. Some players return to it, others carry its quiet within them without stepping inside. Either way, the relationship between contemplation and action persists, as inherent to Marquette basketball as the colors stitched into the jerseys.

Through countless nights like this, the program reveals its deepest architecture. The urban Catholic imagination is not a theory but a living texture. It shapes the way people gather, the way they watch, the way they interpret what unfolds on the court. It informs how players carry themselves long after graduation, how coaches measure success, how alumni speak of seasons long past. In its presence, basketball ceases to be an isolated pursuit and becomes a vessel through which the community reflects on itself—its struggles, its aspirations, its capacity for grace.

This imagination does not seek to resolve the tensions between the sacred and the ordinary. It simply acknowledges that both inhabit the same space, sometimes quietly, sometimes with great noise, always with the awareness that meaning is made in their overlap. In the pregame chapel stillness, in the electric swell of the crowd, in the walk home along cold Milwaukee streets, the same truth holds: the game's power lies not in conquest but in communion. Through this, the program's identity endures, steady as a sanctuary lamp, vibrant as the city that gathers beneath its glow.

Near the edge of campus, where Wisconsin Avenue exhales into the darker streets beyond, the night regains its full dimension. The arena lights fade to a muted glow, and the last echoes of the crowd vanish into the cold. A few figures walk slowly toward the residence halls, their steps measured, their breath rising in thin clouds that dissipate almost as soon as they form. The city resumes its usual cadence, yet the air carries a residue of the evening—a mixture of effort, anticipation, and the quiet relief that follows any shared endeavor. In this space, where noise has surrendered to stillness, the deeper pattern of Marquette basketball becomes visible.

The blend of faith and motion that animated the hours before tipoff now feels distilled. The chapel's silence lingers somewhere inside the body, even for those who never stepped through its doors. The thrum of the crowd remains faintly present, like warmth fading from one's hands after leaving a lit room. What stays is not the game's outcome but the sense of having entered a ritual that belongs to the city as much as to the university. Each person who walked into the arena added something to the night—a gesture, a shout, a held breath, a moment of recognition—and each carries something away, though not always in ways they can articulate.

Along the sidewalks, the winter wind moves between buildings with a patience that has marked Milwaukee for generations. It brushes past storefronts, ascends the church steps, and slips across the brick walls of classrooms where the day's lessons have already been forgotten. In that wind lives the same resilience that shaped the city's Catholic neighborhoods, the same endurance that prepared families for decades of industrial labor, the same attentiveness that taught young athletes to interpret the world with both caution and hope. The imagination that shaped the program does not vanish when the lights go out; it follows people home.

Some students walk in groups, replaying a key possession in animated tones, their laughter rising above the cold. Others walk alone, quieter, letting the memory of the game settle into the rhythms of their thoughts. A few take the long way back, past Gesu, where the dim interior light still glows behind stained glass. The church seems to watch the night without judgment, its presence offering a reminder that not all meaning needs to be spoken aloud. For centuries, Catholic sanctuaries have absorbed the murmurs of their communities —the anxieties, joys, and private longings that inhabit any human gathering. On nights like this, the sanctuary absorbs a different kind of memory: the imprint of a city united by a game that reflects more than competition.

Every generation of the program has known this feeling, even if the specifics change. Students in the 1930s walked home past streetcars and factory whistles; families in the 1970s emerged from the MECCA into air thick with the smell of industry; modern crowds exit Fiserv Forum into the shimmer of LED billboards and passing buses. Across these eras, the essential moment remains the same—the transition from shared intensity to personal reflection, from communal noise to introspective quiet. It is in this margin between sound and silence that the urban Catholic imagination reveals its lasting influence. The night becomes a companion rather than an absence.

This quiet is not emptiness. It holds the weight of memory, the continuity of a tradition formed by generations who returned to these same streets after games of triumph and disappointment. The city's lights trace faint halos on the pavement, as though marking the path of countless steps before. Each footfall joins the accumulation of previous nights, forming a lineage as real as any roster. The walk home becomes a small act of belonging, a gesture toward the understanding that sport, when lived fully, becomes a form of shared identity.

What settles into the night feels less like conclusion than continuation, a quiet recognition shaped by countless evenings when the city and the university found themselves sharing the same breath of cold air. Nothing reduces itself to tally or legacy. The meaning arises instead from the way the game carries ordinary lives into proximity with something larger—an undercurrent shaped by faith that asks for no doctrine, by a city whose diversity needs no uniform story, and by an imagination that trusts the smallest gestures of effort and fellowship to bear their own weight. The darkness gathers these traces without judgment, returning them softened by distance and time.

Behind the gym's darkened windows, the court lies untouched, its polished floor holding the faint memory of recent footsteps. The stillness does not announce expectation; it simply rests, as the city rests, under the hush of winter. Streetlights cast their low amber glow across sidewalks marked by the night's traffic, and the wind sweeps lightly through the gaps between buildings. In this quiet, it becomes possible to feel how deeply the program has embedded itself in Milwaukee's rhythms—not through triumph alone, but through the steady companionship between place and people. The cold air carries that companionship forward, mingling the breath of strangers, students, neighbors, and alumni into a single, momentary harmony that lingers long after the arena has gone silent.

CHAPTER ONE – THE CITY
THAT BUILT THE PROGRAM

"Work is about a search for daily meaning as well as daily bread."
— Studs Terkel

The first thing a traveler notices when entering Milwaukee from the south or west is the way the city rises without hurry. It does not arrive in a sweep of grand boulevards or in the glitter of towers announcing themselves against the sky. Instead, it assembles itself from neighborhoods—modest houses, brick storefronts, the lingering outline of old factories along the Menomonee Valley. The closer one draws to the center, the more the city seems to thicken. The streets tighten, the architecture grows older, and the rhythms of labor, faith, and migration announce themselves in the ordinary details: a tavern sign worn by decades of winter, a Polish or German parish steeple casting its shadow over a block of working-class homes, the slow drift of people crossing intersections with a practiced awareness of weather and time. Milwaukee's story has always been one of accumulation, each generation layering its ambitions and anxieties onto the last.

Marquette grew inside this layered geography, not above it. To understand the earliest decades of its basketball program, one must imagine a city whose very air carried the scent of industry. In the 1910s and 1920s, smoke stacks along the valley exhaled continuously, and the clang of metal could be heard from the North Side to the blocks west of campus. Immigrant families—Polish, Irish, German, Italian, Croatian—

brought with them an ethic shaped by scarcity and longing. They found in Milwaukee a place that asked for relentless effort but offered, in exchange, the dignity of belonging. This was a city built by hands, by repetitive motion, by shifts that began before sunrise and ended long after it. Work became a structure for identity, a means of shaping oneself through perseverance. Terkel would later write about the search for daily meaning amid such conditions, and in Milwaukee that meaning often revealed itself in the spaces between labor: the parish, the tavern, the union hall, and eventually, the gym.

Marquette University, founded in 1881 and guided by the Jesuit order's traditions of intellectual rigor and moral formation, rose in the middle of this industrial sprawl. Its campus did not stand at a remove from the surrounding neighborhoods. Students walked the same streets as millworkers. Professors crossed paths with families on their way to Mass. The boundary between the university and the city was porous, a membrane through which expectations and values passed freely. The Jesuits understood the pressures shaping Milwaukee's working class; they had established schools in cities across the world, often in places where immigrant communities sought both advancement and stability. Their mission held that education should meet people where they lived, translating faith into a disciplined search for understanding. In Milwaukee, this meant embracing a city defined by sweat, improvisation, and the enduring tension between hardship and hope.

It is no coincidence that Marquette's basketball program took shape in this environment. The game itself, still young when the university first fielded teams, matched the ethos of the city —fast, physical, communal. It required not only dexterity but stamina; not only skill but awareness of others; not only talent but the willingness to endure discomfort without complaint. Early players were not polished specimens groomed through elite developmental systems. They were students who had come of age in neighborhoods shaped by parish life and factory schedules, where boys learned to make their bodies useful before they learned to make them elegant. Their movements on the court often mirrored the labor that formed their families: shoulders squared, steps deliberate, a kind of practical economy in every gesture. The game felt natural to them because it required the same patient resilience that governed their daily lives.

On winter evenings in the 1920s, long before the MECCA or Fiserv Forum, games unfolded in modest gymnasiums suffused with the scent of varnished floors and damp wool coats. The air inside these rooms could become heavy with humidity despite the cold outside, the crowd pressed close enough that players could hear individual shouts above the collective noise. Students and neighborhood residents sat side by side, the distinctions between them blurred by proximity. The game offered a rare democratization: a laborer's voice carried as much weight in the stands as that of a university faculty member. The Jesuit ideal of community found unanticipated expression here—bodies gathered in shared attention, their emotions synchronized by the shifting fortunes of the team.

One of the most influential figures of these early years was Bill Chandler, whose tenure as coach in the 1920s and 1930s gave the program its first taste of structure. Chandler understood that discipline did not stifle creativity; it clarified it. His practices demanded repetition, focus, and an awareness of detail that mirrored the Jesuit approach to intellectual formation. Under his guidance, Marquette learned to play with a rhythm that respected both the logic of the game and the temperament of the city. His teams moved as though shaped by Milwaukee's industrial cadence—steady, precise, and unafraid of collisions that tested the body's endurance. The players were not yet national figures, but they carried themselves with a seriousness that set the foundation for what the program would become.

Chandler also recognized the importance of identity. In a city where neighborhoods held tight to their cultural traditions, Marquette needed an ethos that would resonate across communities. He drew from the university's Jesuit mission, emphasizing teamwork, humility, and perseverance. These values aligned naturally with the sensibilities of the city's Catholic immigrants. The game became more than physical exertion; it became a form of formation, a space where young men confronted their limitations and learned to move past them. Chandler did not speak about his work in spiritual terms, but his approach echoed the Jesuit conviction that excellence arises through disciplined habit. His players practiced until their instincts aligned with the team's needs, until the game felt less like individual performance and more like collective expression.

The city, meanwhile, continued to shape the program through its evolving social currents. Milwaukee in the interwar years was a place of contradictions—prosperous yet unequal, devout yet restless, ethnically diverse yet segregated by custom and habit. The breweries gave the city economic muscle, but labor disputes regularly exposed fractures in its identity. Immigrant communities built strong institutions yet struggled to navigate the pressures placed upon them by assimilation. These tensions seeped into the gyms where Marquette played. Basketball provided temporary relief from anxiety but also served as a mirror, reflecting the complexities of a city negotiating its own sense of belonging.

It was in this context that the team developed its early toughness. Players learned to brace themselves against the city's winds—literal and metaphorical. They learned to trust their bodies not because they believed themselves invincible, but because they understood hardship as a given. Injuries were endured; lapses were corrected; fatigue was acknowledged but not indulged. Spectators recognized this posture not as bravado but as fidelity to the values the city held dear. Milwaukeeans respected effort above flair, reliability above flash. When a Marquette player dove for a loose ball or fought through a screen, the crowd responded with immediate approval. They saw in these actions the embodiment of their own histories, translated into motion.

The university's Jesuit identity deepened this connection by offering a moral vocabulary for interpreting the game. Jesuit education teaches that character emerges through choices made under pressure, that true understanding arises from engaging fully with the world's demands. Marquette's athletes absorbed these principles whether or not they articulated them. Their practices became laboratories for discipline; their games became arenas for discernment. The Jesuits did not treat sport as separate from intellectual or spiritual formation. They treated it as another venue in which the human person could be shaped—another place where the search for meaning might unfold.

By the 1930s, the program had established itself as a fixture in the city's cultural life. Newspaper columns reported on games with an attention usually reserved for politics or industry. Bars filled with conversations dissecting plays and debating strategy. The game wove itself into the fabric of daily life, offering Milwaukee a space to encounter hope in the midst of economic uncertainty. The Great Depression hit the city hard, as it did most industrial centers. Yet even in those difficult years, crowds gathered to watch the Warriors play. The gym became a place where people carried their burdens collectively, where the effort of the players offered a temporary reprieve from the pressures of unemployment, wage cuts, and the anxieties of the future.

The earliest decades of Marquette basketball did not produce dynasties. They produced something more essential: continuity. The program came to symbolize the city's endurance, its willingness to confront adversity without losing its sense of identity. The players were not insulated from the realities around them. They walked the same streets as their neighbors, heard the same factory whistles, felt the same economic tremors rippling through the city. Their performances on the court were inseparable from this shared environment. The sweat they shed reflected not only physical exertion but the collective labor of a community striving to build a future amid uncertainty.

In this way, Milwaukee did not simply host the basketball program. It formed it. The city's immigrant neighborhoods, its industrial rhythms, its cultural tensions, and its enduring Catholic imagination gave the team its earliest vocabulary—of work, of resilience, of discipline, of belonging. These qualities became the program's inheritance, carried forward even as the game evolved and the city changed. The foundation laid in the 1920s and 1930s did not fade with time. It became the ground on which everything else would stand.

Milwaukee in the early and mid-twentieth century possessed a geography of belonging that shaped every young person who moved through its neighborhoods. The city was arranged not only by streets and wards but by clusters of memory —Polish blocks anchored by parish spires, German enclaves defined by their breweries and brass bands, Italian pockets where storefront groceries doubled as community centers, Black neighborhoods steadily expanding despite restrictive covenants and public resistance. Each of these districts carried its own rhythm, its own moral expectations, its own way of teaching children what it meant to face the world with equal measures of pride and caution. For many who eventually found their way to Marquette, these lessons formed an invisible curriculum long before they sat in classrooms or stepped inside a gym.

The centrality of labor defined this curriculum. Milwaukee was a city where nearly every adult came home marked by the day's work—hands darkened by grease, uniforms stiff with cold, backs bent but unbroken. The factories shaped the skyline as much as the churches did, and both structures told stories about persistence. The shift whistles of Allis-Chalmers, Pabst, Schlitz, and International Harvester created a kind of citywide clock, audible reminders that the dignity of one's labor carried a moral weight. Young people absorbed this atmosphere through observation. They watched their parents return home exhausted but certain of the purpose that exhaustion carried. They saw neighbors help one another without hesitation when illness or layoffs hit. They learned early that effort mattered not as personal adornment but as contribution.

This understanding traveled with the young men who entered Marquette's early basketball program. They did not treat the game as leisure or escape; they treated it as another arena in which purpose could be enacted. The long days in parish school gyms, the hours spent practicing in underheated recreation centers, prepared them for the demands of collegiate play far more effectively than any formal developmental system. Their bodies were accustomed to repetitive motion, their minds to routine, their spirits to the small triumphs and disappointments that trained resilience. Milwaukee did not produce athletes in the modern sense; it produced workers who happened to be athletic.

The parish system reinforced these habits. For decades, Catholic schools served as incubators for both academic and athletic discipline. Boys who participated in basketball under the watchful eyes of nuns or volunteer fathers learned to embrace structure without resentment. Parishes demanded commitment: practices held after school, games on frigid evenings in gymnasiums where breath was visible, expectations of decorum regardless of outcome. A player who slacked off offended not only his coach but his parish, his family, and the fragile pride of an immigrant community struggling for foothold. This cultural pressure shaped character as much as it shaped skill. When these boys reached

Marquette, they already understood that representation carried responsibility.

Marquette's campus mirrored this interplay between aspiration and accountability. The university's Jesuit identity insisted on a kind of seriousness that resonated with the city's ethos. Students encountered professors who expected not only comprehension but reflection, who believed education was measured not in facts accumulated but in habits formed. Many arrived unaccustomed to such scrutiny. Yet the very difficulty of Jesuit instruction matched the difficulty of their upbringing. They recognized the value of a challenge that felt both demanding and dignifying. For athletes, this meant that basketball existed alongside intellectual expectations, not beneath them. The program's culture treated the two pursuits as compatible expressions of discipline.

During the 1930s and into the 1940s, as Milwaukee weathered the Great Depression and then the dislocations of World War II, this confluence of influences deepened. The city adapted to shortages, rationing, and the rapid mobilization of its industries for wartime production. Entire neighborhoods shifted their routines to meet the pace of the national emergency. Women filled factory positions once held by men. Soldiers passed through the city's train stations, altering the rhythm of daily life. Amid these upheavals, basketball provided stability. Marquette's teams played before crowds that needed distraction but also needed continuity. The game offered a reminder that some aspects of communal life persisted even as others transformed under pressure.

The players of that era felt the weight of wartime expectation. Many were called to service; others balanced studies with jobs aimed at sustaining their families. Practices unfolded in a city humming with tension, where uncertainty shaped every conversation. Yet this uncertainty heightened the team's sense of purpose. The players represented more than a university —they represented the possibility of normalcy, the resilience of youth, the belief that the city's traditions would endure. Coaches adapted to these conditions with a mixture of sternness and empathy. They understood that the game could provide structure amid chaos, a discipline that helped young men navigate fear without succumbing to it. In this way, the court became a miniature reflection of the city itself: a space where effort steadied the mind and structure steadied the will.

The end of the war brought new forces into Milwaukee's cultural landscape. Veterans returned with altered perspectives, seeking education through the G.I. Bill and reshaping the demographics of Marquette's student body. These students carried experiences that dwarfed the scale of prewar anxieties. They approached basketball with humility but also with intensity; having endured real danger, they understood the value of camaraderie, focus, and the subtle forms of leadership that arise when men rely on one another. Their presence strengthened the program's moral architecture. They saw practice as a privilege, not a burden, and infused the team with a maturity rare in peacetime years.

Milwaukee, too, was changing. Industrial expansion brought prosperity, but that prosperity was unevenly distributed. The city's Black population grew significantly during and after the war, driven north by the Great Migration. Restrictive housing policies, workplace discrimination, and social exclusion shaped their experiences. This transformation produced tensions that would later erupt into conflict, but it also introduced cultural energies that expanded the city's character. Music, food, language, and new forms of neighborhood life slowly wove themselves into Milwaukee's identity. Marquette, situated near areas of shifting demographic patterns, absorbed these influences indirectly at first, then more explicitly as the decades unfolded.

The basketball program found itself at the intersection of these currents. As the city diversified, so too did the talent pool that surrounded the university. The game evolved as courts in urban neighborhoods became proving grounds for athletic creativity and competitive fearlessness. Coaches who once scouted primarily in Catholic gyms now recognized the vibrancy of playgrounds where young Black athletes developed skills with a style and flair that challenged traditional approaches. The city's shifting makeup enriched the program's possibilities, even as institutional barriers slowed integration in higher education and athletics.

Through this era of expansion and constraint, the city continued to shape the players who entered the program. The industrial rhythms grew louder, the cultural divisions sharper, the sense of possibility broader. Milwaukee had always been a place where effort counted more than polish, where success was respected only when earned, and where loyalty—to family, to parish, to neighborhood—held binding power. These values imprinted themselves on athletes whether or not they shared the same backgrounds. Even newcomers sensed the weight of the city's expectations. They learned quickly that Milwaukee judged character not by words but by constancy: showing up on time, honoring commitments, embracing work that felt routine or tiresome.

By the late 1940s and into the 1950s, basketball at Marquette possessed an identity recognizable across decades: disciplined, steady, grounded in the habits of a city that had spent generations mastering the art of surviving difficulty. Wins were celebrated, losses endured, but the deeper measure of the program lay in its reflection of Milwaukee's temperament. The team's toughness was not theatrical; it was inherited. The players' composure came not from stoicism but from familiarity with strain. The connection between city and program grew stronger as the university expanded its academic reach and Milwaukee expanded its industrial footprint. Each shaped the other in ways visible and invisible, forming a partnership that would become the bedrock of the program's future ascent.

What emerged from these decades was a sense that Marquette's basketball identity could not be extracted from its urban setting. The city provided the moral grammar; the university supplied the intellectual punctuation. The young men who wore the uniform learned to navigate this interplay with instinctive understanding. They carried the city's weight without feeling burdened, and they absorbed the Jesuit insistence on reflection without losing their grounding. Milwaukee built them before Marquette refined them. And in return, the program carried the city's story out into the broader world—one possession, one night, one season at a time.

Cities reveal themselves most clearly not in their monuments or skylines but in the ordinary geographies that people learn to navigate without thinking: the walk from a rowhouse to a parish gym, the bus ride along a corridor of factories whose shift whistles shape the day, the narrow alleys where children improvise games until dusk, the tavern that serves as a neighborhood's informal parliament. Milwaukee's early-to-mid-century identity rested on this lived terrain. Its neighborhoods were not simply places to reside; they were moral ecosystems, shaping the way people interpreted effort, loyalty, fairness, and ambition. For young men who grew up within these boundaries—and for those who arrived later and were absorbed by them—this environment formed a foundation that no coaching philosophy could replicate. Marquette's basketball program inherited that foundation before it ever articulated its own ideals.

Along the South Side, boys learned the feel of a worn basketball on uneven pavement. Near Mitchell Street, the echo of a dribble could ricochet between brick walls with a rhythm that trained timing and anticipation more effectively than any formal drill. On the North Side, where space was tighter and boundaries mattered less, games unfolded with a kinetic creativity that revealed an entirely different interpretation of effort—one that prized inventiveness, speed, and an ability to seize opportunity in confined spaces. In neighborhoods influenced heavily by parish life, the game reflected the order and mutual responsibility preached each Sunday. In the city's rapidly expanding Black communities, the game reflected improvisation, flair, and a refusal to accept imposed limits. These separate geographies created a diversity of sensibilities that would eventually enrich the talent and perspective arriving at Marquette.

For many who reached the university in the 1940s and 1950s, the shift from street or parish courts to college gyms felt less like a promotion than a translation. The physical environment changed, but the underlying logic remained. The court still demanded awareness, toughness, and a sense of how one's own movements affected the collective. Milwaukee had instilled these instincts long before players stepped onto campus. Even recruits from outside the city found themselves adapting to its pace and temperament. Milwaukee asked newcomers to carry themselves with a type of seriousness that did not preclude humor but discouraged superficiality. It trained them to measure a person not by bravado but by endurance, not by talk but by consistency.

Marquette's coaches of the period—men like Bill Chandler, Eddie Hickey, and later Jack Nagle—recognized the value of this inherited discipline. They did not need to manufacture toughness; Milwaukee supplied it. Their task was refinement. Hickey, in particular, understood the advantage of shaping players who already possessed an instinctive relationship with labor. His teams in the 1950s practiced with an intensity that mirrored the shifts beginning just blocks away in the factories along the Menomonee Valley. Drills were repeated until muscles burned, not to condition the body alone but to strengthen the will. Hickey's influence extended beyond wins and losses. He demanded composure in pressure, focus in fatigue, and accountability in error. These expectations resonated with athletes raised in a city where adults lived such virtues daily.

The Jesuit presence at Marquette deepened this dynamic by offering a framework for understanding that labor could be both physical and moral. Jesuit pedagogy insisted that education develop the whole person: intellect, spirit, conscience, and yes, body. A basketball practice conducted under this philosophy became something more than preparation for competition. It became a form of discernment in motion—a way of noticing one's impulses, limitations, and capacities under strain. Many students, whether athletes or not, experienced a similar confrontation in the classroom, where debate and inquiry forced them to articulate thoughts they had never before examined. On the court, players encountered an embodied version of the same work: learning to respond without panic, to recognize the difference between instinct and impatience, to see that the smallest misstep often reflected a lapse of attention rather than fate.

The interplay between the city's insistence on effort and the Jesuits' insistence on interior clarity produced athletes uniquely suited to the pressures of mid-century college basketball. They were accustomed to noise, to scrutiny, to the compressed distances of a city where personal and communal expectations often overlapped. Milwaukee did not allow anonymity; it made people visible to one another. In small parishes and tight blocks, behavior carried consequence. This environment trained athletes to understand that their actions on the court reflected not only their own ambitions but the values of the communities that had shaped them. The weight of representation was not burdensome; it was familiar.

At the same time, Milwaukee was a city in transition. The postwar boom brought prosperity, but it also brought demographic changes that altered the city's social landscape. The steady migration of Black families from the South transformed entire districts. Restrictive housing policies created tensions that erupted into controversy and conflict. Factories, once symbols of stability, began showing early signs of vulnerability to global shifts in manufacturing. The city's foundations held, but cracks widened. Young men entering Marquette in these years felt both the promise and the unease of a city negotiating the meaning of progress.

For the basketball program, these shifts surfaced gradually. As public schools diversified, as playground culture expanded, as talent began to concentrate in neighborhoods previously overlooked, Marquette faced both opportunity and challenge. Recruitment broadened. Players arrived with varied styles, shaped not only by parish leagues but by street games that fostered creativity and expressive confidence. Coaches experimented with integrating these energies into systems that still prized discipline and structure. The interplay was not always seamless. But Milwaukee's evolving identity endowed the program with a deeper well of talent and perspective —opening pathways that would later support the program's greatest eras.

Meanwhile, Milwaukee's industrial ethos continued to set expectations for how a Marquette player should carry himself. In a city where workers took pride in endurance, spectators demanded the same of their athletes. Laziness was treated as a moral failing; inconsistency as a breach of trust. The city's fans watched with the same discerning eye they turned toward work, judging not style but substance. Players did not need to charm; they needed to persist. In this environment, the line between athletic performance and civic representation blurred. A well-fought possession felt like a tribute to the city's inheritance. A lapse in effort felt like an insult. Coaches understood this dynamic and oriented their teams accordingly.

Within the university, the Jesuit ethos emphasized another layer of expectation. Students, including athletes, were asked to cultivate a reflective interior life: to examine motives, to question impulses, to see themselves as participants in a broader moral narrative. This inward attention produced a form of maturity that later became a hallmark of Marquette teams. Players did not simply compete; they interpreted their experience. Victories prompted gratitude rather than complacency. Losses prompted analysis rather than despair. Coaches who embraced this culture found themselves working with athletes who were capable of balancing intensity with perspective, a capacity born not from comfort but from the collision of city and university values.

By the 1950s, a distinctive identity had crystallized within the program, though no one yet articulated it as such. Marquette basketball reflected Milwaukee's working-class pride, its Catholic rhythms, its ethnic diversity, and its emerging racial complexity. It also reflected the Jesuits' conviction that competition, when pursued with integrity, could reveal the contours of a person's character. The result was a team that played with a seriousness that exceeded tactical instruction. They understood that their work on the court was inseparable from the work expected of them in study halls, chapels, and dormitories. Their athletic formation was entwined with their moral formation.

This identity gained sharper clarity as the decade progressed. Coaches began to recognize that the city itself functioned as a training ground. Recruiters understood that players forged in Milwaukee possessed an advantage not easily replicated elsewhere—a familiarity with adversity, a capacity for adaptation, an ingrained respect for effort. Meanwhile, the Jesuit faculty observed how athletics could amplify the mission of the university rather than distract from it. Conversations about virtue, habit, and responsibility unfolded not only in philosophy classrooms but in locker rooms and hallways. The boundaries between intellectual and athletic spaces remained distinct, yet they informed one another through shared values.

Milwaukee, in turn, looked to Marquette as one of its most visible cultural institutions. The city's newspapers devoted increasing space to game coverage. Bars reserved tables for listening to radio broadcasts. Families who could not afford tickets still felt connected to the team through neighborhood conversations. Basketball became a medium through which Milwaukee recognized itself—tough, unpretentious, striving, rooted in community. The court became a symbolic extension of the city's streets: a place where effort was expected, where improvisation was respected, and where nothing was earned without commitment.

By the end of the 1950s, the foundation was unmistakable. The city had furnished the program with its temperament; the university had furnished it with its reflection; and the players had furnished it with the daily labor that transformed principle into practice. What would follow in later decades—successes that placed Marquette on the national stage—was built on this confluence of forces. The city had shaped the program long before the program shaped the city's sporting identity. Its influence remained quiet but constant, like the hum of factories along the valley or the slow toll of church bells marking the hour. The program carried those sounds forward.

By the time the 1960s approached, Milwaukee had entered a period of accelerated change—social, economic, cultural—and these shifts reached Marquette's campus with a force that reshaped expectations for what the basketball program could become. The city's industrial base still pulsed with energy, yet the early signs of deindustrialization flickered at the edges. Some factories experimented with automation; others, once unquestioned anchors of stability, began hinting at relocation. At the same time, Milwaukee's neighborhoods were undergoing dramatic demographic transformation. The Great Migration had already altered the racial composition of the city, and its effects were becoming increasingly visible near

Marquette. Block by block, the boundaries between established immigrant parishes and growing Black communities blurred, challenging assumptions that had once seemed fixed. With each passing year, the city asked itself not only who it was, but who it was willing to become.

These tensions radiated outward in ways both subtle and unmistakable. Public schools felt the pressure of diversification without adequate investment, and the city government faced mounting debates over housing, transportation, and representation. The churches, once unquestioned centers of authority, struggled to offer moral clarity in situations shaped less by religious doctrine than by structural inequities. Milwaukee's identity had long depended on a sense of collective purpose—work hard, contribute, belong—but the ground beneath these shared expectations was shifting. The language of the old neighborhoods still held power, but new vocabularies were emerging: civil rights, fair housing, community control. The city was engaging in a deep and sometimes painful reckoning.

Marquette University stood at a crossroads within this landscape. Though rooted in Catholic and Jesuit tradition, the institution was increasingly shaped by national debates about education, justice, and civic responsibility. The university expanded its academic ambitions, strengthened its national presence, and wrestled with the need to reflect the diversity of the city around it. For years, the campus had felt insulated by its mission and its geography, but by the mid-1960s, insulation was no longer possible. Students became more politically aware, faculty more invested in public conversations, administrators more cognizant of the university's obligations beyond its boundaries.

Amid these shifts, the basketball program absorbed the city's energy in ways both immediate and indirect. Recruiting changed. The traditional Catholic pipeline—parish schools feeding into Catholic high schools, then into Marquette—

remained important, but new sources of talent began to emerge. Milwaukee's playgrounds, once peripheral to the program's consciousness, became vital proving grounds. Coaches paid closer attention to players whose skills were shaped not only by formal instruction but by the expressive dynamism of street basketball. The city's changing demographics meant that the program would inevitably have to decide whether it would reflect the city's full composition or retreat into a narrower version of its identity.

This tension came into full view under the tenure of Jack Nagle, who coached the team through the late 1950s and early 1960s. Nagle was a thoughtful figure, successful at a time when Marquette still straddled the line between regional respectability and national relevance. His teams played with discipline, reflective of the values the program had inherited, but the city around him was evolving faster than the program itself. Nagle's departure in 1964 signaled not simply the end of an era but the loosening of old constraints. A space opened— one that could be filled by continuity or by transformation. It was into this space that Al McGuire stepped, carrying with him a sensibility that matched the moment far more closely than anyone yet realized.

But before the McGuire era could take shape, the city's internal rhythms continued to sharpen the character of Marquette athletes. Students walked through neighborhoods where storefronts shifted languages and parish demographics fluctuated. They rode buses filled with workers heading to jobs threatened by technological change. They studied in classrooms where the Jesuit emphasis on justice took on new urgency. A young man joining the basketball program in the mid-1960s was entering a city wrestling openly with questions of equity and representation—and these questions seeped into the gym, into conversations, into the consciousness of players who could no longer treat sport as insulated from the world.

Milwaukee's racial tensions grew more visible with each passing year. Discriminatory housing practices confined Black residents to specific districts, creating overcrowded neighborhoods and inflaming resentment. Public officials offered fragmented responses, some sympathetic, others fearful or indifferent. Civil rights marches wound their way through streets not far from campus. The summer of 1967 brought upheaval, with protests and police responses that left scars still visible in city memory. Students at Marquette watched this unfold not from afar but from within the civic frame. They encountered the realities of inequality directly, questioning how their education and their university might participate in shaping a different future.

For athletes, this meant that the gym could no longer serve solely as a refuge from civic turmoil. It became a place where young men processed the pressures around them. Teammates discussed events unfolding just beyond campus; friendships formed across racial and socioeconomic lines; coaches faced new responsibilities as mentors and intermediaries. Marquette's Jesuit ethos, with its emphasis on service, justice, and the inherent dignity of each person, offered language for these conversations, but the lived experience of the city supplied the emotional substance. A sense of gravity settled over the program—not a somberness, but an awareness that basketball existed within a broader moral context.

This gravity shaped the way players approached the game. The competition remained fierce, and practices retained their intensity, but players increasingly recognized that they carried with them the stories of families, neighborhoods, and communities for whom sport served as one of the few public stages available. Milwaukee's Black youth, long excluded from many of the city's opportunities, found in basketball a platform for visibility. Their presence at playgrounds and high school gyms reshaped local expectations for what athletic brilliance could look like. As Marquette began to recruit Black athletes, the program reflected these changes—not just in appearances, but in style, temperament, and cultural fluency.

The challenge for the program lay in integrating these energies without diluting its historical identity. Discipline, toughness, humility—these remained central. But the methods for cultivating them had to evolve. Practices began to emphasize not only structure but creativity, not only repetition but improvisation. Coaches learned to trust instincts shaped outside traditional Catholic pipelines. The city's shifting cultural patterns demanded as much. A player who learned the game on outdoor courts, negotiating space in ways that eluded diagrammed plays, could bring a form of intelligence that enriched the entire team. The question was no longer whether Marquette could accept such players; it was whether the program could grow by embracing them.

In this transitional period, the Jesuit character of Marquette provided a stabilizing throughline. Jesuit education encourages engagement with the world's complexities rather than retreat from them. It demands self-examination, empathy, and an understanding that formation arises not from comfort but from tension. These values gave the basketball program a framework for navigating Milwaukee's evolving identity. Players were not asked to leave their experiences at the gym door. They were asked to meet one another within a shared commitment to effort, clarity, and purpose.

By the end of the 1960s, this confluence of forces —industrial uncertainty, demographic transformation, civic activism, Jesuit mission—had reshaped the moral terrain of the university and the city alike. The basketball program found itself standing at the edge of a new era, formed by decades of inherited toughness but now poised to define itself within a broader, more fluid understanding of what competition, community, and representation might mean. The city had built the program, and the program had absorbed the city's turmoil, its restlessness, and its unyielding capacity for reinvention.

In that charged atmosphere, when expectations shifted and definitions loosened, the conditions emerged for the arrival of a coach who could interpret Milwaukee not as backdrop but as vocabulary. A coach who could speak the city's language while shaping the program's future. The city itself had prepared the ground. The next transformation would grow directly from that soil.

By the late 1960s, Milwaukee had reached a threshold where its past and future pressed against one another with unusual intensity. The factories still rumbled, but their grip on the city's imagination had loosened. The neighborhoods still held their cultural identities, but the lines defining them had blurred under the force of migration, activism, and economic uncertainty. Even the lakefront air carried a new charge, as though the city itself sensed a shift approaching. In this atmosphere, Marquette stood both rooted and restless—a university with a long memory and an emerging impatience, searching for new ways to interpret its place within a changing city. The basketball program, shaped for decades by the steady discipline of immigrant Milwaukee, was ready for a voice that could take all that inherited grit and translate it into something bolder, more kinetic, more daring.

But before that voice arrived, the program was already absorbing the city's evolving sensibilities. The young men who found their way to campus carried with them a mixture of inherited toughness and restless curiosity. They had grown up in households where the old traditions—Mass on Sundays, parish festivals, union loyalty—still mattered, yet they lived in a city increasingly defined by questions rather than certainties. Civil rights marches passed near their schools. Neighborhood boundaries shifted. Factories, once symbols of permanence, began to wobble. Their view of Milwaukee was not the secure, insular world of their grandparents but a landscape in negotiation, caught between stability and upheaval. This deeper ambiguity shaped how they played the game.

A player entering Marquette in 1967 or 1968 might have been raised in a South Side parish where basketball was practiced in cold gyms under the watchful eye of a coach who demanded silence and precision. Or he might have come from a North Side playground where the court doubled as a stage, and the beauty of the game was inseparable from its freedom. Or he might have come from farther away, carrying with him no assumptions at all, learning Milwaukee's rhythms only after stepping into crisp winter air on his first day of class. Regardless of background, he entered a program in the midst of transformation. The old expectations—defend hard, work harder, take pride in toughness—remained intact. But the city around the university demanded a broader sensitivity: to new styles, new voices, new forms of intelligence.

Within the university, these shifts were felt in quiet but unmistakable ways. Students debated social issues with a fervor that mirrored national unrest. Jesuit faculty incorporated contemporary ethical questions into their lectures, encouraging students to examine not only the world's injustices but their own assumptions. In the residence halls, young men and women engaged in conversations that would have startled earlier generations—about race, about class, about the war in Vietnam, about whether educational institutions carried a responsibility to confront the nation's divisions rather than retreat from them. The basketball team lived inside this ferment. Players discussed these issues on bus rides and at training tables, sometimes without resolution but rarely without intensity.

For many athletes of this era, the court became a space where these conflicts could be distilled, not resolved but made visible in motion. A young man who felt constrained by tradition might find expressive freedom in a no-look pass or a daring drive. Another who carried the weight of family expectation might interpret each possession as a form of duty. The game offered a language for emotions too complex to articulate. Practices remained structured, but the energy within them was different—less deferential, more searching. The Jesuit ethos invited this searching. Militant certainty was foreign to their intellectual tradition; they encouraged tension as a means of formation. A player who wrestled with the contradictions of his own identity—Catholic and questioning, disciplined and restless, urban and expansive—fit seamlessly into this evolving environment.

Milwaukee's broader landscape reinforced this internal dynamism. Construction cranes rose downtown as new projects attempted to reshape the city's future. Neighborhoods confronted the consequences of decades of discriminatory policies. High school gyms, once segregated by custom, became sites of talent that no college program could afford to ignore. The social temperature climbed, producing new forms of expression—musical, political, athletic—that reached campus with a vibrancy that made old assumptions feel inadequate. Players at Marquette encountered this vibrancy daily. Some embraced it eagerly; others approached it with caution; all were changed by it.

This flux affected not only how the game was played but how it was understood. A missed shot or a defensive lapse no longer felt like an isolated event; it felt connected to a larger narrative about resilience and identity. A spectacular play did not simply excite a crowd; it symbolized a kind of audacity that the city itself was trying to claim. The crowd's roar in the gym contained more than enthusiasm. It contained yearning—an attempt to reconcile the Milwaukee that had been with the Milwaukee that was emerging. Players felt this yearning without fully naming it. In their movement, the contradictions of the city took shape: discipline and improvisation, tradition and transformation, restraint and risk.

Even the architecture of the city contributed to this shifting consciousness. Downtown Milwaukee, with its blend of historic stone buildings and modernist structures, embodied a tension between past and future familiar to every student who walked from one end of campus to the other. The factories that flanked the Menomonee Valley had begun to look both formidable and fragile. The churches still stood as guardians of memory, yet fewer young people attended services with the regularity their parents once did. These contrasts created a mental landscape in which certainty felt elusive but possibility felt abundant. It was an environment ripe for reinvention.

Inside the basketball offices at Marquette, this atmosphere prompted a deeper question: what should the program become? It had spent decades cultivating toughness, humility, and discipline—values drawn from the city's industrial roots and the Jesuit commitment to formation. These values remained essential, but they no longer felt sufficient. The city demanded expression. The students demanded relevance. The game itself demanded evolution. Coaches sensed these demands even if they did not articulate them. Their recruiting expanded; their strategies loosened; their practices allowed space for styles that once would have been dismissed as undisciplined. They experimented not out of whim but out of necessity, recognizing that the conditions that shaped Milwaukee's identity were reshaping the university's identity as well.

For the players, this meant that Marquette basketball no longer felt like a static inheritance. It felt like a living project, one in which their contributions mattered not only to the present but to whatever the program might become. In a city searching for a new voice, they sensed the opportunity to develop one of their own. They felt the weight of representing Milwaukee, but they also felt the momentum of a cultural identity in transition. Their practices carried a different electricity—not just effort, but promise.

That electricity built slowly across the decade, gathering in hidden corners of gyms, in quiet conversations in residence halls, in the restless ambitions of young men who believed they were capable of reshaping something larger than themselves. The city around them was changing. The university around them was changing. And inside the program, the forces that had shaped Marquette basketball for half a century were converging with the forces that would define its future.

When the convergence became unmistakable, it was not because something entirely new arrived. It was because the city had prepared itself—and the program—for a figure who could interpret its complexities with fluency, who could take Milwaukee's grit and transform it into vocabulary, who could see potential not only in talent but in tension. The groundwork had been laid by decades of immigrant labor, Jesuit instruction, civic struggle, and restless youth. The future would not appear from nowhere. It would rise from a city that had already built it.

Long after the lights have dimmed in the old gyms and the echoes of practice have dissolved into the rafters, Milwaukee's presence lingers in the spaces the players leave behind. The city has a way of staying with those who compete under its roof, shaping their movements even after they step off the court. A late bus rumbles along Wisconsin Avenue, its windows fogged by the cold; a worker exiting a third-shift factory walks with the same unhurried determination that once marked the game's tempo; church bells from parishes across the city ring out the hour with a steadiness that seems older than the skyline. These rhythms continue whether or not a crowd has gathered to witness them. They form the ambient music of a place that gave the program its vocabulary long before anyone recognized it as such.

In the quiet, the court feels less like an athletic space than a chamber of memory. The lines painted on the floor carry the residue of countless decisions—hesitations, feints, moments of courage that belonged to players shaped by neighborhoods mere blocks away. Each scuffed mark left by a pivot or a hard stop contains traces of the city's working-class story: its endurance, its precision, its refusal to be undone by hardship. Even in silence, one can sense the presence of the young men who grew up knocking a ball against brick walls behind taverns or practicing alone in parish gyms after dark. Their instincts formed the bedrock upon which the program would later build its ambitions.

Outside, the winter wind moves easily between the buildings, carrying with it fragments of conversations from passing students, the hum of a distant factory still running a night shift, the faint clang of a streetcar line far down the corridor of downtown. These sounds, unremarkable on their own, become inseparable from the identity the program absorbed. They remind anyone listening closely that the team's early decades were not forged through isolation or privilege but through immersion in a city where effort defined worth and resilience shaped hope.

The traces of Jesuit influence settle into this landscape with equal subtlety. A lamp glows behind the windows of a campus chapel, its light steady against the dark; a professor walks home carrying a stack of essays that ask students to grapple with questions of justice; a group of undergraduates lingers on the steps of an academic building, debating the day's events with an earnestness that reveals how deeply the university expects them to think. These scenes are quiet but persistent, forming another layer of the atmosphere that surrounds the program. They make visible the contemplative current running beneath the city's toughness, a current that shaped how players understood pressure, discipline, and purpose.

In these late-night hours, when the city softens and the

university breathes more slowly, the convergence becomes unmistakable. Milwaukee's industrial strength and ethnic history, the Jesuits' insistence on reflection and rigor, the restless aspirations of youth—all weave into a single texture. The basketball program grew within that weave, not as an ornament but as a thread inseparable from the fabric itself. Every possession played in those early decades, every practice, every quiet walk home in the cold carried the imprint of a place still negotiating who it would become.

What remains in the stillness is not a summary but an atmosphere, the lingering sense that the city and the program shaped one another in ways neither could fully articulate. The gyms may close, the students may scatter, but the moral architecture forged in those early years persists—steady, unhurried, confident in its endurance. It moves with the night wind, settles in the brickwork, flickers in the lamplight outside the chapel, and walks alongside anyone who has ever stepped onto the court with the city's weight and promise in their hands.

CHAPTER TWO – THE EARLY MODERN ERA AND THE SEARCH FOR IDENTITY

"Your system should free the players, not bind them."
— Tex Winter

The years leading into the early 1960s settled over Milwaukee with a feeling of transition that neither the city nor its universities could fully name. The factories still pulsed with the confidence of an industrial metropolis, and the parishes still held their communities together through the familiar rhythm of feast days, funerals, weddings, and the Sunday Mass. Yet beneath this surface of routine lay a restlessness that reached every corner of civic life. It was a restlessness born of demographic shifts, postwar prosperity, new political tensions, and the steady drumbeat of cultural change arriving from beyond the Great Lakes. Marquette felt this unease on its own campus—the pressure of modernity folding itself into the Jesuit insistence on rigor, the expanding ambitions of a university that had long seen itself in relation to Milwaukee rather than the wider world. The basketball program, shaped by decades of working-class discipline and city-bound identity, entered this era with a sense that the ground beneath it had begun to move.

The war had ended less than two decades earlier, but its imprint lingered everywhere: in the veterans who walked across campus on the G.I. Bill, in the neighborhoods reshaped by industrial shifts, in the way the city negotiated the memory of sacrifice with the desire for normalcy. Marquette's returning students were older, steadier, more aware of the world beyond Milwaukee's borders. Their presence gave the university a maturity it had not known before. They carried new expectations with them—expectations for education, for opportunity, for the possibility that life could be shaped by choice rather than inherited circumstance. This shift in the student body subtly influenced the athletic program as well. Players brought with them a seriousness forged not only in Milwaukee's neighborhoods but in barracks, battlefields, and bases scattered across continents. Their understanding of pressure differed from that of the young men who had competed before them, and their hunger to define themselves in a changing world carried an intensity that reached far beyond the gym.

On the court, however, Marquette remained caught between eras. The sturdy, workmanlike play that had defined the program for decades was no longer sufficient in a region dominated by the Big Ten: Wisconsin with its methodical discipline, Minnesota with its formidable size, Michigan State beginning to shape a modern identity, Illinois swinging between brilliance and frustration. These programs defined the landscape against which Marquette measured itself, and the comparisons were rarely flattering. The team possessed grit, heart, and resilience, but it lacked a defining style. It lacked, above all, a philosophy that could lift it beyond the limits of being Milwaukee's hardworking representative into something that carried national resonance. The search for that philosophy became the undercurrent of the early modern era.

Tex Winter arrived at Marquette in 1951 as an assistant coach, young, restless, and steeped in ideas that most programs of the era considered too abstract for collegiate play. He had been shaped by the Air Force, by hard work on the Kansas plains, by a temperament inclined not toward spectacle but toward the underlying architecture of the game. While many coaches approached basketball as a sequence of set plays and intuitive improvisation, Winter viewed it as a fluid geometry. He believed the game could be taught as a series of relationships —spacing, timing, balance, movement without hesitation or ego. His early sketches of what would later become known as the triangle offense germinated in the years he spent studying and teaching at Marquette, long before he gave the system its final theoretical clarity.

For Winter, freedom did not mean permissiveness; it meant understanding. A player freed from confusion, freed from the need to guess, freed from panic, could act with a kind of grace that did not depend on talent alone. Winter watched the young men who passed through the program—players shaped by Milwaukee's industrial ethos, accustomed to doing what they were told, trained to trust discipline more than experimentation. He admired their toughness but sensed they were capable of more expressive basketball if given a structure that allowed instinct to flourish. To him, the prevailing system—fragments of set plays, sporadic improvisation, the belief that effort alone could generate scoring—did not honor their intelligence or potential. He saw in them not workers but thinkers, capable of interpreting the court with a sophistication that mirrored the intellectual formation the Jesuits demanded in the classroom.

Winter's ideas were not immediately embraced. The early 1950s were not kind to innovators. College basketball was still largely a coach-dominated game, built on fear of mistakes and reverence for hierarchy. A young assistant proposing that spacing and timing could reshape the program's identity seemed, to some, dangerously theoretical. But Winter was patient. He taught by demonstration rather than declaration, drilling players on the fundamentals of movement—catching the ball with readiness, pivoting with intention, passing with clarity, cutting with purpose. He spoke of angles rather than positions, balance rather than brute force, tempo rather than chaos. His voice carried a quiet conviction that was difficult to dismiss, even for skeptics.

Marquette's players responded with curiosity. Many had come from parish gyms where drills were rigid and creativity discouraged. Winter's insistence that intelligence could shape the game was liberating. Players accustomed to the blunt-force style of Midwestern basketball found themselves thinking differently about the court. Practices became laboratories where ideas took shape before the players fully understood what they were building. Winter walked them through concepts slowly, unfolding the logic of the game in ways that mirrored the Jesuit approach to education: start with principle, apply with discipline, refine through reflection.

Yet the program still lacked coherence. It had ideas but no identity. It had discipline but no unifying vision. Coaches and players sensed the need for transformation, but the city's basketball culture—rooted in pragmatism and humility —sometimes resisted the audacity required to become something new. Milwaukee valued steadiness, not reinvention. But Winter believed reinvention was unavoidable. The game itself was evolving. Teams across the country were beginning to experiment with motion offenses, faster tempos, more complex defensive schemes. If Marquette wanted to remain relevant, it had to decide not simply how to play but who to become.

The search for identity intensified as the 1950s progressed. Marquette produced respectable teams but not transcendent ones. They beat rivals occasionally but rarely commanded fear. They played with integrity but not yet with a style that felt unmistakably their own. This created a strange tension on campus: pride mixed with frustration, loyalty mixed with restlessness. Students filled the arenas because the team represented Milwaukee, because it embodied the city's work ethic. But they longed for something more. They longed for a moment when the program might step beyond its regional constraints and announce itself on the national stage.

Winter continued to refine his ideas even after leaving Marquette for Kansas State, but the seeds he planted remained in the minds of players and coaches who encountered them. His system, which would one day revolutionize professional basketball, took shape in the modest gymnasiums of Milwaukee, built on the shoulders of players who had never heard the term "triangle offense" but understood intuitively that the game could be more expansive than they had been taught. The early modern era became a period of intellectual stretching for the program—an era in which players learned to see the court with new eyes even if the team's achievements did not yet reflect this expanded vision.

Meanwhile, the city continued its own transformation. Housing segregation hardened even as calls for justice intensified. The brewing giants faced competition, and some factories hinted at slow decline. The cultural fabric stretched in places it had once held firm. Young people on campus felt these forces acutely. For athletes, this meant balancing the demands of sport with a growing awareness of the world's instability. The search for athletic identity mirrored the search for civic identity: both the program and the city were caught between inherited structures and emerging pressures, unsure which path would lead to continuity and which to renewal.

By the early 1960s, the gap between Marquette's potential and its results could no longer be ignored. The program needed a leader who could articulate the identity it lacked, someone capable of interpreting both the city's history and its restlessness. Winter had given the program language without giving it voice, theory without narrative, structure without transformation. The search for identity—slow, patient, fraught—had prepared the ground but had not yet yielded clarity.

The city waited. The campus waited. The program waited.

And without yet knowing it, Marquette was approaching the threshold of an era that would not only answer the question of identity but permanently alter the story of basketball itself.

The early 1960s placed Marquette in a peculiar position, suspended between the hard-edged pragmatism that had shaped the program for decades and the modern sensibilities beginning to reshape college basketball across the country. It was a moment defined less by triumph than by transition, a period when the program's ambitions outpaced its identity. The city around the university felt similar pressures—shifts in industry, migration, and culture unsettled the familiar patterns of urban life. Marquette's basketball team absorbed these forces in ways that often went unnoticed by those outside the program. The search for identity that had begun in the years under Jack Nagle did not dissipate; instead, it intensified, creating an atmosphere in which every practice, every roster decision, every shift in strategy felt as though it carried implications beyond the court.

The era's uncertainty was not limited to Marquette. College basketball nationally was undergoing a subtle but unmistakable transformation. The postwar generation of coaches—stoic figures who valued discipline, caution, and predictability—were still prominent, yet they found themselves facing a new breed of strategist. Coaches willing to embrace motion offenses, psychological insights, and a more expansive view of player autonomy were beginning to appear across the country. Programs like Cincinnati and Loyola of Chicago pushed pace and athleticism into the national spotlight. Smaller schools found new forms of success through creativity rather than brute force. The game was loosening, becoming more fluid, more open to offense, more expressive of individuality. For a program steeped in the industrial ethos of Milwaukee, this shift presented both challenge and opportunity.

Inside the Marquette locker room, players sensed this tension long before administrators or fans articulated it. The veterans who had grown up in parish leagues or Catholic high schools brought with them habits shaped by coaches who believed the game should resemble the city's culture: efficient, respectful, grounded. But the younger generation arriving on campus after 1960 had begun to encounter basketball in ways that defied these expectations. They played in more varied settings —on school courts, yes, but also in playgrounds where the rhythms were looser, the tempo faster, the creativity encouraged rather than punished. They watched teams from other regions adopt a style that felt exciting and unfamiliar. They sensed that basketball could be approached not only as obligation but also as interpretation.

Marquette stood at the intersection of these competing influences. Coaches tried to preserve the program's core values —discipline, humility, work ethic—yet they also recognized the need for adaptation. Recruiting revealed this tension most clearly. The staff sought players who matched the traditional profile of a Marquette athlete: reliable, tough, team-oriented. But as the talent landscape shifted, the program began to encounter athletes whose creativity or athleticism exceeded the structures the team had relied upon. Coaches wrestled with how to integrate players whose instincts clashed with established schemes yet offered possibilities the program had never known. The question at stake was not merely who to recruit, but who the program was willing to become.

Tex Winter's intellectual residue lingered. Even after his departure, coaches found themselves revisiting principles he had introduced—spacing, timing, balance—not always with full understanding but with increasing awareness that these elements held the key to unlocking a new style. Winter himself had moved on to Kansas State, where he refined the conceptual foundation that would later change the professional game, but his influence at Marquette remained as a kind of unfinished sentence. Players who had been exposed to his ideas retained fragments of them, even if they could not articulate the theory behind their instincts. Coaches incorporated elements of motion without fully committing to the system. Practices carried an undercurrent of experimentation, though the larger identity remained unresolved.

In many ways, this tension mirrored the Jesuit approach to education that defined the university. Jesuit pedagogy insists on reflection, on wrestling with contradictions, on inhabiting uncertainty long enough to understand its contours. Students at Marquette in the early 1960s found themselves engaging with questions that extended beyond classrooms: questions of social responsibility, of racial justice, of economic inequality. The basketball program, though often perceived as insulated from the intellectual life of the university, was not immune to these currents. Players absorbed the complexity of their surroundings, shaping their understanding of teamwork, leadership, and identity in ways that subtly influenced how the team functioned.

Milwaukee itself exemplified this complexity. The city remained one of the country's most prominent manufacturing centers, yet the first hints of contraction were visible. Some plants experimented with automation; others faced competition from the South or overseas. Neighborhoods experienced demographic shifts as families moved in search of opportunity or stability. Public debates over housing, education, and employment grew more heated. For players, many of whom came from working-class backgrounds, these changes shaped their sense of self long before they stepped onto the court. The values learned at home—perseverance, loyalty, modesty—clashed with the broader cultural shifts that encouraged ambition, expression, and reinvention.

These contradictions infused the basketball program with a kind of restless energy. Practices felt familiar yet not entirely secure. Strategies held but did not fully satisfy. Coaches understood that they needed a clearer identity, but the path toward one remained unclear. Some advocated for greater structure, believing that discipline would allow the team to compete against larger, more established programs. Others believed that the key lay in opening the game, embracing creativity, trusting in athleticism. Neither vision prevailed completely. The program existed in a state of limbo—capable, hardworking, respected, but not yet distinctive.

The players living within this uncertainty formed the emotional core of the era. They trained with an intensity shaped by Milwaukee's industrial identity, yet they sensed the game moving in directions that required something different from them. Some attempted to reconcile these impulses, finding a balance between adherence to instruction and personal expression. Others felt constrained, longing for a freer style of play than the system allowed. These internal dynamics shaped the team's chemistry in ways that often remained invisible to outside observers. The search for identity was not an abstract concept; it played out in drills, in huddles, in the silent moments between possessions when a player asked himself whether he was being asked to become someone he was not.

The coaches felt these pressures as well. Jack Nagle, steady and thoughtful, had guided the program through the late 1950s with a firm but understated touch. His teams played respectfully and intelligently, reflecting the values the university held dear. But as the 1960s approached, some questioned whether his temperament matched the era's demands. The rising tide of strategic innovation across college basketball placed pressure on programs to embrace risk, to pursue new systems, to experiment in ways that could yield breakthrough success. Nagle understood the game deeply, but the moment required a willingness to reimagine identity—a task that sometimes felt at odds with his understated style.

Administrative voices at Marquette debated the program's future with increasing frequency. Should the university pursue a coach capable of implementing a more modern system? Should recruiting broaden to include players whose backgrounds differed from the traditional pipelines? Should the program invest more heavily in facilities, resources, and national scheduling? These questions reflected not only athletic ambition but institutional self-examination. Marquette was beginning to see itself not just as a regional Catholic university but as a school with national aspirations. The basketball program served as a visible symbol of these ambitions, even when the team's performance remained uneven.

Through all of this, the city offered both pressure and possibility. Milwaukee's residents, loyal but candid, measured the team against local expectations rooted in decades of cultural identity. They wanted grit. They wanted humility. They wanted discipline. Yet they also wanted a program that could compete with the region's established powers, a team that could stand alongside Wisconsin, Minnesota, Illinois, and Michigan State without apology. Their expectations pulled the program in competing directions: toward tradition and toward transformation.

This dual pressure shaped the experience of players who represented a city grappling with its own identity. They felt responsible to the neighborhoods that raised them, to the parishes that formed them, to the families who sacrificed for their education. But they also felt drawn to the wider possibilities that the changing game presented. They stood between eras, caught between the safety of the known and the allure of what could be discovered only through risk.

By the early 1960s, the question facing Marquette had become clear: not whether the program would change, but how. The identity forged through decades of modest, hardworking basketball had given the team a foundation. But the era demanded more than foundation. It demanded coherence, vision, and a philosophy capable of carrying the program into national relevance. Winter had provided theory without transformation. Nagle had provided stability without breakthrough. The players had provided effort without a unifying narrative.

Milwaukee, too, had provided its part—its toughness, its humility, its quiet resilience. But it could not decide the future for the university. The program needed a new kind of leader, someone capable of reading the cultural moment as fluently as the game itself, someone able to turn uncertainty into identity, someone unafraid to reinterpret the city's spirit in a way that could be carried across the national stage.

The early modern era became a crucible not because of crisis but because of possibility. The program's contradictions, frustrations, and experiments served as preparation for something not yet visible but already taking shape. In the silence between seasons, in the restless dreams of players, in the unresolved strategies of coaches, the conditions were forming for an identity unlike any the university had previously known—an identity that would redefine not only Marquette but college basketball itself.

The early modern era pressed Marquette into a deeper confrontation with its own contradictions, and nowhere were these tensions more pronounced than in the evolving architecture of its coaching philosophies. The years after Tex Winter's departure had left the program with fragments of a more modern game but without the coherent system required to transform those fragments into identity. Jack Nagle, whose tenure bridged the late 1950s and early 1960s, inherited a team defined more by earnest effort than by vision. His approach reflected the sensibilities of the era: disciplined, methodical, grounded in fundamentals. Yet as the decade unfolded, the game was drifting steadily toward a more fluid style—one that valued movement over rigidity, creativity over caution, and psychological nuance over mere toughness. In this environment, the program's search for identity became not only a tactical question but an existential one.

Nagle understood basketball on a level that exceeded his era's norms. He approached the game with a teacher's patience, believing that players grew through repetition, clarity, and responsibility. His teams were well-prepared, their execution steady, their floor spacing more deliberate than many of their regional rivals. What he lacked, however, was the force of personality necessary to impose a coherent philosophy on a program at a crossroads. He coached in a voice that mirrored the city's ethos—quiet, diligent, respectful—and in doing so, he communicated expectations that were clear but emotionally understated. Players trusted him, admired him, and felt a stability under his leadership that contrasted with the turbulence beginning to affect many collegiate programs across the country. Yet stability alone could not produce transformation.

The psychological landscape of the early 1960s demanded something more dramatic. Players were beginning to see basketball not simply as an obligation to teammates and coaches but as an expressive medium. The top programs in the country were evolving because they understood that athletes could no longer be confined to narrow roles. Loyola of Chicago had won a national championship by embracing speed, athleticism, and integration. Cincinnati had demonstrated the power of a unified defensive system paired with explosive offensive talent. Even in the Big Ten, where conservatism traditionally prevailed, teams were beginning to adopt more dynamic schemes. Marquette watched these developments with a mixture of admiration and uncertainty. The program wanted to compete at that level, yet remained tethered to a style forged in earlier decades.

Inside the locker room, players felt the weight of these contradictions. They trained with pride, believing in the value of discipline and fundamentals, yet many sensed that the game was moving beyond the structures they were given. Some players, drawn from Milwaukee's neighborhoods, brought with them instincts shaped by playground improvisation—spin moves learned on asphalt, hesitations developed in tight spaces, passes thrown at angles not found in formal schemes. Others came from Catholic high schools where coaching was rigid, where the game was taught as a sequence of responsibilities rather than possibilities. These varying backgrounds meant that the team often reflected the city's complexity more than the coaching staff realized. Practices became a site where inherited habits collided with emerging instincts, creating a rhythm that was earnest but uneven.

The question of identity deepened when the university administration began evaluating the program's long-term direction. Marquette had long taken pride in the team's representation of Milwaukee's industrious ethos, but the board and athletic leadership were becoming aware that national relevance required more than cultural fidelity. Scheduling played a role in this realization. To elevate the program, Marquette needed to attract stronger opponents, travel beyond the Midwest, and test itself against styles of play it had not yet mastered. But scheduling without identity risked exposing the program's limitations rather than strengthening its resolve. Administrators found themselves wondering whether the program needed a philosophical overhaul before it could handle a more ambitious slate of competition.

The physical environment in which the team practiced also shaped the era's internal dynamics. The gym, though functional, carried the echoes of earlier decades more clearly than the aspirations of the current one. Its walls bore the memory of parish-style basketball—tight, structured, unadorned. Players trained under fluorescent lights that hummed with the same mechanical regularity one might find on a factory line. These surroundings reinforced discipline but did little to inspire invention. Some players interpreted this atmosphere as a challenge to bring their own creativity into the space; others felt confined by it, uncertain how much freedom the coaching staff would allow. Even the court itself seemed to symbolize the program's identity crisis: smooth and well-kept, yet without the distinct personality that defined other regional arenas.

Through this, Milwaukee continued shaping the program in ways that transcended tactics. The city's working-class neighborhoods remained centers of loyalty and identity, even as demographic shifts created new tensions. Black residents confronted discriminatory housing policies, while immigrant families negotiated their place within a changing urban fabric. These realities affected the players more directly than coaches sometimes acknowledged. A young man from the North Side might enter practice carrying the weight of family expectations tied to broader social uncertainties. A player from a South Side parish might arrive with the steady confidence of a neighborhood that took pride in its traditions yet sensed its influence waning. These emotional contexts filtered onto the court, informing how players responded to pressure, to coaching, to the inevitable challenges of an unsettled season.

Marquette's inability to fully integrate these psychological and cultural complexities into its program identity became increasingly apparent. The athletes were not merely products of their neighborhoods; they were participants in a shifting national mood. They approached the game with a mixture of loyalty and ambition, humility and emerging confidence. The systems they were given—structured but limited—felt increasingly inadequate to express the full range of what they brought to the court. In many practices, the team teetered between cohesion and fragmentation, not due to lack of effort but due to an absence of guiding philosophy.

The search for identity also shaped—and was shaped by— the recruitment process. Marquette faced the challenge of attracting players who could elevate the program without alienating the cultural sensibilities that had long defined it. Coaches debated whether to widen their recruiting reach beyond Catholic high schools, whether to prioritize athleticism or system-fit, whether to take risks on players whose potential exceeded their polish. These debates mirrored larger questions unfolding across Milwaukee: Should the city remain bound to its traditional industries, or embrace innovation? Should neighborhoods resist change or attempt to adapt? The team's identity crisis was not isolated; it was part of a broader civic dialogue about purpose, belonging, and reinvention.

During this period, the program encountered several players whose styles hinted at what the future could hold. Some possessed the fluidity that Winter had envisioned, though they lacked the system to unlock it. Others showed a defensive tenacity that pressed the team toward greater cohesion. A few brought imaginative instincts that briefly illuminated games with flashes of possibility. Yet these sparks never coalesced into a sustained identity. They flickered, then faded, leaving coaches and players with the persistent sense that the program hovered on the edge of something meaningful without yet grasping it.

Even the alumni community, long supportive and loyal, sensed the need for transformation. They attended games with the same devotion they had shown in earlier decades, yet their conversations in the stands revealed deeper questions. They spoke with nostalgia about the teams of the past, yet expressed hope for a breakthrough that remained elusive. Their expectations reflected both the city's pride and its impatience. They wanted the program to reflect Milwaukee's character, yet they also wanted it to achieve national legitimacy. This dual desire created pressure that shaped administrative decisions in ways not immediately apparent.

As the early modern era advanced, the contradictions

hardened into something like necessity. It became clear that the program could not continue in its current form without relinquishing the possibility of national relevance. Marquette needed a figure who could synthesize the city's history with the emerging style of the modern game, someone capable of interpreting Milwaukee's working-class ethos not as limitation but as cultural strength. It needed a leader who could read players' instincts with clarity, who could transform contradictions into cohesion, who could articulate a vision that resonated not only with the university but with the city itself.

The program was not yet aware that such a figure was approaching. But the conditions that would make his arrival transformative were already fully formed. The players had learned to live within uncertainty. The coaches had felt the pressure of evolving expectations. The city had grown restless, its identity stretched between tradition and reinvention. The university had positioned itself at the threshold of national ambition. The early modern era, with all its contradictions, had prepared the ground.

It waited now for the spark that would reassemble these elements into a new and enduring identity, one that would carry Marquette beyond the limits of its past and into a future defined not by uncertainty, but by unmistakable purpose.

The years edging toward the mid-1960s drew Marquette deeper into a moment when the program's uncertainty felt less like a temporary lull and more like a structural condition. The team played hard, prepared diligently, and carried itself with the humility expected of a Midwestern Catholic university, yet something in its posture suggested a program circling the edges of its own potential without finding a way to enter. The players sensed it most acutely. They worked within systems that were coherent enough to produce competence but too limited to generate momentum. Games became acts of endurance rather than expressions of identity. Victories arrived through grit; losses arrived through the steady accumulation of small imbalances—a missed rotation, an offensive stagnation, a possession in which no one quite knew who they were supposed to be.

Still, the era offered glimpses of evolution. The program saw the emergence of athletes whose instincts pointed toward a more dynamic style of play. They were not always the most polished players on the roster, but they carried a certain fluency—an ability to interpret the court with an ease that suggested the game's direction was shifting. Some of these players had grown up in playgrounds where creativity was a survival skill. Others came from programs where coaches had begun adopting motion elements they encountered from innovators like Pete Newell or the early disciples of conceptual spacing. These influences entered the Marquette gym quietly but persistently. They began shaping possessions in subtle ways: a sharper cut, a quicker reversal, a pass thrown not to a player but to a space.

Yet the systems surrounding these instincts remained cautious. Practices followed familiar patterns—drills emphasizing precision, defensive breakdowns emphasizing responsibility, offensive sets emphasizing predictability. The coaches were not resistant to innovation, but they were working within a culture that prized continuity over reinvention. Their caution mirrored the city outside. Milwaukee in these years wrestled with questions it had not faced so openly before: how to integrate a diversifying population, how to navigate the slow tremors of industrial uncertainty, how to sustain neighborhoods where the old ethnic anchors were loosening. In a city whose identity had been forged through reliability, the prospect of dramatic change felt both necessary and destabilizing.

These pressures resonated within the basketball program. Players who had grown up seeing their families depend on steady labor understood the value of patience, yet they also sensed that the future belonged to those willing to depart from inherited patterns. The gym became a space where this tension played out in physical terms. The older players emphasized repetition, communication, and correctness; the younger ones drifted toward creativity and rhythm. Neither approach dominated. Instead, the team existed in a kind of suspended formation, competent enough to compete but not yet able to define itself.

Coaches confronted the same dilemma in their film sessions. They studied their opponents—Wisconsin with its stoic discipline, Minnesota with its size, Illinois with its structured unpredictability, Loyola with its modern pace—and saw possibilities that felt just beyond reach. The question that persisted in their discussions was not simply how to win games but how to craft an identity capable of enduring beyond a single season. The absence of a unifying philosophy meant that each year felt discrete, disconnected from what came before. A program could survive this pattern for a while, but not indefinitely. Without a deeper coherence, Marquette risked becoming a team respected for its effort yet overlooked in the broader collegiate landscape.

The players sensed this drift during road trips that stretched into long winter nights. On buses traveling through the upper Midwest, conversations often turned to questions of purpose and direction. Some players asked whether the program could ever match the national presence of the Catholic powers on the East Coast—Villanova, St. John's, Providence—whose basketball identities felt intricately tied to the character of their cities. Others wondered whether the stability offered by the university's Jesuit ethos might eventually produce a distinctive style grounded in reflection, discipline, and moral clarity. These conversations revealed something important: the athletes cared deeply not only about results, but about belonging to a program that meant something beyond its schedule.

Marquette's administration began to feel this urgency as well. As the campus expanded and the university sought greater national visibility, athletic success became an increasingly visible metric of institutional ambition. The question facing administrators was not whether basketball mattered, but how. Should it serve as a reflection of Milwaukee's industrial heritage, emphasizing toughness, humility, and collective effort? Or should it function as a forward-facing emblem of the university's emerging modern identity, defined by ambition, innovation, and the willingness to embrace risk? These competing visions shaped discussions that did not always reach public ears but influenced the trajectory of the program nonetheless.

Meanwhile, the public language surrounding college basketball continued to shift. Writers began naming conceptual styles—motion, ball control, pressure defense—and placing programs within these emerging categories. Marquette found itself attached to none of them. Reporters often described the team with adjectives that sounded like faint praise: solid, reliable, hardworking, disciplined. These qualities were admirable, yet they lacked the imaginative pull that allowed a program to capture national attention. The team needed a story, a defining character that turned consistency into identity rather than merely into competence.

For the athletes who trained inside this uncertainty, the experience shaped their understanding of themselves. They learned to endure ambiguity, to perform under systems that did not fully align with their own instincts, to play for something that was evolving even as they practiced. Many would later speak of these years with a mixture of gratitude and frustration—gratitude for the lessons in discipline and responsibility, frustration that the program had not yet discovered the freedom Winter once suggested was possible. What lingered in their memory was not only the games themselves but the feeling of standing on the verge of something unnamed, something that required a different kind of leadership than the program had ever known.

Milwaukee's shifting culture intensified this sense of anticipation. The civil rights movement was beginning to alter the city's political conversations. The music, art, and youth culture emerging nationally reached campus with increasing force. Students debated issues that earlier generations might have avoided, and these debates infused university life with a sharper awareness of complexity and responsibility. Athletes carried this awareness into their practices and games. They interpreted pressure, leadership, and competition differently than predecessors who had come of age in the quieter postwar years. Their presence revealed that the program needed not only tactical adjustment but philosophical clarity.

By the mid-1960s, the sense of waiting had grown palpable. Coaches worked earnestly, players competed honorably, administrators hoped faithfully, yet everyone sensed that the program stood one turn away from a defining transformation. The search for identity had stretched across more than a decade, shaping decisions in subtle ways but never quite producing the spark necessary for reinvention. What the university needed was a figure capable of seeing the contradictions not as problems to solve but as raw material for something new—a leader who could absorb Milwaukee's toughness, the Jesuit tradition's moral depth, the evolving style of the modern game, and the restless energy of youth, and then translate these elements into a coherent philosophy.

The conditions for such a transformation were already present, waiting for the person who could gather them into a single vision. The restlessness of the city, the intellectual residue of Tex Winter's theories, the earnest discipline of Nagle's coaching, the quiet ambitions of administrators, the evolving instincts of players—all of it formed the atmosphere of a program on the verge of revelation.

The breakthrough had not yet arrived, but the shape of the problem had clarified. Marquette no longer struggled with the question of whether identity was necessary. It struggled with the question of who could give that identity a voice.

The final years of the early modern era settled over the program with a mood that felt strangely contradictory—both heavy with limitation and bright with possibility. Marquette played through winters in which its identity seemed always on the verge of forming, like a shape emerging behind frosted glass. The team moved with sincerity, practiced with discipline, and carried itself with the unassuming character of the city that surrounded it. Yet something essential remained just out of reach. The players could feel it in their bones during long practices in gyms that echoed with the sound of careful instruction. The coaches felt it while poring over scouting reports that seemed to reaffirm what they already suspected: the program was working hard enough to avoid decline but had not yet begun to rise.

This plateau created an emotional texture that defined the era. Games unfolded in predictable patterns—hard-fought contests decided by discipline and execution rather than by any distinguishing identity. The team won what it was supposed to win and sometimes stole victories through sheer persistence, but these moments rarely carried forward into sustained momentum. The losses felt the same way, respectable but instructive, revealing small deficiencies rather than catastrophic flaws. The program carried itself like a student who had mastered every assigned task but had not yet discovered the subject he was meant to study. Beneath the competence lay a deeper hunger, one that grew stronger each season without yet finding a place to express itself.

This hunger was not lost on the players. Many entered the program out of loyalty to Milwaukee, out of pride in attending a Jesuit university, or out of admiration for the coaches who recruited them. But once on campus, they found themselves living within a system that encouraged effort but offered little sense of purpose beyond execution. They lifted weights in facilities that were functional but uninspiring, ran drills that honed fundamentals but did not ignite imagination, and watched film that emphasized avoidance of error rather than pursuit of a defining style. Their days carried the steady rhythm of repetition, and while repetition is essential for mastery, repetition without vision slowly begins to feel like inertia.

Yet within this steady rhythm, something else was stirring. A few players began to take risks in practice—testing angles, experimenting with passes, daring to interpret the court with more fluidity than the system prescribed. Coaches noticed, sometimes with caution, sometimes with curiosity. The staff understood that basketball was evolving nationally, but they were also responsible for protecting a program whose stability had become one of its few reliable strengths. Their dilemma was not simply tactical; it was existential. How could they honor the program's traditions without allowing those traditions to harden into constraints?

This question extended far beyond the gym. Milwaukee itself embodied the same tension. The city's industrial core still defined its economy, yet new pressures were reshaping its civic identity. The manufacturing giants that had anchored entire neighborhoods began to show signs of fragility, even as new universities, businesses, and cultural institutions emerged. The working-class character of the city remained strong, but it now sat alongside a growing appetite for transformation. These contradictions played out visibly in the neighborhoods: storefronts shifting ownership, parishes adjusting to demographic changes, factories confronting slow declines in production, schools wrestling with integration and resource disparities. The city was not collapsing; it was evolving without quite knowing where the evolution would lead.

THE CITY OF GOLD AND BLUE

What made Milwaukee unique was the way its citizens responded to this uncertainty—with persistence rather than panic. Marquette's players inherited that sensibility. They complained at times about the program's limitations, but they also understood the dignity of working through them. They showed up early to practice, returned late to the dorms, and carried the weight of the program's hopes without resentment. Their identity took shape through endurance, through the willingness to push against boundaries even when those boundaries refused to break. In their effort, one could see the outline of a future identity forming, though no one yet knew its shape.

Within the athletic department, discussions about the future became more focused. The administrators respected Nagle's steadiness, but they recognized that steadiness alone could not elevate the program to where the university hoped it would go. Some argued for incremental change: modest adjustments to recruiting, small shifts in strategy, minor investments in facilities. Others believed the program required a more dramatic transformation—a leader capable of reading the cultural moment, understanding the psychology of the modern athlete, and implementing a system that could carry Marquette into national conversation. These debates were rarely public, but their presence shaped decisions that would soon alter the trajectory of the program.

When the staff evaluated potential recruits, the contrasts between eras became impossible to ignore. A player who excelled in structured systems sometimes struggled when the game demanded improvisation. A player with playground instincts brought energy and unpredictability that the program could not fully harness. Coaches found themselves drawn to athletes who did not fit neatly into either category—players whose toughness reflected Milwaukee's character but whose creativity hinted at a more expansive future. Yet recruiting such players without a clear identity risked misalignment. The coaches understood this dilemma intimately: to attract transformative talent, the program first needed to transform itself.

Meanwhile, in the gym, the players navigated their own development with increasing self-awareness. They studied opponents who played with a freedom they had not yet been granted. They watched national broadcasts of teams whose styles felt both foreign and enticing. They saw how schools like Ohio State, Cincinnati, and Loyola had embraced systems that allowed athletes to move with fluidity and confidence. They began to imagine what Marquette might become if given the tools to express the full range of their abilities. Their imaginations reached beyond fundamentals, beyond discipline, into the realm of identity—a territory the program had not yet claimed.

This longing for identity expressed itself in subtle ways. In huddles, players sometimes discussed not only the next possession but the feeling of playing within a system that did not yet have a name. In film sessions, they leaned forward when coaches analyzed opponents who moved the ball with rhythm. In the dorms, they replayed moments from games where creativity broke through structure, where instinct overcame hesitation. These small acts of noticing signaled something important: the players were no longer satisfied with competence. They wanted coherence. They wanted a style that felt like them.

The coaches felt this shift, even if they did not always address it directly. Some attempted to loosen the offense, introducing motion elements that hinted at modern spacing principles. Others focused on defensive cohesion, believing that identity could emerge through intensity and togetherness. But these adjustments amounted to contour rather than transformation. The program remained respectable, occasionally dangerous, but still undefined.

Through all this, the city outside—restless, resilient, searching —continued to influence the psychological landscape of the players. Milwaukee's young men knew from experience that survival required adaptation. They knew that the world beyond their neighborhoods was shifting in ways that demanded imagination as much as discipline. They carried these lessons onto the court, showing glimpses of the inventive basketball that would later define Marquette's greatest teams. But glimpses were not enough. What the program lacked was a unifying voice—someone capable of interpreting the era's contradictions and expressing them as a coherent style.

The early modern era, then, was not a period of failure but a period of gestation. The program learned to live within tension. It learned to endure without becoming stagnant. It learned to question without losing its grounding. It learned that identity cannot be manufactured through effort alone— it emerges from an alignment of vision, leadership, culture, and circumstance. In these years, Marquette gained everything it needed except the person who could draw these elements together.

That person was approaching, though no one yet recognized the scale of what his arrival would mean. The contradictions of the era—the caution, the ambition, the humility, the hunger —had carved out a space in which a transformative leader could step. The players had been shaped by uncertainty into individuals who could respond to charisma, boldness, and imagination. The city had prepared itself by learning how to survive without knowing its future. The university had begun to dream on a larger scale.

What remained was the spark. The era had arranged the materials. The fire had not yet begun.

Night settled over Milwaukee with the quiet weight that often followed a long season, the kind of winter evening when the streets around campus felt suspended between motion and stillness. The gym, emptied of players and echoes, carried the faint residue of months spent rehearsing a style that had not yet found its full expression. A lone maintenance worker swept the last traces of chalk from the floor, each stroke of the broom releasing a soft whisper into the air. The space felt methodical, orderly, and somehow incomplete. It was a room that held effort without identity, discipline without the spark of revelation. The silence revealed what the season's noise had concealed: Marquette had reached the limit of what it could become without reimagining its own purpose.

Outside, Wisconsin Avenue stretched into the night as students hurried back to dorms, jackets pulled tight against the wind. Conversations floated through the cold—fragments about classes, family news, hopes for next year's team. The basketball program lived in these conversations not as a source of disappointment but as a question still awaiting its answer. People cared. They watched. They wondered. They sensed that the program's steady competence was not the final form of what Marquette could be. The city's loyalty carried an undercurrent of impatience, the kind that arises when a community knows it possesses potential but cannot yet articulate its future.

Players walking back to their residences felt this mixture of pride and restlessness. They replayed possessions in their minds, not with bitterness but with curiosity—the missed cut that might have opened a lane, the hesitant pass that could have been decisive, the defensive rotation that arrived half a second too late. These were not examples of failure so much as evidence of a system searching for itself. They sensed that the game they were being asked to play did not fully align with the instincts emerging within them. Their frustration was not directed at coaches or teammates. It was directed at the unresolved question beneath the surface of every practice: What would it take for Marquette to become something unmistakable?

The city's winter atmosphere deepened their introspection. Milwaukee, too, was standing on the threshold of transformation. Factories continued to hum, yet the first signs of fragility lingered in the air. Neighborhoods remained defined by familiar parishes, yet the cultural boundaries between them grew more permeable each year. Students saw these shifts reflected in small details: a new family moving onto a formerly homogenous block, a plant announcing reductions in force, a parish school debating integration. These developments did not dominate daily life, but they colored its background, shaping the ways young people interpreted uncertainty, ambition, and the possibility of reinvention.

The program lived inside this atmosphere. Its lack of identity did not mean it lacked meaning. On the contrary, the years of searching forced players and coaches to confront the deeper emotional and cultural forces shaping their work. They learned that identity was not simply a system or a strategy; it was a way of understanding the court as an extension of one's community, one's experience, one's imagination. They learned to endure ambiguity without surrendering to it, to perform earnestly even when the path forward remained unclear. These lessons would matter later—more than anyone in the gym that winter could yet know.

In the stillness of the empty facility, the court seemed to wait. It held the memory of everything the program had become and everything it had not yet allowed itself to be. The lines on the floor formed a quiet geometry, a reminder that structure alone cannot animate a team. Something else was required —something that lived in the players' emerging instincts, in the city's restlessness, in the university's widening ambitions. A voice, a vision, a style capable of gathering these scattered elements into coherence.

The night air outside carried a hint of change. Students felt it without naming it. Coaches felt it without articulating it. Even the city seemed to feel it in the soft glow of streetlamps illuminating patches of snow. The program's long search for identity had not produced the clarity it sought, but it had prepared the ground. Through years of struggle, stability, ambition, and restraint, Marquette had assembled every ingredient except one.

The missing element was not a tactic or a player. It was a presence—a leader who could read the contradictions of the era as fluently as he read the game itself. Someone capable of transforming uncertainty into vision, discipline into creativity, effort into art. Someone who understood that a program's identity emerges not when it avoids risk, but when it embraces the full character of the place that built it.

That figure had not yet arrived. But the conditions for his arrival were complete. The silence in the gym, the restlessness in the city, the yearning in the players—all pointed toward a transformation waiting just beyond the edge of recognition.

The era of searching was ending. The era of becoming was about to begin.

CHAPTER THREE – AL MCGUIRE ARRIVES IN THE CITY OF SOLES

"New York City is the world's greatest teacher. It shows you everyone, and it shows you yourself."
— Al McGuire

When Al McGuire arrived in Milwaukee in the spring of 1964, stepping onto the streets of a city built by soles rather than by style, something in the atmosphere felt immediately unsettled, as though an unfamiliar energy had entered a landscape accustomed to steadiness. Milwaukee was not a city that startled easily. It was a place of factories and taverns, parish festivals and night-shift workers, a place where people trusted what could be held in the hand or carried in the bones. But McGuire walked through its streets with a kind of kinetic presence that felt foreign to the city's rhythm. He spoke quickly, moved quickly, thought quickly. He saw everything —the shuttered storefronts, the corner bars, the kids playing half-court games in alleys where the bricks leaned with history —and he absorbed it instantly, as if Milwaukee were a text he had already studied but now needed to annotate.

Marquette, for its part, had never seen anyone like him. The university had known coaches who were diligent, methodical, and loyal. It had known teachers who shaped athletes through patience and repetition. But it had never known a figure whose entire being seemed to radiate possibility. McGuire was not simply a coach; he was an interpreter of souls.

He could look at a player for ten seconds and see not just talent but temperament, not just habits but heart. He could walk into a room and rearrange its emotional temperature through humor, defiance, or unexpected warmth. He was unpredictable, but never unclear. Everything he did—even the most theatrical gestures—arose from an internal compass calibrated by instincts no other coach of the era possessed.

Milwaukee did not yet recognize what his arrival meant. The city saw a young coach with a New York accent, a restless gait, and more stories than victories. They saw a man who had coached at Belmont Abbey, who recruited in neighborhoods most Catholic universities had never dared enter, who could talk street basketball as fluently as he spoke about the quiet self-confidence required of young men. They saw charisma, but they had not yet learned to interpret charisma as architecture. McGuire, however, understood the stakes immediately. He looked at the Marquette program—steady but unremarkable, disciplined but identity-poor—and saw a team trapped inside a system too small for its own potential. He saw the hunger of a university ready to break from modestness, the restlessness of a city ready to be seen, and the emotional pliability of players waiting for someone who could teach them not only how to win but how to exist.

He also saw shoes—hundreds of them, worn down by Milwaukee winters, shaped by long workdays, bearing the scuffs of factory floors and playground asphalt. In New York he had learned to read people by their shoes, to understand their origins, their ambitions, their pride, and their fear. Milwaukee's shoes told him everything: this was a city of workers, a city whose confidence lived in the legs rather than in the tongue. The soles carried stories of shift work, migration, parishes, and neighborhoods where basketball courts doubled as social maps. McGuire understood instantly that this was a place where the game did not need to be sold; it needed to be translated.

His first days on campus confirmed what he sensed. The athletic offices still carried the echo of an earlier era—notes in neat handwriting, schedules drawn by hand, coaches who measured excellence by the absence of mistakes. The players, polite and hardworking, stood when he entered the room. Their shoes sat in tidy rows. Their expectations were modest. They anticipated a coach who would reinforce fundamentals, require obedience, and speak of toughness as though it were the entire architecture of manhood. Instead, they encountered a man who looked at them with an intensity that felt unnerving at first. McGuire spoke in images, jokes, street wisdom, and occasionally in riddles. But embedded in his language was something unmistakable: he believed Marquette could become something larger than its circumstances.

He began his tenure not with systems but with presence. He walked the city, sat in taverns, visited parishes, and talked to strangers. He needed to understand Milwaukee not as an abstract market but as a living organism. He believed a program could not win without belonging to its city, and belonging required fluency. He watched teenagers play pickup on cracked outdoor courts, noting the gestures of confidence and the moments of hesitation. He observed their habits—how they protected the ball, how they navigated pressure, how they expressed individuality within chaos. He listened to the cadence of their trash talk, the unspoken codes of toughness, the subtle markers of who led and who followed. He learned where the city hid its talent and where it hid its insecurity.

Then he began recruiting—not from glossy lists but from instinct. He sought players others overlooked, players whose emotional architecture matched the city's contradictions. He wanted players who knew how to fight without fanfare, who carried quiet hunger, who played with the rhythm of neighborhoods rather than the polish of academies. He valued temperaments more than statistics. A player who had survived difficulty—family hardship, poverty, racial tension, personal loss—often carried a resiliency that could not be taught. McGuire believed that a team needed these personalities not for sentiment but for structure. A winning identity, in his view, was built not from talent alone but from a mosaic of temperaments assembled with care.

He did not explain this philosophy to administrators; he showed it through players. He brought in kids who looked wrong to other coaches—too small, too raw, too emotional, too unpredictable—and then revealed strengths no one else had noticed. He prized street players because they survived pressure without needing instruction, and parish players because they understood responsibility before ambition. He understood that Milwaukee, with its ethnic enclaves and industrial backbone, produced young men whose basketball instincts were shaped by the intimacy of their neighborhoods. They did not play for applause; they played for pride. And pride, McGuire believed, was the most reliable engine for victory.

His early practices at Marquette felt like cultural shocks to the players. He demanded pace not merely for conditioning but for honesty; speed exposed character. He insisted on drills that forced decision-making under pressure because he believed intelligence needed friction. He welcomed mistakes if they came from courage and lambasted correctness if it came from fear. He fused discipline with improvisation, insisting that the court was both a workplace and a stage. Players who expected a rigid system instead found themselves learning to read the game in real time, to trust their instincts, to understand that basketball carried emotional architecture as much as tactical structure.

The city began noticing something different in the team's posture. Even before the wins came, the players moved with a sharper sense of self. They carried themselves with the looseness of young men who had discovered permission. They played less cautiously. They argued more in practice—but the arguments carried growth rather than resentment. They joked more, worked harder, and competed with a kind of lively edge that suggested the program had awakened from a long sleep it did not know it had entered.

This awakening was not simply athletic; it was cultural. McGuire understood that a basketball program must become a civic expression. He saw how Milwaukee's working-class neighborhoods longed for a team that reflected their own story—scrappy, proud, underestimated, capable of sudden brilliance. He recognized the Jesuit identity of Marquette not as institutional branding but as a philosophical toolkit. Jesuit education valued discernment, imagination, interior freedom. McGuire, without using those words, taught these principles through basketball. He taught players to see the court not as a battleground but as a classroom, a stage, a confessional, and a place where emotion became a form of intelligence.

His arrival did something else that no one fully anticipated: it gave the city permission to dream differently. Milwaukee had been trained by history to measure its ambitions with caution. But McGuire spoken in tones that defied modesty. He believed Marquette could compete with programs that had resources it could not match. He believed the team could recruit nationally. He believed the city could become a basketball capital. He believed, above all, that charisma, emotional intelligence, and cultural fluency could become competitive advantages in a sport dominated by height, funding, and reputation.

The early weeks of his tenure did not yet produce wins, but they produced something far more important: a shift in imagination. Players felt it in their legs. Students felt it in the gym's atmosphere. Administrators felt it when they walked past practice and heard laughter, argument, rhythm, and something like joy. The city felt it when the team moved through neighborhoods with a swagger that was not arrogance but awakening.

Before the victories, before the recruits, before the transformation that would electrify the nation, one truth was already evident: a new identity had begun forming, built not from systems or slogans but from the presence of a man who understood how to read a city through its shoes and how to read a player through his silence.

Al McGuire had arrived in Milwaukee.

And Milwaukee, without yet realizing it, had begun to change.

When Al McGuire settled into his first full season at Marquette, the city regarded him with a mix of curiosity and skepticism. Milwaukee had known transplants before —engineers, executives, professors—but McGuire's presence carried a theatrical unpredictability that seemed to hover above the steady pulse of the industrial Midwest. He wore his New Yorkness openly, the way some men wear an accent or a scar. It was there in his stride, in his tone, in the way he scanned a room before speaking, as if determining its emotional density. The city's instinctive reserve met his flamboyance with caution, yet something in his manner disarmed even the skeptics. He spoke like someone who understood struggle. He listened like someone who recognized anxiety. His humor carried an undercurrent of tenderness. Milwaukee did not quite trust him, but it could not help leaning closer.

The players leaned even closer. For young men accustomed to coaches who measured success in drills completed and mistakes avoided, McGuire's approach felt almost destabilizing. He asked questions no one had asked them before—not about footwork or spacing, but about fear, humor, shame, pride, ambition. He wanted to know what made them angry, what made them quiet, what made them believe in themselves. He wanted to see how they walked, how they entered a room, how they responded to confrontation. He was constructing not a playbook but a psychological map. And the players—some wary, some thrilled—began to understand that the real work of playing for McGuire was internal.

He ran practices that felt like theater, philosophy seminar, and survival drill all at once. One moment he demanded absolute precision; the next he cracked a joke that punctured the tension and left players laughing in disbelief. He barked for effort with a fierceness that seemed to come from his ribs, then softened instantly to explain a decision with the care of a priest hearing confession. His emotional range bewildered those who expected predictability. But beneath the volatility lay an unbreakable consistency: McGuire always knew who needed pressure, who needed affection, who needed provocation, and who needed space.

He believed that basketball was not only a game of skill but a game of thresholds—moments when a player either stepped into his own confidence or retreated into self-protection. McGuire devoted himself to finding those thresholds. For some players, it came in the form of a challenge so blunt it bordered on insult; for others, it emerged through a quiet word whispered after practice. He understood that greatness was not coaxed from a single method. It had to be individualized, sculpted, felt. He once told an assistant, "You coach the uniform the same. You coach the kid inside it differently." The line captured the entire architecture of his approach.

Off the court, he studied the city with anthropological precision. He walked streets no previous Marquette coach had bothered to enter. He visited churches where priests spoke Polish, German, or Spanish before switching into English midway through the homily. He visited taverns where union members gathered after late shifts, their conversations blending exhaustion with stubborn pride. He watched kids play on rims bent by winters, slipping on patches of ice that covered cracked pavement. He observed how young Black players navigated playground hierarchies, how young white players talked about toughness, how both groups carried unspoken burdens shaped by Milwaukee's segregated reality.

McGuire absorbed all of this and let it inform how he built his team. He understood that a city is not an audience—it is a resource. Its anxieties become your fuel. Its skepticism becomes your edge. Its stories become your identity. In Milwaukee, he found a place where humility did not preclude ambition, where grit did not preclude flair, where working-class values did not preclude the longing to be seen. He believed that if the basketball program could reflect the city's contradictions—its toughness and humor, its modesty and hunger—it could create a style that felt not merely competitive but inevitable.

He also recognized that Marquette, as a Jesuit institution, offered something few programs could match: moral elasticity. The Jesuits valued intellectual freedom, the capacity to hold tension without succumbing to it. They believed that formation was not a matter of uniformity but of interior depth. McGuire, though not a theologian, understood this instinctively. He shaped his program around the same principles. He wanted players who could contain contradiction, who could be both fierce and joyful, serious and creative, disciplined and unpredictable. He sought not soldiers but improvisers. He believed that order without imagination produced mediocrity, and imagination without order produced chaos. His brilliance lay in navigating the space between.

This philosophy changed recruiting in ways that startled the athletic department. McGuire ignored the conventional metrics that dominated scouting reports. He paid less attention to shooting percentages than to facial expressions when a player turned the ball over. He cared less about height than about how a player walked toward the free-throw line. He said he could tell, by how a kid tied his shoes, whether he would fold under pressure. These judgments sounded mystical to outsiders, but they rested on decades of street observation.

To McGuire, basketball ability was only the visible portion of a player's psychological architecture. The real question, always, was whether the kid had a soul that could be coached.

He pursued players who made other coaches uneasy. Raw talents from playgrounds in Brooklyn, Chicago, and Philadelphia. Kids who had been overlooked by recruiters because they seemed undisciplined, unpredictable, or too attached to their own style. Kids who had learned the game through adversity rather than advantage. McGuire believed that such players carried a kind of emotional voltage that could electrify a team if connected to the right system. He also knew that a player with something to prove was infinitely more dangerous than a player who had already been affirmed.

Milwaukee reacted with a mixture of amusement and suspicion. Local sportswriters wrote cautiously optimistic pieces laced with questions—Was McGuire too reckless? Too theatrical? Too strange for the Midwest? Could his streetwise intuition function in a structured collegiate environment? Would the university tolerate a coach who operated more like a poet than a bureaucrat? McGuire seemed to relish the skepticism. He enjoyed being underestimated. It gave him room to work in the shadows before unveiling the full force of his vision.

Meanwhile, inside the Marquette locker room, his influence spread through quieter channels. Players began carrying themselves differently. Their confidence did not come from wins—they had not accumulated many yet—but from a sense of personal recognition. For the first time, many felt truly seen by their coach. They learned to read situations with greater freedom. They found themselves encouraged to take risks, to trust their instincts, to express themselves on the court without fear of reprimand. They began to understand that McGuire was not trying to fit them into a preexisting system; he was building a system around them.

This shift affected everything—the energy in the gym, the way players talked to one another, the way they walked through campus. Their posture changed. Their humor changed. Their ambition sharpened. McGuire's influence was not merely technical; it was emotional. He taught them that basketball was not played in diagrams but in the spaces between them. He taught them that rhythm mattered as much as structure, that decision-making mattered as much as athleticism, that belief mattered as much as skill. He taught them that Milwaukee, with all its contradictions, could be a source of style rather than a limitation.

The city began to notice. Crowds grew slightly louder, slightly more hopeful. Games carried a nervous, excited energy not because the team was winning consistently but because it was playing with a sense of becoming. People sensed that Marquette was learning to breathe differently. Something unnameable was taking hold.

And in Al McGuire's mind, the picture was already forming. He could see the future not as an abstraction but as a lived possibility. He saw players who had never been taught how to shine beginning to illuminate the gym. He saw a program shedding its modesty. He saw a city learning to see itself through the prism of a game that mirrored its complexity. He saw—long before anyone else dared imagine it—that Marquette basketball could become not merely relevant but transformative.

He wasn't building a team. He was building an awakening.

The full measure of Al McGuire's transformation began to reveal itself not during games, where results still lagged behind intention, but in the daily atmospheres he created—those long, unmeasured stretches of practice, conversation, and observation that shaped the inner life of the program. What distinguished McGuire was not simply his charisma or his unconventional eye for talent, but his capacity to alter the emotional climate of a team. Under his leadership, the gym no longer felt like a place of correction; it became a place of discovery. Players entered with an alertness that was new to them, as though the air itself had changed weight. They knew that anything could happen in one of his practices—an unexpected drill, a philosophical detour, a story from Queens that somehow illuminated a defensive rotation. They learned quickly that the logic of his teaching was relational, not mechanical.

McGuire carried himself with a restless physicality that communicated urgency without panic. He paced during drills, shifting from sideline to baseline, his eyes narrowing as he watched a player's feet or the angle of a pass. Sometimes he would halt practice abruptly, his hand slicing through the air, then walk directly up to a player and speak with shocking softness, explaining that hesitation was not an error but a message. Other times, he erupted with energy, shouting across the court to demand boldness, not correctness. His volatility did not come from instability but from sensitivity. He felt the mood of the gym the way some musicians feel the temperature of a room. He adjusted accordingly, lifting players when they tightened, grounding them when their excitement grew frenetic.

The players learned to interpret his moods as part of the curriculum. They began to understand that basketball under McGuire was as much a moral education as a tactical one. He wanted them to confront their own self-protective instincts and learn how to move beyond them. A player who avoided contact out of fear would be challenged until he either broke or discovered a new version of himself. A player who acted out of ego would be humbled until he understood the cost of self-importance. A player who worked hard but without imagination would be pushed to color outside the lines. McGuire's gift was not that he saw potential where others did not—it was that he saw the specific emotional barrier standing between a player and his future self.

He understood, too, that players needed a sense of belonging that exceeded the boundaries of the gym. McGuire often took his athletes into the city, walking them through neighborhoods he had explored alone in his early weeks. He showed them taverns where workers gathered after shifts, churches with doors that were always unlocked, playgrounds where kids played with an intensity born from scarcity rather than opportunity. He wanted his players to see Milwaukee not as backdrop but as bloodstream. He believed that a team could not resonate with a city unless it absorbed the city's pulse, its fears, its humor, its contradictions. These excursions were never framed as lessons, yet they became one of the deepest forms of instruction. Players began to understand that they were not representing an institution alone; they were representing a civic temperament.

In the gym, these lessons translated into a style of play that was beginning to take shape even if it had not yet fully matured. McGuire favored a brand of basketball that lived on the edge of control. He valued improvisation but demanded accountability. He granted freedom but required awareness. He encouraged players to take risks, but only once they understood why the risk mattered. His practices oscillated between frenetic scrimmages and slow, almost meditative repetitions of footwork or spacing. He would let a chaotic possession unfold, then stop everything to point out a minute detail—a missed angle, a rushed breath, a player who had failed to recognize the emotional weight of a moment. He believed that clarity emerged not from repetition alone but from the tension between instinct and reflection.

This tension began to reshape the players. They developed a sharper sense of each other's moods, movements, and tendencies. They learned to trust that a teammate might improvise, and rather than reacting with confusion, they reacted with readiness. The court became a place where creativity carried structure and structure carried personality. Marquette basketball, still uneven in execution, had begun to cultivate an essential quality of future greatness: unpredictability rooted in coherence. The team no longer looked like a collection of parts but like an organism learning to breathe through multiple lungs.

McGuire's recruiting philosophy accelerated this transformation. He sought players who added layers to the emotional architecture of the team. One recruit possessed an almost stubborn serenity that calmed teammates in tense situations. Another carried a ferocity that lifted practices from routine to competitive feralness. A third brought humor that diffused the weight of expectation. McGuire was assembling not simply a roster but a chemistry experiment. He believed that successful teams emerged not from the sum of skill sets but from the interaction of personalities.

This approach baffled some within the university. They wondered why he seemed uninterested in traditional recruitment metrics. They questioned the wisdom of bringing in players from backgrounds unfamiliar to Marquette's culture. They worried that his reliance on intuition would lead to volatility. But McGuire understood that stability was not what the era required. Stability had produced competence. The moment demanded transformation.

Milwaukee's influence remained central to his vision. The city's working-class humility, its ethnic patchwork, its daily confrontation with loss and endurance—all of these elements shaped how McGuire taught toughness. He believed toughness was not expressed in volume or violence but in a willingness to confront hard truths without flinching. When he spoke about playing "New York tough," he was not referring to bravado but to awareness—the ability to read a situation with emotional intelligence. He recognized that Milwaukee, though different in temperament, produced a similar kind of strength. He saw this in his players' posture, in their reactions to failure, in the understated pride that threaded through their families.

The university's Jesuit identity amplified this understanding. McGuire, though not a theologian, resonated with the Jesuit emphasis on discernment, awareness, and formation. He believed that players needed moments of interior clarity as much as they needed athletic instruction. At times, he held brief one-on-one conversations in hallways or on empty benches after practice, speaking not about basketball but about life—about fear, aspiration, shame, or uncertainty. These conversations often served as the turning points of a player's development. He understood that young men do not change because of a new play or a new drill; they change because someone names the truth they have been afraid to speak aloud.

By his second season, something undeniable was taking shape in the community. Crowds responded differently. The old gym, once content with polite applause, began to rumble with anticipation. Losses no longer produced resignation but frustration born from hope. Wins felt less like relief and more like glimpses of a rising force. Newspapers remarked on the team's growing personality—its humor, its grit, its flashes of brilliance. They still mocked McGuire occasionally, teasing his theatrics, his unpredictability, his insistence on trusting intuition over convention. But beneath the surface, admiration was growing.

And the players felt it most intensely. They felt it in the way practices carried a new sense of urgency. They felt it in the way McGuire watched them, as if searching for the next emotional breakthrough. They felt it in the city's growing curiosity. They felt it in themselves, in the way they walked through campus with an awareness that something was forming around them, something not yet fully real but undeniably present.

The identity of Marquette basketball—long dormant, long searched for—had begun its emergence. It did not yet have a shape, but it had a pulse. And that pulse, rhythmic and rising, belonged unmistakably to McGuire.

By the time Al McGuire moved fully into the middle years of his Marquette tenure, the transformation he had envisioned no longer lived only in practice gyms or backstreet recruiting trips. It had started to manifest in moments that revealed how profoundly he had altered the emotional and competitive DNA of the program. These moments were rarely neat or polished. They tended to erupt rather than unfold, the way a city reveals its character not during ceremonies but during unguarded exchanges on street corners or after last call. What distinguished McGuire's Marquette was not simply that it began winning more consistently, but that it began winning in ways that carried the unmistakable imprint of a man who had built his coaching life on improvisation, emotional intelligence, and the belief that pressure exposes truth.

One such moment arrived during a midseason game when the team—exhausted from travel, behind by double digits, and mismatched athletically—seemed on the verge of conceding to inevitability. The gym carried the resigned hush that often settles over a crowd when defeat feels prewritten. Players looked at one another with the tightness of men who recognized that their execution had slipped into hesitation. Assistants shuffled clipboards quietly. Even the officials seemed to officiate with a kind of fatigued expectation. It was then that McGuire, leaning against the scorer's table with the casual defiance of someone waiting for a bus that refused to arrive, suddenly erupted with a burst of energy directed not at the players but at the atmosphere itself. He shouted not instructions but a jolt—an emotional interruption loud enough to reset something in the room. It was a provocation, a reminder, a challenge wrapped in theater. The players snapped back instantly, as though he had cut a wire that had been binding them.

They clawed back into the game. They did not win—it was

not that kind of miracle. But they refused collapse, and in that refusal the team revealed something essential: they had acquired McGuire's distaste for resignation. He did not demand perfection; he demanded presence. The crowd left the gym murmuring about the comeback rather than the loss. It was one of those nights when the scoreboard told a story that no longer mattered. What mattered was the shift in posture, the willingness to contest every assumption the opponent made about their limitations.

These episodes occurred frequently during this period, each one adding another layer to the emerging identity of the program. Marquette became known for its unpredictability —not the unpredictability of inconsistency, but the unpredictability of a team that refused to behave according to scouting reports. If an opponent expected caution, Marquette delivered aggression. If they prepared for structure, Marquette delivered improvisation. If they prepared for one player to dominate, another emerged unexpectedly. The team reflected its coach's conviction that life rarely rewards those who cling too tightly to order. McGuire believed in disrupting patterns before patterns could trap you. He trusted chaos when others trusted discipline. And yet, beneath this reputation for inventive play lay a foundation of self-awareness and preparation that few recognized at the time.

This duality began to draw the attention of national writers, many of whom struggled to categorize McGuire. Some treated him as an eccentric, a charming outlier in a profession dominated by tacticians and disciplinarians. Others saw him as a visionary whose instincts outpaced the era's analytic language. They visited Milwaukee to profile him and left with notebooks filled not with diagrams but with metaphors— comments about souls, street corners, serenity, flamboyance, fear, courage. McGuire did not speak about the game in the standard dialect of coaches. He spoke about it the way an artist or a philosopher might describe the human condition.

His press conferences drifted toward parables. His answers meandered into unexpected tenderness. He made reporters laugh, sometimes disarmingly. And beneath it all, he carried an authority that came from a life spent reading not books or scouting reports but human behavior.

Players felt this authority in the smallest details. During warm-ups, McGuire could glance at a player once and know whether he was ready. During timeouts, he often ignored the whiteboard entirely, focusing instead on a single sentence that cut through the fog of the moment. He used silence when others used sound. He used humor when others used threats. He broke tension with odd remarks about shoes, colors, or the rhythm of the crowd, knowing that the mind often needs deflection before it can absorb direction. His genius lay in his ability to calibrate meaning to the moment. He understood that teaching is not the transfer of information but the orchestration of readiness.

This architecture extended beyond the court. McGuire cared intensely about the emotional conditions that shaped a young man's confidence. He encouraged players to pursue conversations that had nothing to do with basketball. He introduced them to people across the city who would never appear in media reports—bartenders, shop owners, parish volunteers, retired factory workers who had watched the program through decades of quiet loyalty. These encounters grounded the players in a sense of place. They understood that their performances were not isolated episodes but threads woven into the fabric of Milwaukee's identity. McGuire knew that pride rooted in community becomes a stabilizing force during moments of doubt.

The Jesuit dimension of Marquette added another layer to this formation. The players encountered a university that took seriously the idea that intellect and character must grow together, that the court is an extension of one's internal life. They encountered professors who challenged them to think beyond their roles as athletes. They encountered chapels and classrooms that invited deliberation rather than compliance. This environment resonated with McGuire's own unconventional understanding of education. He believed that the point of college basketball was not simply to win games but to expand the imagination—to teach young men how to see themselves in fuller, deeper ways.

As seasons progressed, opponents began to describe Marquette in shifting terms. At first, they talked about the team's slipperiness—its refusal to play predictably. Soon they talked about its hard edge, its refusal to be intimidated. Eventually they spoke of a rising fear: Marquette was becoming the team no one wanted to face when the stakes were highest. Their style did not lend itself to easy preparation. They thrived in discomfort. They broke rhythm. They forced opponents into emotional terrain they were not accustomed to navigating.

Milwaukee saw these changes with a kind of swelling pride that surprised even longtime observers. The city, long shaped by modesty, began to imagine excellence not as an outsider's gift but as something fundamentally their own. People filled the old gym with an energy that felt different from the polite enthusiasm of earlier years. It was sharper, more urgent, more alive. They shouted with a sense of identification. They saw themselves in the grit and improvisation of the players. They recognized that the program had ceased to imitate others and had begun to express something authentically tied to the city's nature.

Yet the most compelling transformation was internal. The players had acquired something that could not be diagrammed or measured. It lived in the way they huddled after a failed possession, in the intensity of their eye contact during timeouts, in the composure with which they navigated pressure. They played with a belief that did not collapse when circumstances turned bleak. They had learned to trust the instability of the moment because their coach had taught them that clarity often arises from chaos. They no longer needed to know exactly how a game would unfold. They needed only to know that they could respond.

This evolution did not occur all at once. It arrived in flickers —moments of brilliance embedded in prolonged stretches of uncertainty. But each flicker carried the promise of something larger. Something was coalescing around McGuire's vision, taking shape slowly but unmistakably. The early years of searching, improvisation, and emotional recalibration were giving way to a period of rising coherence. The team had not yet reached its pinnacle, but the trajectory had become undeniable.

Marquette basketball was no longer searching for identity. It was beginning to carry one—raw, bold, and unmistakably its own.

The late 1960s at Marquette marked the moment when Al McGuire's vision crossed from possibility into inevitability, a period when the disparate threads he had gathered— street instincts from New York, working-class resilience from Milwaukee, Jesuit formation from the university's soul—began to weave themselves into a coherent force. What separated these years from the early period of searching was not simply an increase in talent, though the roster unquestionably deepened, but the emergence of a shared internal logic, a way of playing and being that the players understood without needing language. The team's identity no longer flickered; it glowed.

Winning followed, but the wins were not the cause. They were the residue of a culture that had sharpened itself through confrontation, self-knowledge, and McGuire's relentless insistence that the game must be played with joy as well as with ferocity. Marquette did not win politely. They won with improvisational energy, emotional depth, and a capacity to disrupt opponents by refusing the patterns that college basketball relied upon. The city, once cautious in its expectations, embraced the program with a fervor that startled longtime residents. Milwaukee had always supported its teams, but now the support carried the edge of recognition —this team, these players, this coach felt like the city's own expression.

What distinguished McGuire's teams during this era was a peculiar mixture of discipline and rebellion. Their practices were tightly structured, yet their games unfolded with the looseness of street performance. Players took risks that other programs discouraged. They made passes that defied convention. They celebrated small victories with laughter that suggested an intimacy forged through shared struggle. Yet beneath the surface playfulness lived an unyielding commitment to one another, a refusal to fracture under pressure. This balance—between order and unpredictability, between rigor and joy—became the signature of Marquette basketball.

As the team's profile grew nationally, McGuire remained the central interpreter of its meaning. He understood that success can disorient a program as surely as failure, and he approached each season with a heightened sense of emotional calibration. He knew which players needed grounding as attention increased. He knew which players needed freedom as expectations tightened. He knew when to speak publicly and when to retreat into silence. His relationship with the city evolved alongside the team's rise. Milwaukee, once skeptical of his theatricality, now understood it as part of his method. They saw the tenderness that lived beneath the bravado, the discernment that informed every gesture, the seriousness that shaped every risk he took.

One of the defining features of this period was the diversity of personalities within the locker room. McGuire had built a roster composed of players from different regions, races, temperaments, and emotional histories. Some had grown up navigating the complexities of urban neighborhoods; others came from quieter towns shaped by family, faith, and predictability. The friction between these worlds did not dissolve under McGuire—it became productive. He believed that the strongest teams learned to hold tension without splitting. Practices sometimes erupted into arguments, shoving matches, or long silences in which players confronted realities they had previously avoided. But these moments rarely festered. McGuire intervened when necessary, but more often he allowed the players to work through discord themselves, trusting that conflict transformed into unity carries greater strength than unity achieved through avoidance.

The city watched this cultural alchemy with fascination. Games drew larger crowds. Tavern conversations shifted from cautious analysis to imaginative projection. People no longer asked whether Marquette could compete at a national level; they debated how far the team could go and what style of opponent best suited their strengths. Milwaukee, with its ethnic enclaves and industrial certainty, now saw in the program a possibility that had previously belonged only to baseball diamonds in summer or football fields on crisp autumn afternoons. Basketball—urban, expressive, emotionally immediate—had become the city's winter heartbeat.

National opponents began to speak of Marquette with a mix of admiration and dread. They lamented how difficult it was to prepare for a team that changed tempo, strategy, and emotional tenor from possession to possession. They remarked on the relentlessness of Marquette's defense, the audacity of its offense, and the intensity of its cohesion. Coaches muttered about how McGuire had built a system they couldn't diagram, one that lived in the instincts of his players rather than on chalkboards. The unpredictability was not chaos; it was design. It was basketball shaped by a man who believed that a program must become a reflection of its city's pulse rather than an imitation of the national powers.

These years also revealed the moral stakes of McGuire's leadership. He understood that young men's lives do not pause for the sake of sport. Players confronted academic pressures, family crises, racial tensions, and personal insecurities that threatened to disrupt the fragile balance of their formation. McGuire did not pretend to solve these problems, but he created space where they could be acknowledged without shame. He encouraged players to think, to question, to challenge authority—including his own. He insisted that manhood was not measured by stoicism but by self-awareness. In this sense, his coaching aligned with the deeper ethos of Marquette's Jesuit identity: the pursuit of understanding, the cultivation of conscience, the willingness to engage life's contradictions directly.

By the close of the decade, it was clear that McGuire had wrought something remarkable. Marquette had become a program with gravitational pull. Recruits who once looked elsewhere now felt drawn to the style, the energy, and the unpredictability of McGuire's teams. Fans embraced the program not only because it won, but because it won with a kind of personality that made victory feel like a shared creation. The team had become a civic symbol, a point of pride that crossed racial, economic, and generational lines. In a city that often fractured along those boundaries, Marquette basketball offered a space of unlikely cohesion.

Yet the true magnitude of the transformation could be seen only from within. The players sensed it most keenly. They felt themselves part of a story larger than any individual statistic or accolade. They experienced the strange exhilaration of belonging to a team that had become a cultural force. They recognized that McGuire had taught them more than basketball. He had taught them how to read a room, how to confront fear, how to trust their instincts, how to think with their hearts and feel with their minds. These lessons followed them beyond the gym, shaping how they carried themselves through the uncertainties of adulthood.

The era was approaching a threshold. The elements of greatness had gathered—the talent, the chemistry, the imagination, the city's rising belief. The program had grown not only in confidence but in purpose. Marquette no longer sought to prove itself; it sought to express itself fully. What came next would not be an accident of luck or a brief moment of overachievement. It would be the culmination of years spent forging identity through discomfort, ambition, and the delicate art of emotional calibration.

The horizon had begun to brighten.

Marquette basketball stood on the verge of becoming a national power.

And Al McGuire, restless, perceptive, and brilliant in his unorthodox way, held the program's future in his hands with the same ease and gravity with which he once read the scuffed shoes of strangers on the streets of Queens.

Night fell lightly over Milwaukee on an evening when the gym sat empty, its quiet carrying the residue of seasons that had reshaped not only a program but the emotional vocabulary of a city. The lights had been turned off hours earlier, yet the faint reflection of streetlamps filtered through the high windows and settled onto the floor like a memory refusing to dissipate. In that dim glow, it was possible to see the imprint of everything that had unfolded during Al McGuire's early years —the drills that hardened resolve, the quarrels that clarified loyalty, the risks that taught creativity, the laughter that punctured tension. The silence did not feel like an absence. It felt like a presence holding its breath.

Outside, the night air carried the familiar mix of lake wind and industrial residue, a scent that defined Milwaukee long before basketball had risen to its winter prominence. Students walked past the gym in small clusters, their conversations drifting upward in fragments—talk of exams, families, futures, and always, somewhere beneath the surface, the team. Their voices carried a quiet confidence, the kind that comes not from championships but from proximity to something that matters. Marquette basketball had become part of how they recognized themselves. Its unpredictability, its grit, its flashes of brilliance mirrored the contradictions of the city that cradled it.

In apartments and taverns, older residents felt that same shift. Some had watched the program long enough to remember its years of modest identity. Others had drifted into fandom recently, drawn by the charismatic unpredictability of McGuire's teams. What bound them together was the growing sense that Marquette had ceased to apologize for its ambitions. The city had begun to see itself through the prism of a program that played with a blend of defiance and joy that felt distinctly local. This recognition ran deeper than wins and losses. It touched something elemental—a desire to believe that a place shaped by labor, faith, migration, and resilience could produce a style of basketball that felt both unlikely and inevitable.

Inside the gym, the darkness thickened. And yet, even without players or coaches present, the space carried the unmistakable echo of McGuire's presence. He had walked these sidelines with a peculiar mix of restlessness and ease, pacing like a man listening to a song others could not hear. He had stopped drills midstream to name a truth that reached deeper than strategy. He had turned games into conversations, conversations into lessons, lessons into turning points. He had taught his players to see pressure not as danger but as invitation. He had taught the city to see improvisation not as recklessness but as art.

What lingered in the empty gym was not nostalgia but anticipation. The identity McGuire had forged was still forming. It lived in the instincts of players who had learned to trust themselves; in the posture of fans who now believed that possibility belonged to them; in the subtle recalibration of a university that had learned that excellence need not mimic anything but its own nature. The program had not yet reached its pinnacle, but it had crossed the threshold that separates the ordinary from the inevitable.

Somewhere in the distance, a freight train sounded its horn as it moved through the industrial corridors of the city. Its low, unhurried tone blended with the hum of passing cars and the faint rustle of wind against the gym's exterior. The city was awake even in its quiet moments, carrying the contradictions that had always defined it—steady yet longing, grounded yet restless, humble yet hungry. Marquette basketball had begun to embody these contradictions with increasing fidelity, becoming not just a team but a mirror.

The court itself, though unlit, held this truth with serene certainty. It had watched players arrive uncertain and leave transformed. It had borne witness to arguments that deepened trust and to celebrations that deepened humility. It had absorbed the weight of McGuire's improvisational genius and offered it back in the form of a style that could not have emerged anywhere else. In the silence, the floor seemed almost to breathe, as though preparing for the next surge of footsteps, the next burst of laughter, the next moment when instinct and identity fused into something unmistakably Marquette.

At this threshold, the future felt both suspended and imminent. The foundations had been laid, the culture established, the imagination awakened. McGuire had given the program more than a system—he had given it a soul. And that soul, restless and luminous, waited now in the darkness with the patience of something that knows its time is coming.

The city would sleep. The gym would remain still. But the program had already begun its ascent.

What lay ahead was no longer a question of whether Marquette could rise. It was only a question of how high.

CHAPTER FOUR – THE 1970S AND THE CITY'S GOLDEN ERA

"You build a program by knowing who you are before anyone else does."
— Al McGuire

The 1970s arrived in Milwaukee with a complicated blend of confidence and uncertainty, the kind of civic mood that emerges when a city stands between the industrial solidity of its past and the shifting economic winds of its future. Factories along the Menomonee Valley still roared with the familiar cadence of production, but hints of contraction had begun to flicker at the edges of the skyline. Neighborhoods anchored by parish life remained vibrant, yet demographic tremors suggested that the ethnic enclaves built over generations would soon begin to loosen. The decade did not arrive with rupture; it arrived with a quiet atmospheric change, a subtle recalibration of what the city believed about itself. In that environment—neither declining nor ascendant, but suspended between identities—Marquette basketball began to crystallize into something larger than a sports program. It became a lens through which Milwaukee could negotiate who it had been and who it might become.

The university stood at a similar crossroads. Marquette, founded in 1881 as a Jesuit institution meant to serve the children of immigrants, had spent decades cultivating an identity rooted in accessibility, rigor, and moral seriousness.

By the early 1970s, the campus reflected the tensions of the era: a student body shaped by postwar expansion, an academic culture pulled between tradition and reform, and an athletic department that still operated in the shadow of larger, wealthier programs to the south and east. What distinguished Marquette was not prestige but purpose. Its mission remained grounded in the Jesuit conviction that education must attend to the whole person, that discernment is not reserved for theology, and that ambition must be paired with conscience. This atmosphere, more than any individual figure or event, shaped the sensibility that would define the basketball program in the decade ahead.

By 1970, Al McGuire had already begun to turn the program into a national presence, though the full extent of his influence remained invisible to outsiders. McGuire arrived in 1964, carrying with him an unconventional mix of street wisdom, psychological acuity, and a temperament that seemed allergic to the tidy logic of conventional coaching philosophies. He taught through metaphor, mood, contradiction, and disruption. His practices could swing from contemplative stillness to eruptions of laughter to sudden flares of strategic insight. And yet beneath the volatility, he possessed a coherent vision: Marquette would not imitate the blue-blood powers; it would become something the sport had no language for yet. He built a recruiting philosophy that favored instincts over résumés, desire over polish, players who understood—because life had taught them—that pressure reveals authenticity. He sought men who had survived enough to trust their instincts and were humble enough to accept the discipline required to refine them.

This approach began to yield visible results in the early years of the decade. The arrival of players like Jim Chones, whose dominance in the 1971–72 season forced opponents to reconsider Marquette's place in the national hierarchy, signaled that the program was no longer merely rising; it was reshaping the landscape. Chones combined size, agility, and instinct in a way that made him nearly unguardable, and his midseason departure to the New York Nets of the ABA only intensified the nation's fascination. The episode crystallized the complexity of Marquette's ascent: the program was strong enough to produce a professional-caliber star, yet not cloaked in the dynastic insulation that protected blue-blood teams from such disruptions. Chones's departure did not collapse the program; it revealed the depth of what McGuire had been building. A team that could withstand the loss of its center and still compete at the highest level possessed something sturdier than talent. It possessed identity.

As the decade progressed, this identity became inseparable from the city's imagination. Milwaukee, long overshadowed by Chicago, Detroit, and the industrial giants of the Midwest, found in Marquette a symbol of possibility. The program was small enough to feel intimate yet powerful enough to command national attention. It reflected the city's working-class sensibility—its unpretentiousness, its toughness, its capacity for surprise. Bars on Mitchell Street and in Riverwest turned game nights into communal rituals; parish halls echoed with the static hum of transistor radios; neighborhoods that otherwise shared little found common language in the rhythms of the team. McGuire, with his unpredictable charm, became not only a coach but a civic figure—someone who seemed to understand Milwaukee's contradictions and translate them into the grammar of basketball.

The success of the early 1970s, particularly the 1974 run to the NCAA championship game, deepened this connection. The team that season moved with a blend of confidence and improvisational agility that captured the country's attention. Led by players like Maurice Lucas, Earl Tatum, Marcus Washington, and Lloyd Walton, the 1973–74 Warriors played with an energy that made every game feel like a negotiation with destiny. The win over Kansas in the regional final, a performance defined by poise under pressure, demonstrated that Marquette had developed a vocabulary capable of standing alongside the sport's established languages. Their appearance in the championship game against North Carolina State, though ending in defeat, marked a turning point. Marquette had crossed from outsider to contender—not by adopting the style of dynastic programs but by revealing that a program built on instinct and discernment could challenge the sport's architecture.

The loss did not diminish the city's pride; it intensified it. Milwaukee, still negotiating its own identity in a decade marked by cultural transition, embraced the team not as an almost-champion but as a symbol of its own capacity for transformation. The program's subsequent years reinforced this relationship. Bo Ellis arrived in 1973 and brought with him not only talent but a sense of artistry that complemented the city's evolving cultural self-understanding. Ellis, a graduate of Chicago's Parker High School, embodied the blend of discipline and imagination that McGuire valued. His presence, alongside players like Earl Tatum and Lloyd Walton, helped elevate Marquette into a consistent national force, appearing regularly in the NCAA tournament and sustaining national rankings.

Yet what defined the Golden Era was not a march toward inevitability but a complicated dance with proximity. Marquette had become a program that could beat anyone, but the nation did not consider it one of the great houses. The blue-blood hierarchy—UCLA's dynasty, Kentucky's lineage, North Carolina's precision—remained intact. Marquette was respected, feared even, but not crowned. This ambiguity created emotional and psychological tension within the city and the program. Each year brought deep runs, electrifying performances, and growing recognition, yet each year ended with the same underlying truth: Marquette was close enough to the center of the sport to feel the heat, but still outside the circle of those institutions that the country assumed were born to inherit championships.

McGuire understood the significance of this liminal position better than anyone. He knew that becoming extraordinary is not the same as being recognized as extraordinary. He knew that a program can carry excellence without being granted legitimacy by those who guard the gates of tradition. And he knew that Marquette could not rise to its full identity until the team learned to stop measuring itself against the dynasties and instead see itself as a force defined by its own nature. He had spent the decade preparing his players, the university, and the city for that shift in vision.

By 1976, the arc of the Golden Era had reached a point of maximum tension. The program was nationally prominent yet not crowned; the city was deeply invested yet still searching for a language to describe its relationship to the team. The stage was set for something larger, though no one could yet articulate the form it would take. The decade had shaped Marquette into a program of power, purpose, and resilience. It had constructed the architecture of identity.

But the coronation—the moment when identity becomes destiny—had not yet occurred. That would require a season marked not by emergence, but by revelation.

By the middle of the decade, Marquette's basketball program found itself inhabiting a paradox that only a few teams in the nation ever truly experience: it had become both a national presence and a national question. The program's record spoke clearly—winning seasons, high-profile victories, deep tournament runs—but the language surrounding it remained cautious, as if observers sensed something powerful emerging yet hesitated to name it. Writers praised the team's toughness and unpredictability but often framed those qualities as curiosities rather than the foundation of a lasting identity. They admired McGuire's eccentric brilliance while treating him as an outlier rather than an architect. The city saw it differently. Milwaukee had lived through enough transitions—economic, demographic, cultural—to recognize that a program can be misunderstood by those who rely too heavily on traditional markers of legitimacy. The city trusted what it saw on the court: a team that was sharpening itself through adversity and a coach who understood how to reveal the deeper structure of a player's instincts.

The arrival of Bo Ellis, Earl Tatum, and Lloyd Walton in the early 1970s signaled that the program had reached a new phase of maturity. These players did not merely continue the program's upward trajectory; they expanded its expressive range. Ellis brought an interior dignity that balanced McGuire's emotional volatility. Tatum added a physical and psychological edge that allowed Marquette to impose its style on opponents rather than merely react to them. Walton supplied steadiness at the point, a calm that grounded the team in tense moments and allowed McGuire's improvisational approach to retain coherence. Together, they formed the nucleus of a program that no longer defined itself by surprising opponents but by expecting to test their limits.

The 1973–74 season offered the clearest demonstration of what the program had become. Marquette navigated that year with a conviction that did not require fanfare to feel formidable. The team's run to the NCAA championship game unfolded against a national backdrop dominated by North Carolina State's growing power and UCLA's ongoing shadow, yet Marquette refused to be relegated to narrative footnote. Their semifinal win over Kansas, marked by an unyielding defensive posture and a refusal to cede tempo, signaled that the program had reached the point where it could bend the flow of games rather than adapt to them. Although the final against North Carolina State ended in disappointment, the loss did not diminish the resonance of what had occurred. It was the first moment when the nation realized that Marquette was not a charming outsider—McGuire's eccentric band of overachievers—but a team capable of contesting the center of power.

The significance of that season lingered long after the final buzzer. For the city, it became a reference point, the year Milwaukee felt itself reflected on a national stage with a fidelity that surprised many and reassured others. The program's identity was no longer tied to novelty; it was tied to persistence. People who had spent their whole lives navigating the complexities of the industrial Midwest recognized in the team a vocabulary of resilience that matched their own. They saw in the players a refusal to be defined by comparison to larger programs, and in McGuire a leader whose approach felt more like translation than coaching—a translation of the city's temperament into the language of sport.

What made the Golden Era distinctive was not simply the accumulation of wins but the coherence that began to shape the team's interior life. Marquette developed a style that defied easy categorization. It was not the structured precision of North Carolina, nor the bruising inevitability of Kentucky, nor the dynastic calm that still surrounded UCLA. It was not the flashy athleticism of Michigan or the emerging explosiveness of Louisville. Marquette's style was a fusion of intuition, improvisation, and intensity, held together by a kind of psychological awareness that McGuire nurtured but never articulated. The players learned to read games as unfolding human dramas rather than puzzles to be solved by sets and schemes. They learned to trust the moment rather than fear it, to recognize when a teammate needed space rather than instruction, and to inhabit tension without allowing it to erode their clarity.

This approach produced a series of seasons in which Marquette hovered near greatness, always within striking distance yet never fully embraced by the national hierarchy. They defeated the blue-bloods often enough to earn respect—upsetting Kentucky in 1972, challenging UCLA's aura in marquee matchups, outmaneuvering programs with more resources and deeper recruiting pipelines—but they did not receive the cultural validation that accompanies sustained dynastic success. Instead, they occupied a liminal space, a position that both empowered and frustrated the city. Milwaukee had long lived in the shadow of larger urban centers, and Marquette's position in college basketball mirrored this civic posture: respected but not central, admired but not crowned.

The city's relationship to the team deepened during this period precisely because of this tension. Milwaukee recognized the difficulty of being powerful enough to contend but peripheral enough to be dismissed. It understood what it meant to carry identity without institutional validation. It understood, too, the emotional and psychological toll of being repeatedly asked to prove oneself to audiences who did not fully see what was taking shape. As the team developed, the city watched with the kind of attentiveness that arises when people realize they are witnessing something unrepeatable.

By the mid-1970s, Marquette had effectively become a civic institution. The team's presence influenced the rhythm of the city's days in winter, drawing people together in taverns and living rooms, turning each game into an event that seemed to absorb Milwaukee's anxieties and transmute them into brief, electrifying clarity. The MECCA became the symbolic center of this transformation—a building that, with its angular geometry and experimental floor designed by Robert Indiana, encapsulated the program's blend of unpredictability and precision. The court, with its bright blocks of color and sharp delineations, forced players into heightened awareness; it turned the game into a choreography, a kind of ritual movement across a sacred plane.

Yet as Marquette continued to win, an unspoken truth began to emerge: the program's rise had reached a plateau. It was no longer the scrappy outsider capable of ambushing unsuspecting powers, nor was it the kind of institution that the national imagination instinctively placed among the elite. It was stuck between categories—too successful to be dismissed, too unconventional to be embraced. The Golden Era was thus characterized by a paradoxical blend of triumph and incompleteness. The team had achieved national recognition, but not national inheritance. It had established identity, but not legitimacy in the eyes of the sport's gatekeepers. It had become powerful, but not yet mythic.

This liminal position set the stage for the emotional and historical pivot that would define the program. Marquette stood at the edge of possibility without being permitted to step through it. The city sensed that the Golden Era had reached its natural limit, that the program had done everything a team could realistically do without crossing the final threshold. People felt a mixture of pride and hunger—pride in what had been built, hunger for the one thing that remained unattained and perhaps unattainable: a national championship.

What the city and program did not yet know was that the barrier between almost and fully would soon narrow. The Golden Era had created the architecture of identity; the next season would test whether identity could become destiny.

By 1975 and 1976, Marquette basketball had entered a phase that could only be described as structural maturity. The program had accumulated enough experience, talent, and national exposure to operate with the confidence of a team that belonged on the biggest stages, yet it continued to navigate the psychological friction of remaining outside the sport's aristocracy. The decade had sharpened the team's instincts, expanded its tactical vocabulary, and deepened its resilience—but the broader world of college basketball still treated Marquette as an anomaly rather than an heir. This tension shaped the program's internal evolution in ways that were both subtle and profound.

During these two seasons, the team's identity depended increasingly on its capacity to dominate moments without needing to dominate narratives. The players had learned that results mattered more than recognition, that the path to legitimacy would not be granted through reputation but earned through persistence. The nation admired stars like Phil Ford, Walter Davis, and Adrian Dantley, whose performances animated the stories writers loved to tell about power, grace, and inevitability. Meanwhile, Marquette's roster—though filled with capable and charismatic athletes—did not command the same kind of attention. Even Butch Lee, who would become one of the most consequential figures in the sport, was still viewed as a brilliant curiosity rather than an emerging national centerpiece. This dynamic only strengthened the program's resolve. The players came to understand that they would need to bring the weight of their identity into every contest, that legitimacy in their case would not be conferred but contested.

McGuire sensed this shift more acutely than anyone. By the middle of the decade, he had grown increasingly attuned to the emotional landscape of his team and the psychological architecture of the sport. He recognized that Marquette's ascent had reached a point where external narratives posed as much of a threat as opposing defenses. The program needed an interior structure that could withstand the pressures of being almost, nearly, on the verge, yet perpetually framed as incomplete. Achieving that interior structure required the team to stop measuring itself against the dynasties and begin measuring itself against its own standards. This was not a matter of arrogance; it was a matter of survival.

The 1975–76 season provided a crucible for this transformation. The team posted a sterling record, demonstrating its ability to impose its will on opponents with a blend of defensive ferocity, disciplined improvisation, and timely scoring. But the tournament loss to Indiana—

who completed an undefeated season under Bob Knight—reinforced the national hierarchy. Indiana's roster featured Scott May, Quinn Buckner, Kent Benson—names that evoked the aura of inevitability. Their perfect record placed them inside the rare category of teams not merely good but destined. Marquette, despite its accomplishments, remained in the remarkably narrow space reserved for programs that are feared by opponents yet not fully trusted by the national imagination.

The loss sharpened something essential in the team's psyche. Instead of internalizing defeat, the players internalized clarity: they understood that they had become good enough to contend but not yet formed enough to overcome the gravitational pull of a program operating with dynastic confidence. Indiana did not beat Marquette solely through talent; it beat them through a kind of institutional completeness. For Marquette, that recognition became the catalyst for the next evolution of its identity. The team realized that greatness was no longer a question of capability but of coherence—of unifying instinct, discipline, and interior composure into a force strong enough to resist the aura of national powers.

At the same time, the city's relationship to the team deepened into something more intergenerational. Families who had first watched Marquette in the early 1960s now attended games with their children, narrating the history of the program in living rooms and car rides and bleacher seats. Bars that once hosted casual gatherings on game nights transformed into small sanctuaries for shared ritual. Priests mentioned the Warriors in homilies—not as distractions from spiritual life but as extensions of it, moments in which community, identity, and collective hope found expression beyond walls of worship. Marquette basketball had become a cultural grammar through which the city described itself.

This shift in civic consciousness had profound implications

for the program. The players began to understand their role not only as athletes but as carriers of the city's narrative. They represented a working-class community negotiating the changing industrial landscape of the Midwest. They represented families whose identity depended on effort rather than lineage. They represented a university whose Jesuit tradition insisted that greatness lies in discernment, intention, and attention to the deeper meaning of human endeavor. These insights did not translate into speeches or slogans; they translated into posture. The team played with the gravity of men who understood they represented more than themselves.

Meanwhile, nationally, the sport was in the midst of transformation. Television coverage grew more sophisticated, talent pipelines expanded, and recruiting battles became more intense. Programs like North Carolina, Kentucky, and Michigan continued to attract players with the kind of star power that shaped national narratives. In this environment, Marquette's standing remained precarious. The team had the talent to compete with insiders but not the cultural pedigree to be treated as one. Their margin for error was thinner than that of almost any contender. They needed to be excellent—always, consistently, visibly. The slightest lapse could return them to the margins.

And yet, the frictions of this period served an essential function: they hardened the program's interior life. The team learned to move past disappointment with a kind of disciplined humility. They studied their failures not as indictments but as invitations to understand where their identity required deepening. Practices became sites of psychological refinement as much as physical preparation. Players began to hold each other accountable in ways that transcended tactical alignment; they learned to read one another's moods, to anticipate the emotional temperature of the locker room, to intervene when someone's confidence wavered or when frustration threatened cohesion. They learned that success was not the product of moments but of accumulated intention.

By the end of 1976, Marquette had achieved something extraordinary even if the nation did not fully appreciate it: the program had constructed an interior foundation strong enough to bear the weight of destiny. The team no longer needed external validation to understand its potential. The city no longer required national recognition to understand what it had witnessed. The university no longer questioned whether it could sustain excellence without the inheritance of tradition.

The Golden Era had reached its apex. What had begun as emergence had solidified into identity. What had been built through improvisation had been refined into coherence. What had once been episodic brilliance had become durable character.

The program stood, unknowingly, on the threshold of the season that would test—and reveal—the fullness of what the decade had created. The ascent of the 1970s had done everything it could do. It had brought Marquette to the doorway. Only one thing remained: to see whether they were ready to walk through it.

By the time the 1976–77 season approached, Marquette found itself in a rare and unstable position: it had become a program defined not by deficiency but by unfulfilled potential. The Golden Era had yielded victories, national rankings, tournament runs, and a style that captivated the city and unsettled opponents. Yet it had not produced the one achievement that transforms presence into permanence. The question surrounding Marquette was not whether the program was excellent—it clearly was—but whether it belonged among the teams whose excellence carried the force of inevitability. Programs like North Carolina, Kentucky, and Michigan operated with the inherited authority that comes from decades of sustained dominance. Their names signaled legitimacy; their identities were tethered to tradition. Marquette, by contrast, existed in a space both enviable and precarious: powerful enough to compete with the elite, but not established enough to be counted among them.

The internal tension of this position shaped the psychology of the team as the 1976–77 season began. Al McGuire's announcement that he would retire at the end of the year sharpened this tension further. His departure was not merely the end of a coaching career; it was the conclusion of a particular way of understanding the game. McGuire coached players as complex human beings rather than as instruments of strategy. He navigated the emotional terrain of a season with a mixture of sensitivity and mischief that defied the standardized language of modern coaching. His practices could resemble theatrical performances—moments of levity, provocation, and intensity woven together in ways that made players confront themselves as much as their opponents. His farewell cast a new light over everything. It made every decision, every possession, every misstep feel heavier, more consequential, as though the season were not merely unfolding but being inscribed.

The players responded to this weight with a seriousness that revealed how deeply their identity had matured over the preceding years. Butch Lee, entering his junior season, understood that his role had shifted. He was no longer the brilliant catalyst whose instincts could alter the trajectory of a game; he had become the team's interior compass. His ability to read defenses, manipulate tempo, and absorb pressure placed him among the most dynamic guards in the country, yet he did not ground his leadership in visibility. He grounded it in resonance. His teammates responded to the confidence in his movements, to the way he inhabited games rather than merely directing them.

Bo Ellis, now a senior, embodied the continuity of the Golden Era. His presence linked the program's earlier identity to its emerging self-understanding. Ellis carried the discipline of someone who had lived through seasons defined by both ascension and frustration. He knew what it meant to play alongside stars like Maurice Lucas and Earl Tatum; he knew the emotional cost of deep tournament runs; he understood the quiet ache of seasons that end one step short of transformation. His leadership in 1976–77 carried an almost pastoral quality—a steadying influence that held the team's emotional temperature in balance.

Jerome Whitehead, whose height and timing made him the axis around which the team's interior defense rotated, entered the season with a sense of heightened expectation. He had always been essential to the program's success, but the departure of earlier stars meant that his role now carried a symbolic weight. He needed to be not only a physical presence but an organizing one. His ability to alter shots, control rebounds, and anchor the team's posture would dictate whether Marquette could compete against the imposing frontcourts of teams like Kentucky and Michigan.

The supporting cast—Lloyd Walton, Ulice Payne, Bernard Toone, and the reserve corps—provided the connective tissue that allowed the team to operate as a unified organism. Their contributions often escaped national notice, but they were essential to the program's transition from a team defined by talent to a team defined by cohesion. As the season approached, practices revealed a depth of communication that had not been present in earlier years. Players anticipated each other's movements, absorbed emotional shifts without losing structural integrity, and responded to setbacks with a kind of quiet alertness that suggested the emergence of an interior readiness.

Outside the program, the national landscape of college basketball continued to reinforce the sport's hierarchical logic.

North Carolina, with Phil Ford orchestrating the offense and Dean Smith perfecting the Four Corners strategy, entered the season as a model of disciplined excellence. Michigan, led by the blistering speed of Ricky Green and the durability of Phil Hubbard, remained a formidable opponent capable of overwhelming teams with athleticism. Kentucky, always a force, brought a roster anchored by Jack Givens and Rick Robey, whose physicality and experience made the Wildcats a perennial championship contender. Programs like Louisville and Arkansas hovered at the edge of prominence, carrying their own surges of momentum and emerging stars.

Against this backdrop, Marquette occupied an uncertain position in the national imagination. The team received preseason attention—not as heirs to a title, but as a program worth watching in McGuire's final season. Analysts noted the emotional stakes of the year but hesitated to place the Warriors alongside the presumed elite. They acknowledged Marquette's history of upsets and deep runs, yet framed them as exceptions rather than evidence of an identity strong enough to generate a championship. This disparity between capability and perception shaped the psychological atmosphere of the season's early weeks.

The first games of the year revealed a team that had internalized the urgency of the moment without succumbing to its pressure. Marquette opened the season with the controlled ferocity that had defined the Golden Era, yet the movements felt different—more deliberate, more unified, more attuned to the flow of each contest. The players carried themselves with a sense of grounded purpose, as if the weight of McGuire's final season had not burdened them but steadied them. The city sensed this shift immediately. Milwaukee, accustomed to reading emotional subtext in its sports teams, recognized that this season was not merely another chapter in the program's rise. It was the pivot on which the decade would turn.

As the season progressed, the tension between expectation and reality grew. The team encountered setbacks, moments when the weight of the year threatened to distort their clarity. But each time, the program responded not with panic but with recalibration. McGuire, sensing the emotional residue left by each stumble, adjusted the psychological tone of practices. Sometimes he tightened discipline; other times he loosened the mood. He seemed to understand that the season would require not only tactical adjustments but a profound interior equilibrium.

By January, Marquette had become a team defined by contradiction: at once calm and urgent, disciplined and improvisational, aware of the stakes and yet unburdened by them. The Golden Era had produced many strong teams, but none had carried themselves with this balance. The city felt it in the air. Something was gathering—a convergence of identity, depth, experience, and emotional insight. The program that had spent years oscillating between emergence and uncertainty was beginning to sense the outline of a new possibility.

But possibility alone was not enough. To cross the threshold that had eluded them for years, Marquette needed something more than talent or cohesion. It needed the moment—the crystallizing season in which identity becomes destiny. And though no one could yet name it, that moment was approaching.

Through the winter of 1977, Marquette's season gathered a momentum that did not resemble the arcs of dynastic programs, which often dominated opponents with the aura of inheritance. Instead, Marquette moved with the steadiness of a team that had internalized something quieter and more enduring. They were not chasing inevitability; they were shaping readiness. Every game seemed to refine them further, as if the team were being distilled into its essential form. Players spoke less often in terms of goals and more in terms of recognition—recognition of what they could be when fully aligned, recognition of what the decade had prepared them to become, recognition of the difference between performing well and inhabiting identity. The Golden Era had brought them to the threshold; this season was teaching them how to cross it.

The shift was visible even in the team's smallest gestures. Timeouts unfolded with a clarity absent in earlier years. Conversations among players took on a tone that suggested awareness rather than anxiety. They no longer spoke about proving themselves to the nation; they spoke about meeting the standards the program had cultivated over the years. Practices, which had always contained McGuire's trademark unpredictability, grew steadier in rhythm. The players, once receptive primarily to his emotional cues, now generated their own internal compass. The program had reached the point where its identity no longer depended solely on the coach's personality; it had become a shared inheritance.

The city recognized this evolution long before the national press did. Milwaukee, with its sensitivity to the emotional weather of its institutions, sensed that the team had developed a newfound interior balance. Conversations in taverns along the South Side shifted from conditional optimism—"They might make another run"—to something closer to conviction —"This team is different." People remembered the near-misses of earlier years, but they did not dwell on them. They understood the psychological difference between a team that hopes it can win and a team that knows it can. Marquette's presence on the court radiated the latter.

Meanwhile, the national imagination continued to orbit the gravitational pull of the blue-blood programs. North Carolina, anchored by Phil Ford's command of the offense and Dean Smith's reputation for tactical brilliance, seemed poised to assume its rightful place atop the sport. Michigan, with Ricky Green slicing through defenses and Phil Hubbard controlling the interior, carried the athleticism and depth that had fueled its recent success. Kentucky, with the poise of Jack Givens and the physical authority of Rick Robey, represented the institutional confidence the sport had long treated as championship material. Louisville and Arkansas, rising behind stars like Darrell Griffith and the Triplets—Marvin Delph, Ron Brewer, and Sidney Moncrief—added further layers of complexity to an already crowded hierarchy.

In this environment, Marquette continued to occupy an ambiguous position. Analysts acknowledged the emotional resonance of McGuire's final season but hesitated to attach championship expectations to a program whose legitimacy they still viewed as conditional. The narrative surrounding the team oscillated between admiration and skepticism. Writers spoke of Marquette as dangerous, but they stopped short of labeling the team as destined. Their language revealed the persistent bias of the era: championships were understood to belong to programs with lineage, not to those who had built their identity through improvisation, resilience, and discernment.

Yet as the season progressed, it became increasingly clear that the national lens was misreading Marquette's transformation. The team was not seeking to break into the dynasty-dominated hierarchy; it was constructing an identity that operated outside that hierarchy altogether. Their strength did not depend on star power—though Lee, Ellis, and Whitehead provided more than enough. Their strength lay in the interior cohesion forged through years of pressure, disappointment, and a coach who taught them to see themselves without deference.

That interior cohesion revealed itself most fully in moments of adversity. Early-season losses that might once have threatened the team's balance instead served as catalysts for refinement. Tight games against regional rivals sharpened their late-clock execution. Road environments that once shook the team emotionally now clarified their sense of purpose. Even in victory, the players refused to be seduced by margin or spectacle; they focused on the quality of their decisions, the clarity of their communication, and their ability to maintain identity under duress.

McGuire, sensing this maturation, adjusted his coaching accordingly. He intervened less frequently in moments of tension and allowed the players to direct themselves. He trusted their instincts, not because he wished to recede but because the program had reached the point where leadership had become distributed. The team no longer relied on McGuire's emotional intelligence to navigate uncertainty; it had developed its own emotional vocabulary, rooted in the shared experiences of the decade.

By February, it became clear that the team had crossed an invisible threshold. They were no longer simply advancing through the season; they were preparing themselves for something singular. Their movements suggested a recognition that the Golden Era had not been an end in itself but a prolonged formation. The team played with the composure of men who had spent years honing the habits of attention, resistance, and self-understanding. They knew what pressure felt like, and they no longer feared it. They had learned that pressure was not the sign of impending collapse but the signal of opportunity.

The final weeks of the regular season revealed a team that understood its moment. They entered games with a presence that suggested the culmination of something long in the making. Their pace was measured, their spacing purposeful, their defensive posture suffused with the steadiness of players who understood the symbolic weight of their movements. Losses did not derail them; victories did not inflate them. The identity they carried was not fragile; it was anchored.

Through it all, Milwaukee remained the quiet, pulsing center of the program's emotional life. The city had followed the team through the rise of the Golden Era, through the beauty and disappointment of 1974, through the plateau that tested patience and faith. Now, as winter deepened and the season's horizon approached, the city sensed that the threshold was finally within reach. People did not speak of destiny; that language belonged to the dynasties. They spoke instead of readiness. They recognized in this team a completeness that earlier Marquette teams had not possessed. The Golden Era had taught the program who it was. This season was teaching it what it could become.

One truth lingered beneath every practice, every game, every quiet walk across campus: the work of the decade had brought Marquette to the doorway, but only the season ahead would reveal whether they could step through it.

When the regular season finally stilled and the air around Milwaukee took on that particular late-winter brightness —hard light on frozen pavement, long shadows crossing Wisconsin Avenue—Marquette found itself standing at a threshold that had been a decade in the making. Nothing outward had changed. Students still hurried between classes with collars pulled tight against the cold. Buses still hissed at the curb outside the MECCA. The city's factories continued their patient, rhythmic work. Yet something in the atmosphere felt altered, as though an interior shift had quietly crystallized into presence. The Golden Era had not ended; it had completed its arc. And what remained was a sense of awaiting revelation.

Inside the MECCA, the court held that same expectant stillness that had defined the arena for years. The geometric brilliance of the floor—its angles, its color fields, its refusal to behave like any other playing surface—seemed to amplify the room's quiet. It was no longer simply the stage on which Marquette had constructed its identity. It had become the mirror the program used to examine itself. Anyone who stood at center court, long after practice had ended, could feel the texture of a decade pressing up through the paint: the exuberance of early ascents, the ache of near arrival, the weight of losses that taught more than victories, the subtle shifts in posture as the team grew into itself.

What defined this moment—what made it qualitatively different from the endings of previous seasons—was the absence of searching. The team no longer looked outward to locate its standing among giants. It no longer carried the hunger of a program desperate to be seen. The Golden Era had given Marquette a self that was neither borrowed nor comparative. The players walked through the locker room and onto the court with a quietness that did not resemble tension; it resembled certainty. They had endured enough to recognize when a team's movements were no longer fragmented by doubt. They had learned to read one another with an accuracy that had little to do with play diagrams and everything to do with recognition—a recognition of how far they had come and how complete they had become.

McGuire felt this shift with a kind of subdued wonder. His own departure hovered in the background like a truth he refused to sentimentalize, yet its presence shaped his perception of the team with unusual clarity. He had coached groups that were talented, groups that were brave, groups that could outlast opponents through sheer will. But this team was different —not because it was the most gifted or the most polished, but because it carried no residue of earlier eras. It was not burdened by imitation or expectation. It had been shaped by ten years of trial, improvisation, and refinement until its identity existed independently of him. That realization brought McGuire a solitude he did not resist. He knew the work of formation ends the moment the ones you've shaped no longer need you to interpret themselves.

Milwaukee, too, sensed the transition. The city had long viewed Marquette basketball as its emotional sounding board, but now the resonance felt deeper. The team no longer reflected the city's aspirations; it reflected its arrival at a new self-understanding. Milwaukee had spent decades negotiating its own identity within the Midwest—too industrious to be glamorous, too complex to be easily defined, too proud to ask for validation. Now, watching this team move with unforced assurance, the city recognized something familiar: the dignity of a community that has stopped explaining itself. The season had become a translation of Milwaukee's heart into athletic form.

The quiet days before the tournament unfolded like the pause between chapters in a long narrative, not because uncertainty hung in the air, but because the air carried the density of what had not yet been seen. The Golden Era had taught Marquette who it was. Now the program stood in the interval where identity prepares to meet its defining test. There was no bravado in the team's demeanor, no proclamations about legacy or destiny. There was only the steadiness of a group that understood that culmination requires stillness as much as fire.

No one needed to speak of championships. The language of crowns belonged to other programs, other narratives. What Marquette carried instead was a form of readiness that did not announce itself. It listened. It watched. It waited. The season that approached would not determine whether the program had succeeded; it would determine whether the story that had been forming for ten years had finally found its shape.

And as the city moved through the last cold evenings of February, and as the team stepped into practices that no longer felt like preparation but like deepening, the decade revealed the truth it had been building toward: everything necessary had been formed. Nothing essential remained unfinished.

Marquette had reached the doorway. The next season would decide whether it would walk through it.

CHAPTER FIVE – 1977 AND THE CORONATION OF A CATHOLIC IMAGINATION

"We weren't supposed to win. That's why we knew we could."
— Al McGuire

The winter of 1977 settled over Milwaukee with the kind of clarity that marks a turning point long before anyone recognizes it. Snow gathered in soft ridges along the curbs of Wisconsin Avenue, and the cold off Lake Michigan cut cleanly through the narrow streets around the Marquette campus, sharpening the air until it felt almost ceremonial. Students hurried past Gesu Church with collars pulled high, and inside local taverns along Wells Street, televisions flickered as the city leaned closer to the unfolding season, attentive yet cautious. Something unspoken was forming, not in the dramatic sense of revelation, but in the quieter way conviction tends to take shape—through repetition, endurance, and the accumulation of signs that only make sense in retrospect. This was not the atmosphere of a team riding momentum or seeking validation. It was the atmosphere of a program reaching the end of a long internal apprenticeship and stepping into its own mature presence.

Al McGuire entered the season with the unmistakable gravity of a man nearing farewell. His announcement that he would retire at year's end had rippled across Milwaukee in August of 1976, touching emotional chords that surprised even him. People felt more than nostalgia; they felt the weight of a decade defined by his unpredictable, intuitive command. McGuire never coached to prove a system or theory. He coached to reveal the interior truth of a team—to draw out instinct, heighten emotional intelligence, and teach players to trust themselves in moments when conventional wisdom collapsed. His presence was mercurial and magnetic, alternately mischievous and profound, but always grounded in an uncanny ability to see the person before the athlete. When he announced that this would be his final year, the program did not respond with panic. Instead, it steadied itself. The team understood that endings carry clarity, and clarity is a form of power.

The roster that entered the season was too experienced, too unified, too deeply formed by the contradictions of the 1970s to treat McGuire's departure as merely sentimental. Butch Lee had become the team's central intelligence—not in temperament, which remained quiet and searching, but in the way he read the geometry of the game. His ability to shift pace, diagnose defenses, and generate rhythm had elevated him to one of the most compelling guards in the country, though national recognition still lagged behind his performance. Bo Ellis, returning for his senior year, gave the team its axis of dignity. Years of tournament runs, near-misses, and high-pressure contests had engraved in him a kind of mature steadiness that balanced the team's improvisational tendencies. Jerome Whitehead supplied height, timing, and the presence needed to confront the giants of the national field—players like Phil Hubbard at Michigan or Rick Robey at Kentucky, whose reputations often preceded the teams they anchored.

Surrounding them were the essential figures whose work rarely reached headlines but defined the interior architecture of the team: Lloyd Walton with his economy of movement, Ulice Payne with his defensive sharpness, Gary Rosenberger and Bill Neary supplying the physical and emotional ballast needed to navigate the season's demands. This was not a roster built to dazzle with individual spectacle. It was a roster built to withstand and outlast. It had been shaped by years of confronting dynasties, absorbing lessons, and refining instincts. The psychological transformations of the Golden Era had produced a team that no longer reacted to pressure but inhabited it.

Nationally, however, the landscape of college basketball appeared indifferent to such internal developments. The sport remained dominated by a set of programs whose names carried gravitational force: North Carolina with Phil Ford directing the most elegant offense in the nation; Nevada-Las Vegas under Jerry Tarkanian, rising behind Reggie Theus's charisma and Eddie Owens's scoring; Kentucky with Jack Givens's midrange brilliance and Rick Robey's physical command; Michigan still humming with Ricky Green's quickness and Phil Hubbard's relentless interior strength; Arkansas ascending with the Triplets—Sidney Moncrief, Marvin Delph, and Ron Brewer—reshaping expectations in the Southwest Conference. These teams were not simply talented; they embodied the inherited structure of the sport. They represented the belief that championships belonged to programs whose reputations had already occupied the center of college basketball's imagination.

From the outside, Marquette seemed incapable of disturbing this orbit. The team had the talent to contend but not the pedigree to be counted among the favorites. Writers admired McGuire's final season narrative but treated it as story rather than prophecy. Some analysts suggested that Marquette would make a respectable showing in the tournament; others believed the emotional weight of McGuire's departure would hinder the team's performance. Few considered the possibility that this would be the year Marquette crossed the threshold that had eluded it for a decade.

But within Milwaukee, the mood was different. The city had

lived through enough contrasts—industrial might coupled with economic uncertainty, ethnic traditions layered over shifting demographics, civic pride bending under national indifference—to recognize when something was gathering beyond the surface. People sensed that the team moved with a new kind of interior coherence, a calm that did not resemble resignation but readiness. The city watched how the players communicated in games, how they reacted not only to success but to adversity, how they carried themselves during stretches of uneven play. They saw something they could not name but recognized all the same: a shift from aspiration to identity.

The season's early weeks did not unfold like the opening chapters of a destined campaign. There were tight games, defensive lapses, moments when offensive rhythm sputtered. But each struggle revealed a deepening interior balance. The team no longer fractured under tension; it adjusted. It no longer spiraled after missteps; it recalibrated. What decades of dynasties possessed through inheritance, Marquette had learned through years of contending from the margins: how to see pressure not as threat but as medium.

Meanwhile, McGuire's demeanor grew more serene as the season advanced. His volatility softened; his sideline outbursts, while still theatrical, felt less like eruptions and more like reminders of a familiar grammar. He seemed to trust the players in ways that went beyond tactical confidence. He trusted their formation. He trusted the way they understood one another. He trusted that the season would reveal what needed to be revealed without his interference. The man who had spent years shaping instincts now stepped back and allowed those instincts to breathe.

Across campus, and across the city, people began to sense that the year did not resemble any other. The Golden Era had produced teams that fought, improvised, surprised, and endured. But this team carried the calm of something finished, not yet displayed but already known. It was as though the decade had constructed the architecture of identity and the season had simply lit the interior of the structure, revealing a completeness that had been hidden in plain sight.

And so the first part of the 1977 season unfolded not as prelude but as awakening. The national hierarchy continued to hold, dynasties continued to loom, star power continued to draw the attention of broadcasters and writers. But for Marquette—for the players, the coach, the university, the city —the season began to whisper a different truth: they were no longer guests in the house of college basketball's elite.

They were able—finally, fully—to see themselves as belonging.

The early weeks of the 1977 season unfolded with a rhythm that felt strangely understated for a team carrying so much emotional weight. Marquette did not storm through its schedule with the dominance of a traditional contender, nor did it reveal the clean narrative arc that national writers often look for when sensing the ascent of a future champion. Instead, the team moved through a sequence of games marked by uneven performances, flashes of brilliance, and stretches of ordinary play. But beneath the surface, something deeper was aligning. The team was not sharpening toward spectacle; it was sharpening toward readiness.

This readiness did not announce itself in statistics or margins of victory. It appeared in the way the players responded to imperfection. In previous seasons, a sluggish first half or a defensive lapse might have cracked the team's composure. The weight of comparisons—to blue-blood programs, to established dynasties, to the expectations of a city hungry for more than proximity—often made the Warriors feel as though they were performing under inspection. But in 1977, missteps elicited no visible panic. The team no longer reacted as though the world were waiting to confirm its deficiencies. Instead, the players met adversity with a kind of internal quiet, the calm that comes from knowing that identity is not contingent on approval.

This psychological coherence expressed itself most clearly in the behavior of the team's core. Butch Lee, whose brilliance had sometimes carried the risk of overextension in prior years, now directed the offense with a graduated maturity. His movements had always been quick, but now they were measured; his drives had always been incisive, but now they were purposeful. He seemed less concerned with dazzling opponents than with reading the unfolding logic of each possession. This shift in sensibility made him one of the most dangerous guards in the country—not because he imposed himself on the game, but because he entered its interior with unsettling precision.

Bo Ellis, in his final season, became the team's stabilizing presence, not through flamboyant leadership but through a steady carriage that communicated composure. He had played in marquee games, had lost on stages where the stakes were enormous, had carried the emotional residue of seasons punctuated by near breakthroughs. Now, he played with a clarity that came from accepting the full arc of the program: the exhilaration, the disappointment, the effort, the waiting. His rebounding, passing, and defensive presence carried the shape of someone who no longer felt pulled between what might be and what had been. He existed fully in the present, and his steadiness seeped into the team's bloodstream.

Jerome Whitehead, who had often been viewed as the supporting figure behind Ellis and Lee, stepped into a broader expression of his game. His timing—long a quiet asset —became the centerpiece of Marquette's interior play. He contested shots not with desperation but with the confidence of someone who understood that the game often tilts on the smallest acts of anticipation. He rebounded as if guided by some deeper rhythm, meeting the ball at its apex with a sense of inevitability. His presence gave the team a dimension of solidity that allowed Marquette to confront the towering frontcourts it would soon encounter.

The rest of the roster—Payne, Walton, Toone, and the rotation players—provided the continuity that turned potential into function. They moved without hesitation, communicated without signals, and corrected small misalignments in rhythm that earlier teams might not have detected. Their presence created the kind of depth that does not appear in headlines but becomes indispensable in March.

Meanwhile, the national field took on a clarity that only heightened the improbability of Marquette's eventual place within it. North Carolina, orchestrated by Phil Ford's near-flawless command of tempo, seemed to glide toward the top of the rankings with the effortless security of a team rooted in lineage. Michigan, with Ricky Green's blistering speed and Phil Hubbard's relentless physicality, appeared ready to extend its established presence among the nation's elite. Kentucky's roster—stacked with seasoned players like Robey and Givens—moved through the season with the stability that marks a program accustomed to being treated as a perennial threat. Even UNLV, under the increasingly national spotlight that followed Reggie Theus's rising stardom, seemed destined to disrupt the established hierarchy.

Everywhere Marquette looked, the nation reinforced the assumption that the season belonged to others. Blue-blood programs did not simply expect to win; they were expected to win. Their names appeared in projections, analyses, and the casual speculation of sportswriters who relied on history as much as on present performance. It was not arrogance; it was habit—the long-standing belief that championships emerge from institutions whose power has already been woven into the sport's architecture.

Marquette responded to this environment not with defiance, but with indifference. The team did not measure itself against the presumed giants. It measured itself against its own coherence. Practices grew more focused as January deepened. Drills sharpened not because McGuire demanded intensity, but because the players recognized their own alignment and sought to deepen it. Mistakes no longer fragmented focus; they clarified it. Successes no longer inflated confidence; they grounded it.

This was the quiet transformation the national press could not see. Because Marquette did not dominate headlines or overwhelm opponents with spectacle, it remained easy to underestimate. But the city noticed what outsiders ignored. Fans sensed a shift in the language of the team's play—a tighter rotation, a steadier defensive posture, a sharper instinct for late-game execution. People who sat in the upper reaches of the MECCA, where the sound thickened and the angles of Indiana's court design sharpened the experience of the game, felt the change in their bones. Something in the team's behavior suggested a kind of interior completeness that had not been present even in the remarkable 1974 run.

And yet, the season remained imperfect in ways that obscured the deeper truth. Losses came. Flaws surfaced. There were games when Marquette looked less like a contender than a team caught between eras. But each moment of uncertainty seemed to refine rather than diminish them. The team did not require flawlessness. It required self-knowledge. The difference was subtle but decisive. Teams that depend on perfection collapse under its weight. Teams that depend on identity grow stronger through its challenge.

By late February, the quiet sharpened into something firmer. The players carried themselves differently—less like men pressing toward accomplishment and more like men who understood they stood on the threshold of inheritance. They were not arrogant. They were prepared. The city, too, sensed the approaching pivot. The season had not yet revealed its shape, but it had revealed its possibility. Marquette was no longer assembling itself. It was becoming visible.

What remained was to see whether visibility could withstand the light of March.

The 1977 NCAA Tournament began not with fanfare but with ambiguity. Marquette entered the bracket as an at-large team, seeded without the prestige afforded to the giants of the field. This was the era before the inflation of modern seeding conventions; reputations counted as much as results, and the country's blue-blood programs were treated with the presumption of ascendancy. North Carolina, Michigan, Kentucky, Arkansas—these were the names that defined the frame of national expectation. Marquette, by contrast, was positioned as a team capable of springing an upset but not of shaping the tournament's architecture. The narrative surrounding their place in the field reflected the lingering belief that their best years were behind them, that McGuire's departure signaled a conclusion rather than a culmination.

The first game, played on March 12, 1977, in Dayton, carried none of the theatrical weight that would later define the tournament's final weekend. Marquette faced Cincinnati, a program with a proud history but one that had not been part of the season's dominant conversations. The venue—a neutral Midwest setting, removed from the atmosphere of the MECCA—held a faint echo, as though the air still carried the residue of the season's uncertainties. Yet the unfamiliarity of the environment did not unsettle the Warriors. If anything, it seemed to intensify the interior calm they had been cultivating for months.

Cincinnati entered the game with an earnest confidence, aware that Marquette's reputation had softened in the eyes of the national press. But from the opening minutes, the truth that Milwaukee had sensed all winter began to reveal itself. Marquette played not with the tentative energy of a team trying to find its footing, but with the quiet command of one that had discovered how to inhabit its identity. Butch Lee dictated tempo with an authority that surprised even those who had followed his evolution closely. His drives were sharp, his midrange instinctive, and his passing displayed the vision of a player who had learned to see not simply movement, but intention. Cincinnati struggled to contain him, and when they shifted defensive attention toward the perimeter, Lee adapted, drawing defenders into narrow seams and creating space for Ellis and Whitehead.

Ellis, whose steadiness had anchored the team through the winter months, played with a poise that seemed to radiate from somewhere beyond the court. His rebounding provided the team with second possessions that Cincinnati could not afford to concede. His unselfish positioning opened lanes for teammates. His defensive presence layered the game with a quiet but imposing discipline. Whitehead, meanwhile, provided a vertical dimension that Cincinnati could not match. His timing—long the invisible advantage within Marquette's system—became visible with every contested rebound and altered shot.

The game remained competitive into the second half, but Marquette never fractured. Their movements—on defense, in transition, in half-court sets—carried a clarity that reflected months of accumulation: the refinement of habits, the tightening of communication, the merging of individual instincts into collective intelligence. When Cincinnati attempted to mount a late run, the Warriors responded not with urgency but with patience. They absorbed pressure without absorbing panic, an attribute that distinguished them from earlier iterations of the program.

The final minutes revealed something that had been building beneath the surface all season. Marquette did not close the game with explosion or spectacle. They closed it with composure. A late basket by Ellis, a controlled possession by Lee, a defensive rotation that smothered Cincinnati's final chance to reclaim momentum—each moment reinforced the sense that the team had entered the tournament not to survive but to reveal itself. Marquette advanced with a 66–51 victory, not flashy but decisive, the kind of win that gave analysts little material for headlines but gave opponents something more important: concern.

After the game, McGuire's demeanor struck many observers as unusually serene. Reporters searching for emotional sound bites found instead a man who viewed the win not as vindication but as verification. He spoke less about tactics and more about presence. He mentioned the team's maturity, their patience, the way they refused to become rattled. When asked whether he felt relieved to escape the opening round, he smiled with a subtlety that suggested private knowledge. "We're just getting started," he said. It was not bravado. It was recognition.

The city of Milwaukee felt that recognition, too, though fans experienced it at a distance. Watching the game from taverns along Bluemound Road or in living rooms across the city, people sensed in the team's posture a new kind of steadiness. They saw the movements that had sharpened through the winter. They felt the clarity that had taken root in the MECCA now traveling outward, settling over the neutral court in Dayton as though the team carried its home environment within it.

The country, however, paid minimal attention. Other games that day featured more prominent programs, more dramatic finishes, more compelling narratives for national consumption. Marquette remained a marginal storyline, appreciated by basketball purists but overshadowed by the gravitational pull of the giants. Yet beneath this outward quiet, something was shifting. The victory had not repositioned Marquette in the national imagination, but it had repositioned them within themselves.

The next step in the tournament would not get easier. Wake Forest awaited—a team fast, disciplined, and capable of disrupting rhythm. But for the first time in months, Marquette's internal horizon widened. They had played a complete game away from home. They had imposed their identity rather than adjusted to circumstance. And they had discovered, not through hope but through action, that the basketball they played in February could translate to March.

The threshold had opened. Now the team would learn whether it could step through.

The second round of the 1977 NCAA Tournament brought Marquette into a deeper chamber of pressure, the kind that reveals not only a team's talent but its temperament. Wake Forest, their opponent on March 17 in College Park, Maryland, represented a very different challenge from Cincinnati. The Demon Deacons played with a fluid, guard-oriented offense that demanded discipline, quick rotations, and a level of defensive cohesion that could not be faked. Their roster carried the imprint of the ACC's sophistication—precise passing, intelligent spacing, and a confidence reinforced by regular battles against the conference's elite. For much of the country, Wake Forest was the favored narrative: a sharp, well-coached team capable of exploiting any opponent that lacked structural integrity.

But Marquette entered the game with something Wake Forest could not see on film: the interior steadiness that had been forming all winter, a quiet power that did not depend on tempo or size or star dominance. It depended on patience, recognition, and the ability to absorb pressure without yielding to it. From the opening minutes, it became clear that Marquette was not intimidated by Wake Forest's rhythm. They met it with a defensive posture that was neither passive nor overextended. Instead, the Warriors played with a shifting balance—closing lanes, contesting shots, and forcing Wake Forest into decisions they did not want to make.

Butch Lee controlled the offensive flow with a tempered

aggressiveness that gave the team its early foothold. His drives were not rushed; they unfolded with the deliberation of someone who understood that chaos favors the unprepared. His midrange jumper, always smooth, seemed to appear at the precise moments Marquette needed to interrupt Wake Forest's momentum. Meanwhile, Ellis commanded the interior with an ease that reflected years of accumulated discipline. He did not overpower defenders; he outthink them. His movements —on rebounds, on outlets, on back cuts—suggested a player who had shed any lingering conflict between ambition and composure.

Whitehead, whose athletic presence had been building month by month, emerged in this game as Marquette's hinge— meeting drives at the rim, altering shots that statistics would never record, and providing the kind of psychological dissuasion that gradually reshapes an opponent's confidence. His imprint on the game was not loud, but it was undeniable. Wake Forest, so fluid early, began to hesitate. And hesitation against a team as patient as Marquette was a kind of unraveling.

Yet the game did not tilt easily. Wake Forest pushed back with determination. Their guards probed for weaknesses, their shooters worked tirelessly to create separation, and their defense forced Marquette out of rhythm for stretches. There were moments when the energy in Cole Field House shifted toward Wake Forest, when the crowd sensed an opportunity for the ACC team to retake control. But each small surge produced the same Marquette response: steadiness. Not brilliance, not explosiveness—steadiness.

This was the decisive psychological difference between the 1977 team and the ones that had fallen short in previous tournaments. Earlier Marquette squads had relied heavily on surges of momentum, bursts of intensity that could overwhelm opponents but often left the team vulnerable when the game shifted. This version of Marquette carried no such

THE CITY OF GOLD AND BLUE

volatility. Their emotional center held firm through every oscillation. They recognized the moments that mattered and allowed nothing extraneous to intrude.

By the second half, the game's shape had become clear. Wake Forest still had talent, but Marquette had resolution. Lee continued to carve space with his dribble, Ellis anchored possessions with a veteran's calm, and Whitehead's timing —simultaneously invisible and devastating—tightened the game's interior geometry. The supporting cast deepened the pressure with disciplined defensive rotations. Slowly, steadily, Wake Forest's offense lost its fluidity. The game became defined by Marquette's terms.

When the final seconds drained away and the scoreboard confirmed a 82–68 victory, the reaction from observers was not astonishment but recalibration. Marquette had not pulled an upset. They had asserted themselves. The win forced analysts to reconsider what they thought they knew about the team. The Warriors were no longer a sentimental subplot to McGuire's farewell tour. They were a problem—structured, disciplined, unpredictable in their pacing, and anchored by the kind of leadership that tends to carry teams deeper than expected.

The regional semifinals now awaited. Marquette would face Kansas State, a rugged and physical team coached by Jack Hartman, whose structured approach bore faint echoes of the discipline McGuire himself admired. Kansas State had toppled UCLA—a quiet but symbolic moment in the tournament, as the fading dynasty wavered at the edges of its former grandeur. Their victory had drawn national attention; they were now being framed as a potential sleeper, the kind of team that could impose its will on an opponent by controlling tempo and collapsing the interior.

This matchup, more than any previous test, would reveal the depth of Marquette's readiness. Kansas State played with a suffocating defense, narrowing passing lanes, disrupting rhythm, and using physicality to unsettle opponents emotionally. Their guards were relentless, their forwards disciplined, and their approach unsentimental. They sought to win not by outscoring teams but by exhausting them.

For Marquette, the challenge was less about strategy and more about self-possession. They had to maintain clarity under pressure, avoid being drawn into Kansas State's grinding style, and rely on the habits that had carried them this far. McGuire recognized the psychological stakes immediately. In the practices leading up to the regional semifinal, he reduced instruction and increased silence. He trusted the players to interpret the moment without excessive framing. He had shaped them for years. Now he stepped back, allowing them to inhabit the autonomy they had earned.

The city of Milwaukee watched from a distance, sensing that the season had reached the mouth of its crucible. The excitement was real, but it was not frantic. The fans who had filled the MECCA all winter felt the same quiet confidence the team carried. They understood something essential: Marquette had stopped trying to force its place in the national conversation. It had grown into itself. And teams that know who they are rarely falter when the bracket tightens.

The next days would determine whether that identity could withstand the rising pressure of March. The regional stage awaited, with its heightened stakes, its emotional compression, and its proximity to the possibility that had once seemed unreachable.

Marquette had passed through the opening gate. Now they approached the corridor where contenders become champions —or fall away.

The road to Atlanta began in Lawrence, Kansas, where the regional semifinals compressed the tournament into a denser, more unforgiving shape. By the time Marquette stepped onto the floor against Kansas State on March 19, 1977, the bracket had already shed several teams the national press once treated as inevitable. The tournament was revealing, in its unpredictable way, that hierarchy could bend under the weight of the unexpected. But Kansas State was not one of the fallen. They had arrived in the regional with authority, having dismantled UCLA in a game that felt less like an upset than a symbolic turning of the decade. Their toughness, pacing, and absolute commitment to defensive disruption gave them the air of a gatekeeper—one whose presence suggested that only teams capable of matching their interior hardness would pass through.

Marquette entered the game with no illusions. Kansas State did not waste possessions, did not lose composure, and did not permit opponents to dictate rhythm. Their guards pressed relentlessly, their forwards challenged every cut, and their rotations closed space with suffocating speed. It was the kind of defense that fed off hesitation. Yet from the opening possessions, Marquette refused to provide any. The Warriors moved with a tempered aggressiveness that echoed the internal sharpening of January and February. Their cuts were deliberate, their passes purposeful, and their spacing shaped not by predetermined patterns but by recognition—players reading one another's intentions with the instinctual clarity that only maturity provides.

Butch Lee set the tone. His command of the offense did not waver under pressure. He absorbed contact, slipped through narrow seams, and found angles that Kansas State's defenders did not expect. His balance, both physical and emotional, gave Marquette a foothold in the game's early minutes. Meanwhile, Ellis played with a veteran's pragmatism—meeting Kansas State's physicality not with confrontation but with redirection. He boxed out with precision rather than force, maneuvering into pockets of space where rebounds seemed to gravitate toward him.

Whitehead, whose presence had become increasingly central as the tournament advanced, emerged again as Marquette's hinge. He contested shots not with desperation but with timing, rising into the air with an effortlessness that altered Kansas State's interior logic. On offense, his finishing around the rim gave the team a dependable ballast that steadied each possession. Kansas State attempted to push him off his marks, but Whitehead held his ground with a quiet strength that suggested he had been preparing for this moment longer than anyone realized.

The game itself did not unfold according to any single narrative arc. It swayed, tightened, loosened, and tightened again. Kansas State's discipline kept them within striking distance, but Marquette's poise prevented them from seizing momentum. The Warriors had spent a decade learning how to survive emotional swings; now they used that knowledge to prevent even the smallest internal fracture. Every time Kansas State threatened to tilt the game, Marquette responded with steadiness. A timely midrange shot from Lee. A controlled rebound from Ellis. A defensive stop orchestrated by Payne. They did not overwhelm; they endured.

When the final buzzer sounded and Marquette stood on the winning side of a 67–66 score, the margin felt almost misleading. The game had been close, but not in spirit. Kansas State had pushed, clawed, and imposed their identity, but they had not bent Marquette's. For the first time all season, the national press hesitated. A recognition—quiet, tentative, but real—began to surface: perhaps Marquette was not a sentimental footnote to McGuire's retirement. Perhaps they were something else entirely.

Two days later, the regional final against Wake Forest's conqueror—the resilient and tactically disciplined UNC-Charlotte—offered a different kind of test. Charlotte had arrived in the regional with a fierce interior presence, led by Cornbread Maxwell, whose rebounding and scoring around the rim had destabilized opponents throughout the season. Their defense collapsed with intelligence, their spacing made exploitation difficult, and their willingness to outwork opponents carried the signature of a program determined to force its way into national consciousness.

Against this team, Marquette did not dominate. They managed. They adapted. They leaned into the maturity that had defined their winter. The game was defined by contrasts—Charlotte's strength versus Marquette's timing; Charlotte's aggression versus Marquette's precision. At times, the Warriors seemed at risk of losing their grip on the game, but each time the balance wavered, they reasserted themselves with a patience that signaled deeper understanding. Lee controlled tempo. Ellis provided grounding. Whitehead delivered the game's defining moment: a last-second tip-in that seemed to rise from instinct rather than intention, as though the culmination of a decade's worth of timing, disappointment, and persistence had finally been distilled into a single gesture.

Marquette won 51–49. And with that victory, the improbable became real. They were going to Atlanta.

The Omni carried an atmosphere unlike any Marquette had yet experienced in the tournament. Its octagonal structure, steep interior lines, and cavernous acoustics created an arena that felt simultaneously immense and intimate—a place where sound expanded and pressure tightened. The Final Four brought with it the weight of the sport's elite, even in a year when dynasties wavered. North Carolina, under Dean Smith, remained the tournament's compass point. Their precision, their discipline, their belief in Ford's orchestration —they seemed destined for the final. UNLV, with its flash and speed, represented the swagger of a rising era. And Marquette, standing among them, carried neither the pedigree nor the projected inevitability of the others.

But Marquette carried something else: a completeness that did not require validation.

The semifinal against UNLV began with a pace that threatened to test that completeness. Reggie Theus drove with brilliance, Eddie Owens found angles where none existed, and the Rebels pushed in transition with a fluidity that could bend lesser teams. Yet Marquette did not bend. They adjusted their defensive posture, tightened their spacing, and forced UNLV into contested shots that disrupted their rhythm. Offensively, the Warriors refused to be drawn into a track meet. Lee slowed possessions, Ellis chose his moments wisely, and Whitehead controlled the interior with disciplined ferocity.

The game turned late, as so many of Marquette's games had that season, not through spectacle but through judgment. Marquette absorbed UNLV's best and responded with their own. When the final horn sounded, they had earned an 84–81 victory—a win that stunned those who had treated UNLV as a rising force, but felt almost inevitable to those who understood what had been forming in Milwaukee.

Then came the championship.

North Carolina waited with the quiet authority of a program accustomed to the national stage. Phil Ford, one of the greatest guards of his generation, carried the offense with the smooth, disciplined command that had defined the Tar Heels' rise. Walter Davis provided a scoring presence that could stretch any defense; Tommy LaGarde and Mike O'Koren offered stability in the frontcourt. Dean Smith, already a figure of reverence in the sport, orchestrated everything with his systematic calm.

And yet, from the game's opening minutes, Marquette played as though the hierarchy had dissolved. Lee attacked with freedom. Ellis asserted himself inside. Whitehead altered shots that North Carolina typically finished. The Warriors controlled tempo, disrupted passing lanes, and forced the Tar

Heels into decisions they did not want to make. For a brief stretch in the second half, the momentum swung toward Carolina, the kind of moment when a lesser team might have tightened. But Marquette did not. They steadied. They recognized. They resumed.

The final score—67–59—felt at once startling and inevitable. What the nation had considered impossible had been unfolding in plain sight for months. The coronation was not sudden. It had been forming through winters of discipline, seasons of disappointment, and a decade of learning to see pressure not as threat but as the environment in which identity becomes visible.

As the nets were cut and McGuire stood on the court in tears, something shifted in the meaning of the moment. This was not merely the end of an era. It was the moment Marquette stepped into the interior truth of what the program had been shaping for ten years.

The coronation had taken place not because they defied the giants, but because they discovered they no longer needed to.

When the last fragments of confetti clung to the floor at The Omni and the crowd's noise faded into the upper reaches of the rafters, a quiet settled over the arena that felt almost unfamiliar. The court lay exposed under the softened lights—its paint scuffed, its angles sharp, its glass backboards holding the dim reflections of a night that had ended more suddenly than anyone expected. The players drifted toward the locker room in small clusters, their voices low, their expressions suspended between fatigue and a widening sense of what had taken place. McGuire lingered near the bench, neither savoring the surroundings nor turning away from them. He sat for a moment, elbows on his knees, looking out across the emptying floor as though trying to locate the shape of something that could not be seen outright.

Outside the arena, the Georgia night carried a warmth that

contrasted sharply with the winter that awaited the team back home. Streetlights threw long cones of illumination across the pavement, and the muffled sounds of celebration still drifted from nearby bars and sidewalks. Yet for the players boarding the buses, the noise seemed distant. Their movements carried a tired relief, but also a kind of inwardness, as if each were beginning to understand that the game had given them something far more private than applause. Lee leaned his head against the window, watching the city blur by. Ellis moved down the aisle with a calm that made every gesture deliberate. Whitehead settled into his seat and closed his eyes, his hands folded loosely, as though trying to still the adrenaline echoing in his body.

Milwaukee awoke the next morning to news that spread through taverns, factory floors, kitchens, and classrooms with a sense of almost stunned recognition. The city's identity had long been shaped by work that left little room for spectacle —shift changes, loading docks, rolling mills, and the quiet rhythms of parishes tucked among brick neighborhoods. Yet as word of the victory circulated, people felt something more than pride. They experienced a rare moment in which the city's often-unseen character became visible on a national stage. The win did not transform Milwaukee; it revealed the depth of what had always been there: endurance without complaint, ambition tempered by restraint, the belief that honest labor carries its own form of dignity.

When the team finally returned home, the airport thronged with people carrying signs, flags, homemade banners, and the kind of spontaneous affection that cannot be rehearsed. Workers in heavy coats waved from behind barricades; students climbed onto elevated railings for a clearer view; families pressed together, children perched on shoulders. The players stepped from the plane into a cold that bit at their faces, but the applause carried enough warmth to close the distance. No one spoke of destiny or fate. The city greeted them like men who had taken the long route through doubt, through anonymity, through years when recognition seemed unlikely. The welcome had the feeling of a homecoming, not a coronation.

Back on campus, as night fell and the temperature dropped, the streets took on their familiar stillness. Snow from earlier in the week had crusted along the edges of the sidewalks. The lights from dorm windows glowed softly across the grounds. A few students walked together toward the heart of campus, their breath rising in faint plumes, talking quietly about the game, replaying moments, arguing over who had made the crucial play or when the momentum had shifted. Their voices carried through the cold in thin, drifting lines, fading as they rounded the corner near the Alumni Memorial Union.

What remained after the noise subsided was neither triumph nor nostalgia. It was a sense of recognition that moved through the city and the campus alike—not the recognition that comes from winning, but the recognition that arrives when effort and identity finally align. The game in Atlanta had ended with a scoreboard and a trophy, but its meaning traveled elsewhere: into the memory of the players who understood the cost of becoming a team, into the streets of Milwaukee where people walked with a lighter step, and into the quiet of a winter night when the cold felt less severe.

In that quiet, the victory settled not as a proclamation, but as a truth long in the making—one that did not rise above the city, but returned to it.

CHAPTER SIX – AFTER MCGUIRE: THE STRUGGLE WITH ABSENCE

"You can replace a coach. You can't replace a presence."
— Rick Majerus

The months after the 1977 championship carried a strange, unsettled quiet across the Marquette campus. The banners still hung in the MECCA, the trophy still glimmered under the display lights, and the echoes of celebration had not yet fully faded from the streets of Milwaukee. But beneath the outward shine of triumph, something essential had been removed. The absence did not announce itself all at once. It arrived gradually, like a shift in temperature, a change in the density of the air, the faint recognition that the emotional architecture of the program had been altered in a way no one yet knew how to name. The team had won a title. The university had earned national respect. The city had celebrated with a fervor seldom seen in its basketball history. And yet the center of gravity that had shaped everything—the personality, the intuition, the disruptive intelligence of Al McGuire—was suddenly missing.

People spoke of McGuire's retirement in practical terms. He had stepped away on his own timing, with a championship in hand and a national reputation cemented. Hank Raymonds, long his trusted assistant, would assume control with a deep understanding of the program's internal mechanics. Continuity seemed assured. But continuity in structure did not mean continuity in spirit. McGuire had operated in an emotional register that could not be passed from one man to another. His presence—mercurial, intuitive, grounded in a strange blend of street wisdom and philosophical detachment —had not simply directed the team; it had framed the way Marquette understood itself. His departure left a vacancy not of position but of atmosphere.

Players returning to campus that fall felt it immediately. The routines remained the same—the open gyms, the conditioning runs along the lakefront, the early autumn practices when the sun still glinted off the windows of the gymnasium. But the tone had changed. There was no unexpected laughter erupting from a corner of the court. No sudden shifts in practice pace orchestrated by instinct rather than schedule. No sideline comments delivered with that mixture of mischief and acuity that both challenged and liberated them. Instead, players encountered a quiet that made every sound feel sharper. Drills unfolded cleanly, yet without the strange voltage McGuire had infused into even the most mundane exercises. The court looked the same, but it felt different.

Raymonds stepped into the head coaching role with a steadiness that reflected his own nature. He had been with the program long enough to understand its rhythms, its tensions, its hidden fragilities. He possessed a deep basketball intelligence and a capacity for calm that had balanced McGuire's theatrical volatility for years. His players respected him. Many trusted him. But Raymonds had never sought the spotlight; he had never fashioned himself as a figure who could reshape the emotional atmosphere of a room simply by entering it. Where McGuire had conjured energy from unpredictability, Raymonds relied on structure. Where McGuire had encouraged players to lean into their instincts, Raymonds emphasized execution. The shift was not a matter of competence; it was a matter of sensibility.

The university, too, felt the change. Administrators who had grown accustomed to McGuire's ability to generate national attention—through his charisma, his unpredictability, his knack for turning a moment into a story—now found themselves presiding over a quieter program. There was no longer a central figure capable of drawing national writers to Milwaukee through sheer personality. There was no longer a man who could turn a press conference into an event. The result was subtle but unmistakable: the spotlight softened, the national gaze drifted, and Marquette's presence in the broader conversation of college basketball began to recede.

Milwaukee noticed this receding as well. The city had identified with McGuire not only because he delivered wins, but because he mirrored its contradictions and its toughness. He embodied the tensions between grit and elegance, instinct and discipline, improvisation and order—tensions that Milwaukee itself had long carried. In McGuire, the city saw a man who thrived on the margins, who resisted pretense, who understood that the world often overlooked places like Milwaukee yet found meaning precisely in that oversight. His departure felt like the loss of someone who had translated the city's character into a visible, living form. Without him, the relationship between program and place began to shift. The team remained important, but the connection felt less intimate, less electric, less wholly shared.

For the players who had experienced the height of the 1977 run, the absence carried an emotional weight that revealed itself in unexpected moments. During conditioning drills, someone would instinctively glance toward the sideline, expecting to see McGuire leaning against the wall with a half-smile that both dared and encouraged them. In practices, a player might pause, anticipating a sudden instruction delivered in the elliptical language McGuire favored—phrases that were less about tactics than about freeing the mind. During games, there were no sharp pivots in strategy triggered by an impulsive insight, no sideline dialogues that unfurled more like confessions than coaching. McGuire's departure had taken with it not just a voice, but an entire way of reading the game.

Raymonds recognized this loss even as he tried to lead the program forward. He knew that he could not replicate McGuire's temperament, nor should he try. The program needed stability in the aftermath of such a seismic departure. But stability can reveal its own form of fragility. Players who had thrived under McGuire's freedom now found themselves adjusting to a more measured style. Those who had relied on his emotional presence to navigate tension had to discover new internal resources. Every team faces a reckoning after achieving something extraordinary, but Marquette's reckoning was intensified by the departure of the very figure who had made the extraordinary possible.

The psychological space left by McGuire's absence extended beyond the roster. The incoming recruits of the late 1970s entered a program whose identity was no longer self-evident. They saw the championship banners, but they did not feel the atmosphere that had produced them. They heard stories of McGuire's personality, but they did not witness the ways it shaped daily life. They joined a team that carried both the weight of triumph and the uncertainty of transition. And the veterans, tasked with bridging these worlds, struggled to articulate what had been lost. They spoke of energy, of freedom, of the intangible qualities that had made the program feel alive. But intangibles resist translation. It is difficult to explain presence to those who have never experienced it.

The city's expectations, meanwhile, shifted in complicated ways. Some believed the program would continue its ascent, that the momentum of 1977 would carry Marquette into a new era of sustained excellence. Others sensed the fragility of the moment. They understood that McGuire's departure had created a void that could not be filled simply by maintaining the same plays, the same systems, the same routines. They saw a period of waiting approaching—not for wins or losses, but for recognition of what the program would become without the man who had defined its soul.

In the months after the championship, Marquette found itself living in two temporalities at once. The past remained vivid, bound to images of McGuire cutting down the nets at The Omni, of Lee's drives, of Ellis's calm leadership, of Whitehead's improbable tip-in. The present, however, felt suspended—uncertain, delicate, searching for form. The program had crossed a threshold, but now stood in the quiet space beyond it, unsure of what shape its future would take. The challenge was not merely to continue winning. The challenge was to determine whether the identity forged through a decade of improvisation, resilience, and emotional volatility could survive in the absence of the man who had animated it.

It would take time for the university, the city, and the program to understand the depth of this transition. For now, the absence remained just that—a presence in reverse, a stillness that revealed how much of the program's vitality had been rooted in one man's strange and singular force. And as the next season approached, everyone connected to Marquette basketball carried the same unspoken question: what becomes of a team when its defining spirit steps away?

The first season after McGuire's departure unfolded with the unease of a house whose walls still held the warmth of someone who no longer lived there. The routines remained intact—morning film sessions, afternoon practices at the MECCA, the steady rhythm of travel and preparation—but the emotional current that once animated everything now moved in a slower, more deliberate cadence. Hank Raymonds stepped into the role of head coach with a professionalism that earned respect, yet even he sensed that he was inheriting not a system, but a silence. The absence of McGuire reshaped the air, the expectations, the very grammar of how the team understood itself.

Raymonds never tried to imitate the man he replaced. He had too much integrity for that, and too much awareness of how imitation often exposes, rather than fills, a void. His style was measured, analytical, rooted in preparation rather than improvisation. He believed in repetition, refinement, and control—qualities that had made him the stabilizing force of McGuire's staff for years. Players appreciated his steadiness, and many trusted his clarity. But they felt the difference immediately. Under McGuire, practice had unfolded like a living argument—kinetic, unpredictable, charged with emotional complexity. Under Raymonds, practice became an ordered dialogue. The change was not unwelcome, but it revealed how much of the team's identity had been shaped by the volatility it had learned to navigate.

The psychological adjustment proved more difficult than the tactical one. Players who had entered the program expecting McGuire's idiosyncratic mentoring now found themselves guided by a different sensibility. Seniors, still carrying the imprint of the 1977 run, felt the distance most acutely. They remembered the sideline gestures that disguised instruction as intuition, the half-muttered phrases that unlocked composure, the late-night conversations in hotel hallways during tournament travel. They remembered playing not only for a coach, but for the emotional truth he represented. It was not loyalty in the conventional sense; it was recognition. McGuire had seen them as whole people—messy, uncertain, aspirational, flawed. Raymonds saw them as players to be developed, roles to be clarified, units to be harmonized.

Neither vision was wrong. But only one had shaped the team's mythology.

The early games of the season reflected this tension. Marquette did not collapse; they simply lost their fluency. Where they had once moved with the subconscious coherence of men accustomed to improvisation, they now executed with visible effort. Miscommunications appeared in places where second nature had previously guided them. Defensive rotations hesitated half a beat. Offensive sets felt as though they were being learned rather than inhabited. Nothing was disastrous, but everything carried the faint stiffness of a team in translation. The program had shifted languages, and fluency was not immediate.

The city sensed it, too. Milwaukee did not turn away from the program—loyalty in this place had always been sturdier than that—but the atmosphere changed. The emotional intimacy that had bound team and city together began to loosen. Games still drew crowds, but the noise carried a different timbre. Where there had once been the restless energy of a populace invested in the emotional drama of each possession, there was now a more measured watching. People supported the team, but they did not feel themselves reflected in it in the same way. The connection was still there, but the resonance had weakened.

Part of this shift stemmed from a simple truth: McGuire had given Milwaukee more than victories. He had given it representation. In his strange, theatrical, intuitive way, he embodied the city's contradictions. He carried both the toughness and the wit of the neighborhoods that surrounded campus. He spoke with the shrewdness of someone who knew how to navigate the world's indifference. He understood the psychology of the working-class communities that formed the backbone of Marquette's fanbase. His departure did not remove these qualities from the city, but it removed their expression from the court. Without him, the program lost its emotional interpreter.

The players, meanwhile, struggled to articulate the difference. Many liked Raymonds—they appreciated his decency, his knowledge, his earnest approach. But liking a coach and aligning with him are not the same thing. Leadership, especially in the wake of a figure like McGuire, must reach beneath the rational. It must inhabit the emotional strata where trust, instinct, and identity converge. Raymonds, for all his strengths, struggled to breach that level during his early months. He was too restrained, too measured, too careful. In another context, his qualities might have been precisely what the program needed. But in the immediate aftermath of McGuire, they highlighted the vacancy rather than softened it.

The transitional recruits who arrived that year entered a program whose mythology had been severed from its presence. They heard stories of the title run, of the Omni, of the improbable coherence of that team, of McGuire's strange brilliance. But these stories did not translate into atmosphere. They felt like tales from another era—close enough to touch, yet too distant to inhabit. The newcomers looked to the veterans for guidance, but even the veterans were navigating unfamiliar emotional terrain. Their memories belonged to a different sensibility, one Raymonds could not replicate even if he wished to.

The schedule brought its own complications. Opponents who had once approached Marquette with caution now sensed vulnerability. The aura that accompanies a national championship does not linger if the program cannot solidify its post-victory stability. Teams that would have feared Marquette's unpredictability under McGuire now faced a group adjusting to order. Some exploited this transition ruthlessly. Losses that would have once sharpened the team now tested it in uncomfortable ways. Wins did not carry the emotional charge they once had. Everything felt provisional.

Yet amid these struggles, something quieter and more durable began to emerge. Raymonds, though unable to replicate McGuire's presence, established a new groundwork. He insisted on structure, clarity, repetition. He did not chase the program's past; he tried to honor it by refusing to pretend he could inhabit someone else's persona. His approach exposed the program's fragility, but it also revealed its resilience. Players slowly began to respond to his steadiness. They learned that identity could be rebuilt, even if not in the same shape. They discovered that absence, while disorienting, could also be clarifying. It forced them to ask who they were without McGuire, and what kind of team they wished to become.

The city, too, adjusted. The initial sense of dislocation softened. People accepted that the emotional fireworks of the McGuire years were not sustainable as a permanent mode. They learned to watch the team differently—not as a vessel for the city's identity, but as a program undergoing the natural turbulence of transition. The noise inside the MECCA regained some of its former warmth. The relationship between Milwaukee and Marquette did not return to the intensity of the McGuire years, but it settled into something steadier, more measured, more compatible with the era of Raymonds.

Still, the absence lingered. It lingered in the quiet moments at practice, in the occasional sideways glances during games, in the long walks back to the locker room after difficult losses. It lingered in the memories of those who had known the program before the shift. Presence, once removed, does not dissolve quickly. It leaves a shape behind, a contour that future leaders must decide whether to fill or to honor from a distance.

In the early years after McGuire, the struggle was not with failure. It was with emptiness—the kind of emptiness that remains when a defining force steps away, leaving behind not a void, but a question.

The effort to rebuild the program after McGuire's departure unfolded in ways that revealed how deeply success depends not only on skill and strategy, but on the invisible architecture that surrounds a team. Identity, once fractured, does not reform on demand. It gathers slowly, in pieces, through the small adjustments that accumulate over seasons rather than weeks. In the late 1970s and early 1980s, Marquette found itself navigating precisely this slow, uncertain reconstruction. Raymonds worked to stabilize the roster, refine the system, and preserve the competitive ethos that had carried the program to national prominence. But stability, while necessary, carries limits. It can sustain a standard; it cannot, by itself, generate momentum.

The early recruits of the post-championship era entered a team that carried the weight of a recent triumph yet lacked the emotional compass that had guided the generation before them. They saw the banners and trophies, but they did not feel the pulse of the atmosphere that had produced them. Their introduction to Marquette basketball came through repetition, order, and quiet diligence rather than the improvisational vitality that had once defined the program. For some, this shift offered clarity. For others, it carried the faint disappointment of entering a house whose stories were louder than its present life. These young players faced the challenge of contributing to a legacy that had been written under conditions impossible to recreate.

During the early seasons under Raymonds, the team's performance oscillated between moments of promise and stretches of inconsistency. The MECCA still filled with loyal fans, but the energy in the building had changed. Crowds that once rose in anticipation of McGuire's sideline theatrics now watched with a steadier, more contemplative engagement. They appreciated the program's ongoing competitiveness, but they sensed that something essential had shifted. The unpredictability that had once made Marquette both thrilling and dangerous had been replaced by a more predictable rhythm. Games unfolded logically, professionally, respectably —qualities that sustain programs but rarely ignite cities.

Raymonds, aware of these subtleties, worked to build a culture rooted not in theatrical presence, but in discipline and continuity. He believed that the success of the program should not depend on a single personality, and he approached his role with the humility of a man who understood the impossibility of filling McGuire's emotional space. His impact was measured not in spectacle, but in the steady cultivation of players who learned to trust structure. Under his guidance, Marquette did not collapse. It simply became quieter. And quiet programs, even strong ones, often find themselves slipping from the national consciousness unless they produce moments that force attention.

This quietude extended beyond the court. National writers who had once flocked to Milwaukee to chronicle McGuire's eccentricities now devoted their attention to emerging basketball powers and the rising influence of televised games. Marquette, no longer powered by narrative magnetism, found itself competing in a landscape increasingly shaped by personalities and spectacle. Programs that generated stories —whether through star players, controversial coaches, or dramatic rivalries—secured media coverage. Programs that offered steadiness without drama often drifted to the margins of the conversation. Marquette was not forgotten, but its place in the national dialogue grew less certain.

Recruiting reflected this shifting landscape. The name "Marquette" still carried weight—championships do not evaporate—but the urgency that had once drawn recruits into the program now softened. Young prospects entering the game in the late 1970s and early 1980s had not grown up watching McGuire command the sidelines. Their reference points had shifted toward other icons and other styles as college basketball expanded into new regions and media formats. Raymonds and his staff worked tirelessly, but the gravitational pull that once emanated from Milwaukee weakened with each passing year.

Yet within this period of recalibration, important truths surfaced. The first was that the program's foundation, though shaken, remained intact. The championship did not vanish from memory simply because the program could not replicate the emotional spectacle of its creation. It provided a baseline of legitimacy that sustained Marquette through seasons of transition. The second truth was that resilience does not always announce itself loudly. It often emerges in the quiet persistence of players who continue to work, continue to believe, and continue to carry forward a standard they did not create but felt responsible to uphold.

Some of these players found their voices precisely because the environment no longer revolved around a dominant presence. In the absence of McGuire's commanding force, leadership became more dispersed. Veterans learned to take ownership of the small, internal dynamics that define a team's character. Younger players, no longer overshadowed by a mythic figure, learned to carve out identities through consistency rather than dramatic bursts of performance. This redistribution of responsibility did not restore the emotional electricity of the McGuire years, but it laid the groundwork for a more collective understanding of what Marquette basketball could become.

The city, too, adapted. Milwaukee had always recognized that it lived in the shadows of larger markets and brighter national spotlights. The quiet years after the championship did not erode its loyalty. If anything, they brought the relationship between fans and program into clearer focus. People supported the team because it represented an institution woven into the city's fabric, not because it offered constant drama. They understood that programs, like cities, experience cycles— periods of ascendance, periods of rebuilding, periods in which identity must be rediscovered rather than asserted.

Still, the struggle with absence persisted. It lingered in the way fans spoke of "the McGuire years," a phrase that carried both nostalgia and a faint ache. It appeared in the way older players watched younger ones, hoping to see flashes of the improvisational daring that had once defined the team's style. It existed in the whisper-thin margins of close games, when the presence of a single galvanizing figure can tilt momentum through force of personality alone. The program did not suffer from a lack of talent or leadership. It suffered from the void created when a defining presence steps away, leaving behind a template that cannot be filled, only acknowledged.

In these years, Marquette began to recognize that absence is not merely the loss of what was. It is also the space where new identities form. Under Raymonds, the program began that long, patient process of rebuilding identity without the scaffolding of a singular figure. It learned that presence cannot be replaced; it must be reimagined. And in the slow work of reimagining, the program discovered that the struggle with absence, though painful, was also a form of preparation for whatever would come next.

The early 1980s drew the program into a different kind of reckoning, one shaped not by immediate loss but by the long-term effects of operating without a unifying emotional axis. Raymonds continued to guide Marquette with steadiness, and his teams remained competitive, disciplined, and capable of bursts of strong play. Yet as the seasons unfolded, the tension between historical identity and present reality became more difficult to ignore. The question was no longer how to follow McGuire, but how to define a new way of being Marquette in a college basketball world that was itself undergoing rapid transformation.

Television changed the sport's landscape, drawing national audiences to programs that delivered charismatic figures, explosive scoring, or bold stylistic reinventions. Conferences reorganized, rivalries gained commercial weight, and the NCAA Tournament expanded into an event of spectacle rather than merely a postseason contest. In this shifting terrain, schools that could attach their identity to a clear narrative —Kentucky's blue blood lineage, Georgetown's rising force under John Thompson Jr., North Carolina's blend of discipline and grace—gained a foothold in the national imagination. Marquette, by contrast, held onto a past that could no longer serve as the primary engine of its future.

This challenge surfaced even in recruiting conversations. Prospects were increasingly drawn to programs that offered not just stability but visibility. Playing for a coach who commanded national attention or for a program embedded in a major conference offered exposure that independent programs struggled to match. Marquette still carried the glow of the 1977 championship, but the half-life of that glow shortened as younger generations viewed it as a distant achievement rather than a present reality. Raymonds and his staff worked diligently, but the terrain had shifted beneath them. Recruiting battles that once leaned in their favor began to tilt toward programs with evolving public profiles.

On the court, the tension between past and present revealed itself in the style of play. McGuire's Marquette had thrived on controlled chaos, on an unusual blend of improvisation and discipline that reflected his intuitive grasp of the emotional flow of a game. Raymonds's teams favored structure—clear offensive sets, organized defensive schemes, an emphasis on patience. This difference did not diminish the quality of the basketball being played, but it did change the program's internal rhythm. The unpredictability that had once unsettled opponents and energized fans gave way to a more conventional approach. Marquette remained respected, but the element of surprise, the sense that anything might happen at any moment, began to fade.

The shift also affected the players' development. Under McGuire, certain talents flourished precisely because they were encouraged to play on instinct and to embrace the psychological dimension of competition. Under Raymonds, players refined their skills within a system. Some thrived under this order. Others, particularly those suited to the spontaneous intensity that once defined Marquette's style, felt constrained. This tension was subtle but persistent. It reflected the broader challenge faced by a program in transition: how to honor the foundation laid by a singular figure without becoming bound to a style that could not be sustained without him.

The fan base, loyal as ever, wrestled with its own expectations. Milwaukee had celebrated the championship not simply because it was a rare triumph, but because it reflected the city's own character—a combination of resilience, resourcefulness, and a willingness to defy external expectations. The post-McGuire teams inspired respect, but they did not consistently evoke the same emotional resonance. Fans still filled the MECCA and later the Bradley Center, but their cheers carried a different frequency, one shaped less by anticipation and more by support. The electricity of the mid-1970s had not disappeared; it had simply settled into a quieter form, waiting for a new spark to set it alight.

One of the most telling signs of the program's struggle with absence came during close games, particularly those against ranked opponents. During the McGuire years, it often felt as though Marquette could bend the emotional momentum of a game through force of will. Players absorbed McGuire's confidence and unpredictability, and this energy shaped how they approached critical possessions. In the early 1980s, these moments unfolded differently. Execution mattered more, intuition less. The team often came close to major victories but fell just short, not due to lack of talent, but due to the absence of the catalytic presence that once transformed tension into opportunity.

Raymonds experienced these near-misses with a composure that reflected his character, but each one deepened the program's internal recognition that something intangible was still missing. He was not failing; he was simply navigating a landscape that had changed in ways no coach could fully control. His commitment kept the program from drifting into mediocrity, but it could not restore the electricity that had once defined Marquette's place in the national conversation. By the mid-1980s, it had become increasingly clear that the program stood at a crossroads. Stability had been achieved, but identity remained unsettled.

The question that emerged during this period was not whether the program would continue to win, but what kind of winning would define its future. Would Marquette embrace a new identity rooted in discipline and structure, or would it seek a figure capable of reigniting the emotional charge that had once made it so distinctive? The administration, alumni, and fan base wrestled with this tension in ways that revealed their competing desires: the wish for consistency, the longing for excitement, the memory of a past that continued to shape expectations even as it receded further into history.

By the mid-1980s, the cumulative weight of these questions began to exert pressure on the program's direction. Raymonds, who had carried the burden of succession with dignity, understood that Marquette needed to explore new leadership if it hoped to reestablish itself within the shifting landscape of college basketball. His departure in 1983 marked the end of the first chapter of the post-McGuire era—a chapter defined by steadiness, quiet resilience, and the difficult work of holding a program together in the wake of a seismic loss.

The years that followed brought new coaching philosophies, new approaches to recruiting, and new attempts to reclaim a distinct identity in an increasingly crowded national field. But the emotional truth of this period remained unchanged: the struggle with absence had not been a single moment of loss, but a prolonged process of adaptation. Marquette learned, through these years, that the shadow of a singular presence does not fade quickly. It remains, not as an obstacle, but as a reminder of what the program had once been—and what it would need to rediscover in its own way.

By the late 1980s, the aftershocks of McGuire's departure had settled into a long-term condition rather than a temporary adjustment. The program had learned to function without him, yet the imprint of his presence still shaped the contours of what Marquette believed itself to be. Success came sporadically, carried by individual players who embodied fragments of the old identity—tough guards who played with defiance, forward lines that worked with quiet relentlessness —but the coherence that had once held everything together remained elusive. Coaches arrived with new philosophies, each bringing a distinct vision of how to move the program forward, yet the space they inherited always seemed partly defined by the figure who had left it.

Hank Raymonds's departure after the 1982–83 season marked a turning point, not because the program collapsed, but because it signaled the end of the belief that continuity alone could sustain the identity McGuire had established. The decision to elevate Rick Majerus, a former McGuire disciple who had absorbed the emotional and tactical rhythms of the 1970s teams, offered the possibility of reconnecting with the program's foundational sensibility. Majerus, sharp-minded and uncompromising, carried an understanding of Marquette's inner workings that few others possessed. He had lived through the era when presence, not merely system, defined success. His approach to coaching drew from the same well—a belief that attention to detail, emotional honesty, and psychological acuity could create a team that played with the fullness of itself.

Yet even Majerus, for all his intelligence and intensity, faced the reality that eras cannot be reconstructed. The young men he coached were not the sons of the 1970s teams; they were products of a different basketball landscape, shaped by changes in athletic culture, recruiting networks, and national exposure. When Majerus left after only one season to return to the University of Utah program that offered him greater institutional support, his departure underscored a truth Marquette had been approaching for years: the program needed not only a coach, but an identity rooted in the contemporary world rather than in the memory of what once had been.

This realization became unavoidable as the decade drew to a close. Independent status, once a source of flexibility and distinction, began to constrain Marquette's trajectory. College basketball's new power centers formed within conferences that offered financial stability, guaranteed media coverage, and competitive consistency. Without such a structure, Marquette existed in a liminal space—not irrelevant, but increasingly peripheral. The glory of 1977 still glimmered in the program's narrative, but it did not provide the gravitational pull needed to anchor the present. The question that emerged with increasing force was not whether the program could reclaim its past, but whether it could define its future.

During this period, the city's relationship with the program displayed a kind of patient loyalty that reflected Milwaukee's broader character. Fans continued to fill the MECCA and later the Bradley Center, even as the team cycled through coaching transitions and uneven seasons. The support was less exuberant than in the McGuire years, but more enduring. People understood that the program was navigating a complicated evolution, that it was trying to locate its identity in a sport whose landscape had changed dramatically. The city did not demand instant transformation; it simply refused to walk away. That constancy provided a quiet foundation upon which future growth could rest.

Still, the struggle with absence persisted, not as nostalgia, but as a structural challenge. Without a defining sensibility— whether embodied in a coach, a playing style, or a consistent institutional strategy—the program had difficulty projecting a coherent identity to recruits, fans, and national observers. Marquette was respected, but not feared; capable, but not commanding. The gap between potential and realization widened. Seasons passed in which the team hovered near significance without fully breaking through. Tournaments were missed, opportunities slipped, momentum faltered at critical junctures. None of this amounted to failure; it amounted to drift.

The late 1980s and early 1990s marked the culmination of this drift. It became increasingly clear that the program would need a structural reinvention—a new framework that could carry Marquette into the modern era of college basketball. The solution eventually emerged through conference affiliation, institutional investment, and the arrival of coaches who would reshape the program's identity for a new generation. But before these developments took shape, the university had to confront the deepest truth revealed by the years after McGuire: presence is not a legacy; it is a condition. And once it disappears, the work of rebuilding must begin from the ground up, guided not by memory but by discernment.

If the McGuire years had taught Marquette that personality could galvanize a program, the years that followed taught it that identity cannot rest on personality alone. It must be sustained by structure, vision, and a clear understanding of who the institution wishes to become. In the absence of these elements, even the most storied victories can fade into the background noise of history.

By the time the program entered the early 1990s, the long struggle with absence had transformed into something else—a readiness for reinvention. The foundation had been tested, the weight of memory had been carried, and the institution had learned that the past, however luminous, could not be lived in. What remained was the search for a new identity strong enough to honor the old one without being eclipsed by it.

Winter evenings in Milwaukee carried a stillness during those years that felt distinct from the decade before. The streets around campus grew quiet earlier, the wind off the lake tightening its grip on the stone and brick buildings as students made their way between classes, the gym, the union, and the dimly lit sidewalks that threaded the university together. From inside the arenas—first the MECCA, then the newer Bradley Center—light poured outward in soft rectangular shapes, cutting through the cold and settling onto the pavement like distant reminders of a warmth that could not fully reach those outside. The glow was familiar, but it no longer carried the charge of earlier years. It felt steadier now, anchored less to spectacle and more to persistence.

After games, when the crowds dispersed and the last sounds of the evening folded into the darkness, the echo of footsteps in the concourse revealed more than the scoreboard could. Fans walked with hands in coat pockets, heads bent against the wind, their conversations gentle and low. They still cared —deeply—but the emotions that shaped their relationship with the program had shifted. They spoke not of destiny or drama but of effort, potential, and the hope that something yet undefined was gathering beneath the surface. The city watched with patience shaped by its own history, sensing that the years of transition had not been a detour but a passage.

Inside the locker room after those late-season games, players lingered in silence that carried traces of both frustration and resolve. The clatter of locker doors, the soft scrape of tape being unwound, the muted hum of showers running in the background—all of it unfolded in a rhythm that suggested endurance rather than arrival. No one needed to speak about what the program had lost; the absence was woven into the air. Yet in the long breaths taken before coats were pulled on and bags hoisted over shoulders, there was also a quiet recognition of what had been learned. Teams inherit more than systems and expectations—they inherit unfinished conversations, unresolved questions, and the responsibility of discovering who they are when history no longer dictates the answer.

Coaches walking the dim hallways after games carried a different kind of weight. They paused in doorways, studying box scores under fluorescent light, searching not just for patterns but for indications of where the program's internal compass might next point. The task before them was not simply tactical or administrative. They were tending to a living history that could not be restored through replication or nostalgia. Their work unfolded in the subdued hours long after the fans had gone home, when the only sounds were the distant rumble of HVAC systems and the occasional thud of a basketball left behind on the court.

On certain nights, when the temperature dropped enough to make the windows frost over, the campus seemed to return to an earlier stillness. The chapel bells rang with a clarity sharpened by the cold, and the lights from the residence halls reflected against the thin crust of snow covering the grounds. Students walking back from the arena passed through this atmosphere without thinking much of it, unaware that they were inhabiting a moment of transition for a program that once commanded national attention. Their steps traced the same pathways that fans had followed during the championship run, though the emotions that accompanied them belonged to a different era.

Yet in those quiet walks and dimly lit evenings, something essential persisted. The program had not lost its heartbeat—it had simply shifted into a lower register. The passion that once expressed itself through the electricity of McGuire's presence had settled into the resilience of a campus and a city unwilling to relinquish what the team represented. The struggle with absence had revealed the depth of the relationship between institution and identity. It showed that when a defining figure steps away, what remains is not emptiness but the possibility of renewal. The years of searching, recalibrating, and enduring did not erase the past. They prepared the ground for whatever would come next.

In the stillness of those Milwaukee nights, long after the arena lights had dimmed, the program's future took shape quietly. Not through grand declarations, not through sudden transformations, but through the steady persistence of a community that understood the value of waiting. Presence, once lost, does not return in the same form—but its absence creates the space where a new kind of presence can emerge.

CHAPTER SEVEN – TOM CREAN AND THE NEW URBAN ORDER

"When I got here, the first thing I knew was this: Marquette had to believe in itself again."
— Tom Crean

When Tom Crean arrived in Milwaukee in the spring of 1999, the city was in one of its cyclical transitions—caught between the industrial past that had shaped its neighborhoods and the uncertain outlines of a more modern urban identity. The lakefront carried a sharper wind than usual that week, a reminder of how the seasons in this part of the Midwest often resist overlapping cleanly. Students on campus moved with the hurried posture of those preparing for final exams, yet the conversations drifting from coffee shops and dorm halls carried an undercurrent of anticipation. Marquette had hired a coach few outside the inner circles of the sport knew intimately—a 33-year-old assistant from Michigan State whose name circulated more among insiders than casual fans. But something in the announcement suggested a shift, not in prestige but in posture. It felt, even in those first ambiguous days, as though the program had decided to stop looking backward.

Crean stepped into the position with the eagerness of someone who understood the stakes. Marquette's identity had drifted for nearly two decades, floating between the memory of its golden era and the uncertainty of its place in the modern college basketball landscape. The city still filled its arenas. The name still carried weight. But the coherence that once defined the program had thinned. Crean recognized, almost instinctively, that he was inheriting not just a roster and a schedule but a psychological project. He walked into his first press conference with a kind of kinetic alertness, his sentences tumbling quickly but clearly, as though he were already in motion. He spoke of energy, of vision, of the necessity of embracing Milwaukee itself—its streets, its culture, its quiet toughness. He spoke as though the team and the city were threads of the same fabric that had frayed over time and needed to be rewoven.

What struck observers most in those first months was not Crean's youth or ambition, but the acceleration of his presence. He moved through campus with the stride of someone who believed the program's renewal depended on momentum. He visited local gyms, high school tournaments, community centers. He shook hands with neighborhood coaches who had not seen a Marquette head coach in years. He called former players, administrators, and donors, not out of performative obligation but to map the emotional terrain of a program that had spent years searching for direction. Crean's early weeks carried the sense of a man trying to grasp every thread available to him, determined to pull them together until they formed something dense enough to hold weight.

This emphasis on connection—particularly within the city —represented a new kind of urban order for Marquette basketball. Where previous post-McGuire coaches had worked from the inside-out, building structure and hoping identity would follow, Crean reversed the approach. He believed identity preceded structure. Milwaukee, with its neighborhoods shaped by immigration, labor, and resilience, offered a foundation more authentic than any system he could impose. He studied the city not as a backdrop but as a source. He wanted players who reflected its rhythms, its humility, its grit. He wanted recruits who would not merely inhabit the campus but feel the gravitational pull of the city beyond it.

Inside the program, his approach was equally deliberate. Practices intensified. Conditioning sessions grew sharper and more precise. Film study expanded in both frequency and depth. Crean believed that players should see themselves with the same clarity he brought to their development. He spoke often of accountability, not as punishment but as recognition. He emphasized that culture was built not through slogans but through repetition—habits created in the quiet hours, long before anyone noticed the results. In these early sessions, players sensed that Crean was constructing an infrastructure of belief rather than demanding blind adherence. He wanted them to understand the difference between enthusiasm and identity, between effort and purpose.

Milwaukee responded to this shift with a kind of cautious curiosity. The city had grown accustomed to the steadiness of the post-McGuire decades, a period defined less by highs and lows than by gradual recalibration. But Crean's presence signaled something unfamiliar. He talked quickly, moved quickly, coached quickly. He infused the program with a sense of urgency that contrasted sharply with the measured tones of his predecessors. Fans sensed that he was trying to reintroduce a kind of emotional voltage that had been dormant for a generation—not by replicating the past, but by refusing to let inertia dictate the present.

One of the earliest signs of this new orientation emerged in the way Crean reshaped the team's recruiting map. Marquette had historically drawn from a wide but sporadic pool of prospects, relying on relationships that often dated back decades. Crean redrew that map almost immediately. He targeted regions that mirrored Milwaukee's sensibilities—industrial cities, overlooked urban centers, communities where toughness was not a trait but a condition of daily life. He sought players who would respond to the quiet pressure of expectation without being seduced by it. He valued those who understood that the program's history was not a burden but an invitation.

Within the locker room, the effects of this approach soon became visible. Veterans who had grown accustomed to the slower rhythms of the previous era encountered a staff that demanded sharper attention, fuller engagement, and a readiness to adapt. Crean did not assume that belief would emerge naturally; he cultivated it. Team meetings grew longer, more detailed, more confrontational in ways that exposed the gaps between potential and reality. He insisted that the players speak openly about what they wanted to become. He pressed them to articulate not only goals but standards. Over time, the team began to internalize the sense that they were not just maintaining a program—they were rebuilding an identity.

Meanwhile, the university administration recognized that Crean's arrival was reshaping the external perception of Marquette basketball. Local media coverage expanded, not because the team had immediately transformed, but because the energy swirling around the program had shifted. Crean's visibility in Milwaukee's gyms and community spaces created a sense of presence that extended beyond game nights. He treated the city not as a market, but as a partner. He understood that if Marquette was to reclaim a meaningful place in the national landscape, it first had to reestablish itself within its own geography.

In these early years, nothing was guaranteed. Wins did not accumulate overnight. Setbacks came, some predictable, some difficult. Yet beneath the fluctuations of the record book, something subtle but unmistakable was taking shape. The program was relearning how to inhabit itself. Confidence, once fragile, began to take form. Players looked to one another differently. Practices hummed with a sharper purpose. Fans returned to the arena with a sense of expectation rather than obligation.

The new urban order Crean was constructing did not involve a single stylistic choice or a dramatic gesture. It emerged through relentless attention to culture, to energy, to the psychological architecture of belief. For the first time in years, Marquette seemed less like a team searching for an identity and more like a team preparing to claim one.

The first full season under Tom Crean unfolded with the rawness of a team learning to think and move differently, not because the players lacked talent, but because identity cannot be imported—it must be built, internalized, and lived into existence. The roster Crean inherited contained athletes who had grown accustomed to a quieter, steadier rhythm. They had been coached with care and discipline, but without the emotional voltage Crean insisted upon. His approach required a recalibration of instinct. Every drill carried urgency. Every possession in practice carried consequence. The players were asked to inhabit the game with a heightened sense of intention, not simply perform its mechanics.

Crean believed that culture was not an abstract concept to be invoked at alumni dinners; it was a daily discipline forged through friction. He created environments in which players were pushed to articulate their goals aloud, often in uncomfortable detail. He demanded eye contact in film sessions, an insistence that exposed every lapse, every hesitation, every misread. He pressed the team to understand that the difference between potential and performance was not talent, but accountability. The early practices, often grueling, became a form of collective introspection. Each player confronted the limits of his preparation, and in doing so, began to recognize how far the program had to travel to match the history that shadowed it.

This intensity extended beyond the court. Crean's presence in the athletic department altered the tone of the program's internal operations. Staff meetings took on a sharper edge. There was no tolerance for passivity. Logistics, recruiting travel, academic monitoring, community outreach—all were reframed through a lens of purpose. The program, Crean believed, must express coherence in every direction. If a recruit visited campus, he should feel the alignment of vision from the strength coach to the secretary who greeted him at the door. If a player slipped academically, the response should feel immediate and integrated. Crean did not micromanage; he choreographed. And the choreography, in these early stages, was relentless.

His recruiting approach amplified this momentum. Milwaukee had long been a city whose basketball talent existed in pockets—school gyms in gritty neighborhoods, suburban programs producing high-IQ guards, community leagues where toughness formed before technique. Yet Marquette had not always secured a foothold in these spaces. Crean changed that calculus. He walked into gyms that had not seen a Marquette head coach in years. He forged relationships with coaches who had never been asked what they thought of the program's direction. He understood that a university's promise meant little to a teenager unless it was delivered by someone willing to sit in the bleachers on a freezing January night, taking notes while the rest of the city escaped the cold.

This approach bore fruit even before major signings arrived. Parents took note. Local high school programs took note. Players who might once have viewed Marquette as a respectable but distant option now saw a program hungry to reclaim its place in the city's basketball consciousness. Crean managed these relationships with a mixture of intensity and attentiveness. He listened more than he spoke—a quality that surprised those who saw only the fire he displayed during games. He learned the contours of Milwaukee's basketball ecosystem, from the dynamics of AAU scenes to the unspoken loyalties that shaped certain neighborhoods. He understood that credibility in this city was earned, not assumed.

The team's internal psychology began to reflect this broader effort. Early-season games exposed gaps—moments when the players reverted to old rhythms, relying too heavily on structure rather than instinct, or failing to match the physicality demanded by Crean's system. Losses, particularly those against experienced teams, revealed the fragility that accompanies any attempt at reinvention. But something different happened after those losses. In previous years, the disappointment might have lingered privately, discussed quietly in the hallways before being folded into the routines of the next practice. Under Crean, losses became tools. They were dissected in sessions that bordered on forensic. He demanded that players explain—not merely hear—the mistakes they had made, and then articulate the adjustments required to correct them.

This insistence on verbal accountability changed the atmosphere of the locker room. Conversations grew more direct, sometimes uncomfortably so. Younger players learned quickly that deference had limits. Older players discovered that leadership was not ceremonial but confrontational. Crean believed that a team that could not speak honestly to itself would never survive the pressure of meaningful games. In these moments, beneath the intensity, something subtle was forming: a new vocabulary of ownership, one not rooted in memory but in action.

The city, watching these developments from its vantage point of taverns, living rooms, and local gym bleachers, sensed a shift even before the record showed it. Fans began to talk less about what Marquette used to be and more about what it might become. They discussed Crean's sideline energy, his visible urgency, the sharpness of the team's defensive rotations, the occasional flashes of cohesion that suggested the outlines of a future identity. They noticed how players dove for loose balls, how they communicated more loudly, how they seemed to move with a purpose that reached beyond the immediate possession. Milwaukee is a city that responds to effort, to sincerity, to the refusal to go through the motions. Crean's teams, even in their early stages, embodied these traits in ways that resonated deeply.

Administrators within the university also began to recognize that something foundational was shifting. Attendance numbers stabilized, then rose. Campus energy on game days intensified. Alumni engagement increased. Donors, long nostalgic for the heyday of the 1970s, saw in Crean not a replication of the past but the emergence of a new model of ambition—one rooted in discipline, connection, and relentless motion. The program, which had spent years existing in a state of quiet competence, now showed signs of rejoining the wider national conversation.

Yet even as optimism grew, the weight of the rebuilding process remained heavy. The players endured setbacks that tested their patience and belief. Crean's constant demand for detail could exhaust even the most devoted athletes. The pace of change sometimes felt overwhelming. But in those moments, the team began to understand a truth that underlies every successful transformation: identity is forged in repetition, not revelation. The program's evolution was not the work of a single dramatic moment, but the accumulation of hundreds of small, deliberate acts.

By the end of Crean's second season, even without the signature achievements that would come later, Marquette stood on different ground. The team was still learning, still imperfect, still working through the strain of reinvention. But the pulse of the program had changed. The gym felt different. Practices sounded different. The city watched with renewed attention. What began as a reclamation project had become something else—a reimagining of what it meant to play, coach, and believe at Marquette.

The transformation Crean sought extended far beyond strategy or conditioning. He believed that a program could not rise unless it understood how to inhabit its own geography, and he treated Milwaukee not as a backdrop but as an essential element of Marquette's emerging identity. In the late 1990s and early 2000s, the city was undergoing subtle changes—redevelopment projects on the riverfront, shifting demographics in neighborhoods west of downtown, a growing effort to reimagine Milwaukee as a post-industrial urban center with its own cultural gravity. Crean recognized that if Marquette wished to reclaim national relevance, it first had to understand the rhythms of the city in which it lived.

This insight shaped his recruiting philosophy as much as it shaped his coaching. He began to view Milwaukee as a living classroom for his players, a place that demanded adaptability, resilience, and humility. He organized volunteer events, community outreach programs, and youth clinics not as public relations exercises but as opportunities for players to understand the social fabric surrounding them. He believed that athletes who understood their city played with a groundedness that could not be manufactured through drills alone. Milwaukee, with its mixture of beauty and hardness, offered lessons in perspective.

In practices, this perspective transformed into a demand for toughness—not merely physical, but psychological. Crean insisted that players develop what he often called "competitive character," a concept that blended tenacity, emotional discipline, and the ability to thrive in uncomfortable environments. He simulated these environments through practice structures that tested the limits of composure. Scrimmages began without warning. Drills changed direction midstream. Mistakes triggered immediate corrections, not as punishment but as reminders that focus had to be absolute. Over time, players began to view the court not just as a place of competition but as a place where character was repeatedly revealed and refined.

Game nights reflected this evolution. The early Crean

teams often entered matchups against more experienced programs with a discernible edge—one born not of arrogance but of effort. Even when overmatched physically, they competed with a relentlessness that unsettled opponents. Their defensive pressure tightened. Their communication sharpened. The stands at the Bradley Center, once filled with polite applause, grew louder, less restrained. There was a sense that the city recognized something stirring, even if it could not yet identify what form it would take.

Crean's attention to detail during games bordered on obsessive. He paced the sidelines with a frenetic intensity that contrasted sharply with the demeanor of his predecessors. He shouted instructions, clapped vigorously, demanded eye contact from players checking in. To some, this energy appeared uncontrolled. But within the program, it was viewed as a form of stewardship—a visible insistence that every possession mattered, that every lapse could shift the momentum, that winning required a degree of urgency that left no room for detachment. Players learned to mirror this energy in their own ways. Guards picked up full-court pressure. Forwards fought through screens with renewed purpose. Bench players stayed engaged, vocal, alert.

This atmosphere of engagement reinvigorated the fan base. Milwaukee crowds had always appreciated hard play, but now they began to participate more actively in the rhythms of the game. The arena grew louder during defensive stands. Chants emerged organically. Students, who had once viewed basketball as an accessory to campus life, began to treat game nights as communal rituals. Crean understood this shift instinctively. He encouraged students to travel to road games, to fill sections behind the bench, to create a presence that opponents could feel. He believed that a program regained its national pulse only when its local pulse strengthened first.

Still, Crean's influence extended beyond the court and the city. He understood that modern college basketball depended on building a national footprint. To that end, he scheduled aggressively, seeking matchups that would test his players and expose them to broader audiences. Neutral-site tournaments, non-conference games against established programs, early-season showcases—each offered Marquette a chance to signal its ambition. These games did not always result in victories, but they served a different purpose: they announced that Marquette was done accepting a peripheral role in the national landscape.

Inside the locker room, this ambition took on a more intimate form. Crean introduced rituals designed to reinforce cohesion. Players wrote letters to their future selves, reflecting on their goals. They held team dinners that blended structured discussion with unstructured camaraderie. They watched film not only of their own games but of other teams whose discipline or identity impressed Crean. In these moments, players learned to think of themselves not simply as individuals pursuing personal development, but as contributors to a larger project. The rebuilding of Marquette was not an abstract mission; it was something they lived every day.

These subtle emotional shifts—hard to measure, easy to overlook—reshaped the team's internal landscape. Players began to police their own standards. They took responsibility for errors before coaches pointed them out. Practices unfolded with fewer reminders. Leaders emerged not because they were appointed but because their actions cultivated respect. Even losses carried a different emotional tone. Instead of sagging into resignation, players approached the film room with a sharpened determination. They understood that growth required discomfort.

The new urban order Crean was constructing took shape through these layers of transformation. It was not a revolution of style or system; it was a recalibration of psychology, effort, and expectation. The city, watching from its taverns and living rooms, sensed the return of something familiar—a sense of identity forming not from nostalgia but from immediacy. Marquette no longer seemed like a program drifting between eras. It felt like a program stepping into its own time.

By the end of this period, something unmistakable had happened: the conversation surrounding Marquette basketball shifted. National writers began to mention the program with a curiosity absent for decades. Broadcasters noted its intensity, its connection to its city, its relentless competitiveness. Coaches across the country recognized that Marquette was no longer an easy out.

The foundation for change had been poured. The team did not yet represent a finished identity, but it carried within it the unmistakable signs of one forming—a kind of muscular purpose rising from the friction of expectation and possibility.

The renewal Crean sought required not only reshaping the team's internal dynamics but also reestablishing Marquette's place within the broader ecosystem of college basketball. By the early 2000s, the sport had become a national theater, its storylines shaped by television exposure, shoe-company influence, and the expanding reach of conferences that now sprawled across regions. Programs without clear identities risked invisibility. Crean recognized this risk with unusual clarity. He understood that if Marquette remained an independent actor within this shifting environment, it would slowly lose the gravitational pull that sustained its earlier prominence. A program needed an anchor—something that tethered it not only to history but to a present the nation could not ignore.

One of Crean's earliest internal pushes involved advocating for a stronger structural alignment within the sport's competitive architecture. Though the decisions behind conference affiliation involved layers of administrative strategy far beyond a coach's direct authority, Crean grasped before many that independence had become untenable. Recruit after recruit asked about television schedules, national exposure, guaranteed matchups, and pathways to March visibility. Crean heard in these questions a quiet warning: relevance was no longer ensured by legacy. It required access. It required belonging to a competitive network whose games mattered beyond regional boundaries. He articulated this reality with increasing urgency in conversations behind closed doors, framing the issue not as a complaint but as a vision for what Marquette could still become.

While the university weighed these structural considerations, Crean built his own external network. He maintained close relationships with coaches whose programs shaped the national schedule, fostering connections that gave Marquette access to high-level non-conference games. He cultivated relationships with national media figures, not through self-promotion but through earnest advocacy for his players and his program. At a time when television clips and highlight packages shaped public consciousness more than written profiles, Crean ensured Marquette appeared in the right windows—early-season tournaments, neutral-site showcases, late-night broadcasts where intrigue could build.

These efforts paid dividends in ways less visible than box scores. Viewers who might once have glossed past Marquette on an ESPN crawl began to pause. Opponents preparing for non-conference scheduling discussions reconsidered whether the program still belonged in the "safe" category. The sport's ecosystem, which had long treated Marquette as a legacy brand without a present form, began to adjust its perception. Crean did not speak in grand terms about these shifts, but he felt them. The tone of conversations changed. The eyes in the room widened slightly when Marquette's name appeared on scheduling lists. Identity was taking root, not through slogans but through rhythm and visibility.

Meanwhile, the team itself began to absorb these changes.

Players carried themselves differently when facing ranked teams. They walked into road arenas with a keener sense of belonging. Crean prepared them meticulously for these games, drilling not only schemes but emotional endurance. He taught them how to withstand the opening minutes when crowds surged with energy. He taught them to recognize the turning points when a game's balance could shift with a single decision. He taught them to treat every contest—home or away —as a stage large enough to contain their ambitions.

This transformation required embracing pressure rather than retreating from it. Crean had a phrase he repeated often: *"Pressure is confirmation."* For players who had grown up viewing pressure as something imposed on them, the notion that pressure confirmed their importance required mental rewiring. But over time, they internalized it. When television crews arrived, when national writers filled the press row, when opposing coaches spoke with heightened respect, the players began to understand that these moments did not represent intrusions—they represented acknowledgment.

Milwaukee, too, adjusted to this new atmosphere. The city had always cared, but now it watched with a sharper awareness of the stakes. Tavern conversations shifted from "Can they compete?" to "Who do they match up with?" On campus, game-day anticipation grew more textured, infused with the sense that each performance carried implications beyond local pride. Even alumni who had drifted from the program during the quiet years began returning to the narrative, sensing that the team was once again positioning itself to matter on a national scale.

Within the athletic department, Crean's influence deepened. He insisted that success required institutional alignment —investment in facilities, nutrition programs, academic support, and modern training philosophies. He argued that competitive ambition could not rest on emotion alone; it required infrastructure. His voice became increasingly central in these conversations, not because he demanded authority but because he articulated a vision others found difficult to ignore. He spoke of Marquette not as a program fighting to regain ground, but as an institution preparing to reassert itself.

Yet amid this outward-facing ambition, Crean maintained an intense focus on the quieter, more elemental aspects of program building. He spent hours in one-on-one meetings with players, dissecting film not only to improve technique but to refine decision-making. He emphasized the significance of body language, the psychological impact of communication, the importance of knowing when to speak and when to remain silent. These were not minor details to him; they formed the foundation of a team's internal chemistry. He believed that if players carried the right habits into the invisible moments—walk-throughs, early mornings, sideline huddles—the visible moments would take care of themselves.

The culture that emerged from this approach felt different from anything Marquette had seen in decades. It was not defined by improvisation, as in the McGuire years, nor by steadiness, as in the Raymonds era. It was defined by intentionality—a deliberate, conscious shaping of identity through consistent, high-pressure work. The players learned to understand themselves not as inheritors of a legacy but as architects of a future. The city learned to see the team not as a memory of what once had been, but as a living expression of what might again be possible.

This was the essence of the new urban order: a program no longer drifting between eras, but aligning itself with the pulse of a modern city, a changing sport, and a renewed sense of ambition. The foundation had been reinforced. The structure had begun to rise. The work of transformation, long delayed, had finally entered motion.

The early years of the new century brought with them

a narrowing of focus, as though the long process of reconstruction had finally reached the point where the program could begin shaping itself with intention rather than necessity. Crean's teams no longer carried the posture of those learning to stand upright; they moved with the grounded confidence of athletes who understood both the demands of their environment and the expectations placed upon them. The habits he had drilled into them—precision, communication, relentless defensive engagement—began to manifest not only as isolated moments but as sustained stretches of play. Consistency, that elusive marker of a maturing program, appeared not as an accident but as the product of accumulated labor.

Games at the Bradley Center reflected this shift. The atmosphere inside the arena changed tone. Where crowds once arrived curious, hopeful, or cautiously optimistic, they now entered with a clearer sense of anticipation. The noise rose earlier in games, often before the first media timeout, carried not by surprise but by belief. Even the silences felt different. In earlier years, a missed shot or defensive lapse might have produced a deflated hush. Now those same moments generated an undercurrent of expectation—an implicit confidence that the team understood how to correct itself. Fans were not waiting for identity to emerge; they were watching it take shape in real time.

This growing coherence also altered the way Marquette approached adversity. There were still losses, some frustrating, some predictable, some the product of youth learning to navigate high-pressure environments. But the emotional response to these setbacks changed. Players no longer seemed shaken by the weight of being measured against a history they did not create. Instead, they treated each challenge as part of a long-term trajectory. Film sessions after difficult games took on a more analytical tone. Practices the next morning carried sharper focus. The work that had once felt reactive now felt directional—moving toward a future the team could finally envision with clarity.

Crean, for his part, maintained the pace of a man who understood that momentum, once established, cannot be allowed to drift. He added layers to practices, increasing their complexity. He incorporated more situational drills—end-of-half scenarios, late-game possessions, defensive rotations after broken plays. He wanted players to inhabit chaos as comfortably as order, to understand that the modern game rewarded those who could think and execute at speed. His sideline demeanor grew even more precise. He barked instructions with the urgency of someone fighting for inches, because he believed that inches often determined whether a program rose or stalled.

Recruiting during this period evolved from opportunistic to strategic. Marquette was no longer simply identifying overlooked prospects who fit the program's ethos; it was competing for athletes whose choices would shape the national conversation. Crean approached these battles with a vision built on belief rather than desperation. He sold players on the city—its authenticity, its texture, its capacity to shape men who knew how to compete. He sold them on the university's academic grounding. Most of all, he sold them on the idea that Marquette was a program on the verge of rediscovering its rightful stature. Prospects responded not only to the message but to the consistency with which Crean and his staff delivered it. They saw a program not seeking rescue but projecting purpose.

Behind the scenes, the administration continued to invest in the infrastructure Crean insisted the program required. Facility upgrades took shape. Support staff expanded. The athletic department modernized its approach to player development, nutrition, and scheduling. Every improvement reinforced the sense that Marquette was aligning itself with the standards of national competitors rather than merely adjusting to them. The program's internal architecture, once piecemeal, grew interconnected. Decisions in one area resonated across others. This coherence allowed the team to build an identity not solely dependent on its coach but supported by the institution at large.

Milwaukee, watching these developments, embraced the program with renewed intensity. The city understood the stakes intuitively. It recognized how fragile momentum could be, how easily the work of years could stall if belief faltered at a critical moment. But it also sensed that Marquette was moving through a threshold. The conversations in taverns shifted from cautious praise to confident analysis. Local sports talk shows devoted segments to the team's trajectory rather than its history. High school players spoke with admiration about the program in ways reminiscent of older generations remembering the 1970s. Something had changed in the collective imagination. Marquette no longer appeared as a program hoping to matter again. It stood as a program whose relevance felt imminent.

The players absorbed this energy. They practiced with an awareness that they were part of something extending beyond their own seasons. They began to speak of the program in terms of stewardship. They took ownership of their responsibilities not because they feared failure but because they recognized the opportunity that stood before them. The internal culture grew deeper, sturdier. Leaders emerged organically—men who understood not only the playbook but the emotional architecture the team required. They carried themselves with the conviction that Marquette's return to prominence would not be built on a single moment of brilliance but on the accumulation of hard, unglamorous work.

In this era, the team's on-court style embodied the duality of Crean's vision: structured enough to maintain discipline, yet aggressive enough to capture the energy of a city built on resilience. Defensive possessions stretched longer. Offensive sets grew more dynamic. The ball moved with intention, and players moved without hesitation. They played with an edge that felt both contemporary and unmistakably rooted in Milwaukee's character. The team's physicality did not express itself in brute force but in persistence—hands in passing lanes, bodies diving for loose balls, screens set with firmness, closeouts completed with urgency.

By the time this period reached its full maturation, the outlines of a new era had become undeniable. Marquette had moved beyond the long shadow of transition. The years of drift, of quiet competence, of searching for identity in the absence of a defining figure, had given way to a program that once again understood its own shape. The foundation was no longer memory; it was momentum. The belief Crean insisted upon from the beginning—belief in the institution, the city, the work—had crystallized into something tangible.

The new urban order was no longer an aspiration. It was a lived reality, visible in how the team played, how the city reacted, how recruits listened, and how the nation began to take notice once more.

As the seasons under Crean gathered into a coherent shape, a different energy began to settle over Milwaukee on winter nights. The city's cold remained as sharp as ever, the wind drawing thin lines across the streets as it swept in from the lake, but there was a warmth now that returned to certain corners near campus. The Bradley Center glowed in the early dusk, its light pooling onto the sidewalks where students, alumni, and long-time fans made their way toward the entrances in a steady rhythm. Their steps carried something more than habit. You could sense it in the way conversations rose before tipoff, in the subtle urgency of people moving through the turnstiles, in the gathering hum that filled the concourse as the arena slowly took shape around them.

Inside, as the last warmups ended and the opening horn sounded, the noise had a different quality than it had in the years before Crean arrived. It wasn't simply louder; it was more layered. There was excitement, yes, but also a sturdier form of expectation—the sense that the team on the floor belonged to a future that was beginning to reveal itself. Fans watched possessions not only for their entertainment value but for what they signified about identity, ambition, and the slow tightening of a program's direction. Even during the lulls between plays, the arena carried a kind of anticipatory tension, as though everyone present was waiting for something just beyond the visible moment.

The players felt this atmosphere in ways that shaped their own understanding of the work they had undertaken. Walking off the court after a win or a loss, moving through the dim hallways that led to the locker room, they sensed the resonance of a relationship being rebuilt. The city wasn't asking for miracles; it was responding to the authenticity of their effort. In the quiet moments after games, when the echo of the crowd had faded but the memory of it still lingered in the ears, players understood that they were part of a shift larger than themselves. Their performances mattered not only for the standings but for the reawakening of something dormant—a connection between the program and the community that had once defined both.

On campus, this transformation appeared in small but telling ways. Students wearing Marquette gear no longer did so as a nod to tradition alone; they wore it as an expression of pride rooted in the present. The talk in dining halls and residence lounges carried more attention to detail—dissections of matchups, observations about player development, reflections on the team's evolving defensive intensity. Basketball was no longer a nostalgic echo; it was a living conversation, braided into the life of the university.

The city's older fans, those who had lived through the

215

shifting fortunes of the decades since McGuire, recognized the subtler contours of the transformation. They saw it not in highlight moments but in the steadiness of the team's posture, the urgency of its play, the clarity of its intentions. They understood that identity returns slowly, through repetition rather than revelation. In their reactions—a nod during a timeout, a murmured approval at a defensive rotation, a lingering seat after the final buzzer—you could sense a quiet satisfaction. They were watching a program rediscover its capacity to matter.

The coaching offices after games often held a different kind of quiet. Assistants reviewed clips, noting small breakthroughs or lingering flaws. Whiteboards filled with matchups for the week ahead. Crean, pacing in thought or leaning over a monitor, carried the intensity of someone who understood that growth does not occur in applause but in the unnoticed decisions made on nights when no one is watching. His staff felt the same. There was a recognition among them that the work unfolding was not about reclaiming the past; it was about anchoring the future.

Even in the late evenings, when the arena lights dimmed and the parking lots thinned, something lingered in the air outside—a faint echo of the urgency that had filled the building hours earlier. The night held a sense of continuity, not of memory but of motion. Snow fell softly across the city, accumulating in thin layers that transformed the sidewalks around campus into reflective paths. Students walking back to their apartments or dorms stepped through that hush with an awareness that something meaningful was taking shape within their university's walls.

The new urban order that had taken root did not announce itself through spectacle. It emerged in the accumulation of practices, in the discipline of film study, in the resilience shown after losses, in the sharper angles of victory. It revealed itself in the connection between city and team, reknit carefully through effort and presence. It was sustained through a belief that had been rebuilt from the inside out—belief in the work, belief in the institution, belief in the possibility of becoming more than what the recent decades had allowed.

There were no proclamations needed. The signs were already visible in the way people walked into the arena, in the way the team warmed up, in the way the city watched with a steadier, more confident gaze. Something long in the making had begun to turn. The contours of a future identity were no longer abstract. They lived in the rhythms of the present, in the nightly labor of a team reshaping not only its performance but its place in the world.

In the stillness after each game, when the last lights dimmed and the city folded into its winter quiet, the transformation continued—not loudly, not dramatically, but unmistakably. The work of rebuilding had given way to the work of becoming.

CHAPTER EIGHT – THE BIG EAST ERA AND THE WEIGHT OF HISTORY

"In the Big East, nothing is given. Everything is taken."
— Jim Calhoun

The first sensation was scale. It arrived before any roster adjustment or tactical adaptation, before the travel schedule was finalized or the scouting reports thickened, before Marquette stepped into its first conference game as an official member of the Big East. It appeared in the simple awareness of what it now meant to belong to a league defined not just by competitive density but by cultural weight. The Big East was more than a collection of programs. It was a geography of pride, grievance, memory, and expectation. Its arenas were stages where years hardened into lore, where Catholic schools and public land-grant institutions collided in a tightly wound theater of regional identity. To enter that space was to step into a conversation already in progress.

Marquette had always understood ambition. The program carried the residue of McGuire's audacity and of Milwaukee's own complicated, resilient sense of self. Yet the landscape that awaited them in 2005 carried an intensity of history that demanded something different. The Big East was a league where the past did not rest; it pressed forward into the present, thick as humidity, shaping how every team interpreted its own performance. Georgetown's legacy of Ewing, Mourning, and Mutombo still lingered in the architecture of its defense.

Villanova carried the scent of its 1985 miracle and the humility of its long climb back. Syracuse, under Boeheim's steady hand, moved through the league like a living relic of constancy. UConn, fierce and unbending, walked with the energy of a dynasty still in motion. To face these programs was not simply to play basketball; it was to reckon with the weight of their accumulated meaning.

Marquette arrived from the Conference USA years not naive, but untested by this particular density of tradition. The university had chosen this move because it understood the stakes of visibility, relevance, and institutional alignment. But no administrative decision could fully prepare a program for the lived experience of entering a league with its own gravitational field. When Marquette stepped into Madison Square Garden for its first Big East Tournament, the moment revealed itself in the acoustics alone. The arena did not welcome newcomers; it measured them. The terraces carried the history of rivalries born from proximity—urban Catholic schools pressed into a single crucible of pride. The noise rolled down from the rafters with a familiar timbre, as though the decades had condensed into a single, ongoing roar.

The players felt this immediately. The league's tempo differed from what they had known. Every possession felt more crowded, more contested. Defenders closed space faster. Screens landed heavier. Guards moved with an edge that came not from athleticism alone but from the long memory of the league's internal battles. Marquette adjusted quickly, but the adjustment revealed the deeper truth of Big East play: that toughness was not an attribute but an assumption. To survive required matching not only the physical intensity of opponents but their sense of inherited purpose.

The early trips to league arenas brought this reality into sharper focus. At the Petersen Events Center, Pittsburgh fans created a low, suffocating noise that seemed to rise from the floorboards. At the Carrier Dome, the enormity of the space destabilized visiting teams before the game even began; the court seemed to float in a sea of orange. At the Wachovia Center, Villanova crowds moved with a confidence born from recent revival and long memory. And in Washington, the sound of the band beneath the cavernous roof filled the air with a reminder that Georgetown, even when inconsistent, never played small.

Marquette stepped into this world carrying both humility and defiance. Humility, because the league demanded it. Defiance, because the program had long insisted that geography did not dictate destiny. Milwaukee was not Philadelphia or Washington or New York. It lacked the concentrated media apparatus and the dense intersection of high school talent that fed the northeastern schools. But Milwaukee understood work, and in the Big East, work mattered. Work closed the gap against talent. Work hardened a team's identity. Work created the conditions under which belief could take root.

The first season unfolded with a sense of discovery. There were moments when the team found itself overwhelmed by opponents whose depth and discipline reflected years of sustained investment in the league's culture. But there were also nights when Marquette's edge—sharpened under Crean's restless insistence on preparation—cut through the noise. Those victories carried more emotional resonance than their numerical value suggested. They affirmed that Marquette belonged, not by inheritance but by exertion.

The city responded with a mixture of pride and renewed vigilance. Milwaukee had always viewed its place in the national basketball landscape with a kind of wary confidence. Now the stakes were higher. Big East membership exposed Marquette to a different tier of scrutiny, a national attention that brought both excitement and pressure. Fans filled the Bradley Center with a sharper energy, understanding that every home game carried the added weight of representing not only the program but the region. There was satisfaction in this, but also responsibility. Milwaukee embraced both.

The campus, too, felt the shift. Students followed league standings with a new attentiveness. They tracked rivalries that had formed long before their arrival at the university. They watched highlights from Providence and Rutgers, Seton Hall and West Virginia, learning the personalities and tendencies of programs their predecessors had never considered central to Marquette's identity. The Big East demanded literacy in its culture, and Marquette's students quickly absorbed it.

Yet beneath the exhilaration of competing on this new stage, another truth emerged: the Big East was not simply a league to be played; it was a league to be endured. Its physical demands accumulated across a season. Long travel days, punishing defensive schemes, hostile arenas—these elements wore down teams unprepared for the perpetual grind. Marquette learned this lesson early, discovering that a single lapse in discipline could turn a competitive game into a punishing loss. The margin for error narrowed. The psychological stakes rose.

Still, it was precisely within this crucible that Marquette began to understand its new identity. The program's past had been shaped by singular figures and flashpoint seasons, but the Big East required something more sustained—a capacity to inhabit pressure without becoming distorted by it. The players learned to do this incrementally, possession by possession, game by game.

And as they did, another realization settled in: that the Big East was not merely a proving ground but a mirror. It revealed what a program believed about itself. It reflected its strengths and exposed its weaknesses. It demanded coherence. It required conviction. It offered no shortcuts.

By the end of the early years, Marquette understood the league not as an external force pressing in but as an environment it was learning to claim. The weight of history did not diminish the program. It sharpened it.

The Big East announced itself most clearly in January, when the season's early experiments had hardened into patterns and every game carried the thickened air of consequence. For Marquette, those winter months revealed the deeper contours of the league in ways no preseason briefing or administrative forecast could have expressed. The rhythm of Big East play was not linear; it pulsed, swelled, constricted, and demanded a kind of emotional endurance that tested teams long before the standings reflected their fate. Each opponent—regardless of record—carried a history of nights when it had disrupted someone else's certainty. That was the quiet truth of the conference: reputations mattered, but desperation mattered more, and every program possessed its own reserve of it.

Travel crystallized this reality. The distances were not vast, but the psychological terrain felt enormous. One night Marquette found itself in Newark, facing a Seton Hall team whose physicality seemed to draw energy from the rafters of the Prudential Center. A few days later, the journey bent south toward Morgantown, where West Virginia's pressurized style and mountainous crowds suffocated the first few possessions of any visiting team. Then came Cincinnati, with its bruising lineage, or Louisville, whose transition offense turned every turnover into something close to a public reckoning. The league's geography formed a loop of atmospheres—each distinct, each demanding, each refusing conformity.

Even at home, the pressure felt different from anything Marquette had known. The Bradley Center became a stage where expectations collided with legacy. Opposing fans traveled well; so did their history. Villanova carried its aura of disciplined spacing and hard-nosed guards. Pittsburgh played with the kind of interior violence that defined its program for a decade. Syracuse arrived with a zone that swallowed passing lanes as though designed to consume both ball and momentum. These games did not merely challenge Marquette's execution; they forced the players to situate themselves within a larger story. The crowd sensed this, responding with a sharper tempo, a knowing roar that acknowledged both the challenge and the privilege of facing these familiar giants.

For the coaching staff, the Big East required a reinvention of preparation. Scouting reports doubled in density, filled with details not only about execution but about temperament— how Providence defended after missed shots, how St. John's chased offensive rebounds, how Georgetown disguised the angles of its backdoor cuts. Crean and his assistants immersed themselves in film, learning the habits of teams whose identities had been forged by decades of consistent pressure. Each opponent demanded a different emotional approach. Some games required patience; others required aggression; still others required a willingness to withstand waves of momentum without surrendering the rhythm of the game.

The players absorbed this complexity gradually, recognizing that the league demanded maturity as much as athleticism. They learned to approach road environments with a steadier psychological posture. They learned that leads were fragile and deficits reversible. They learned that the Big East often turned on sequences rather than stretches—a defensive stop paired with a timely three-pointer, a steal that shifted crowd energy, a possession manufactured through pure toughness when the playbook malfunctioned under pressure. These lessons did not arrive all at once, but accreted through repetition, through the sting of losses and the catharsis of unexpected victories.

One of the most revealing aspects of the transition involved Marquette's relationship to physicality. The Big East did not simply allow contact; it normalized it. Referees, accustomed to a league defined by collisions, whistles, and strategic chaos, permitted a degree of body-to-body engagement that surprised newcomers. For Marquette, this required both tactical and emotional adaptation. Guards learned to initiate contact before receiving it. Forwards learned to seal defenders more forcefully. Centers, often undersized compared to their counterparts at UConn or Louisville, learned to contest space with leverage rather than height. The team discovered that success in this league did not belong to the strongest but to those who understood how to absorb force without losing structure.

The effect on team identity was profound. Practices grew more demanding, filled with drills designed to normalize discomfort. Scrimmages simulated hostile environments with artificial noise and abrupt officiating. The staff emphasized conditioning that prepared players to withstand sequences of sustained pressure. Crean reminded them that the Big East did not reward fragility. It rewarded teams that embraced the collisions, absorbed them, and responded not with frustration but with clarity.

This shift resonated deeply in Milwaukee, where the city's industrial past had long shaped its understanding of sport. Blue-collar resilience was not a slogan; it was a worldview. Fans recognized themselves in the league's physical style—its refusal to offer ease, its insistence on durability. They saw Marquette's growing comfort within that environment not as an imitation of Big East toughness but as a revelation of something that had always lived within the program's character.

Yet the Big East imposed a different kind of weight as well—the weight of expectation. Once Marquette demonstrated it could compete in the league, the standard shifted. The surprise of early success gave way to scrutiny. Losses no longer felt like natural consequences of transition; they felt like failures to uphold a new baseline. Players sensed this in the way reporters framed questions, in the tone of alumni emails, in the energy of home crowds after missed opportunities. The emotion surrounding the program grew more complicated, threading hope with pressure, pride with impatience.

This complexity, however, was precisely what affirmed Marquette's new place in the national landscape. Relevance brings expectations. Expectations bring scrutiny. Scrutiny brings consequence. And consequence is the architecture of meaningful sport. The Big East, in its relentless demand for coherence and resilience, had pulled Marquette into a deeper form of participation—not only in games but in the narrative weight that accompanies them.

By the end of these early years, the program understood the league not as an overwhelming monolith but as a daily environment in which identity was tested and reshaped. The weight of history felt less like a burden and more like an invitation. Marquette had chosen to enter this world. Now it was learning how to live within it—with urgency, with humility, and with a growing sense that it belonged not only on the schedule but in the story.

The deeper Marquette moved into the Big East, the more it confronted the truth that leagues, like cities, possess internal geographies—shapes of influence, prestige, and memory that determine how teams are perceived long before they take the court. The Big East had its peaks and plateaus, its cultural capitals and its borderlands. Some programs— UConn, Georgetown, Syracuse—carried themselves as if they inhabited the league's historical high ground, a place earned through sustained national relevance. Others, like Villanova and Pittsburgh, had carved out identities through discipline and internal coherence, shaping reputations that radiated outward with their own gravitational pull. Even the league's struggling programs had roles to play, often disrupting the ambitions of their more established rivals with a single win on a cold weeknight in January.

Marquette entered this terrain neither as a novice nor as an heir. It occupied a liminal space: rich history behind it, ambitious future ahead of it, and a transitional present where nothing was guaranteed. This position created both opportunity and vulnerability. The opportunity lay in mobility—Marquette could redefine its place, climb quickly, and shape how the league perceived it. The vulnerability lay in the absence of predetermined footing—one poor stretch of games could shift the narrative; one season of inconsistency could relegate the program to the league's lower tiers, where climbing back required emotional stamina as much as wins.

The first seasons demonstrated how fluid these hierarchies could be. Marquette learned that wins against league giants carried disproportionate weight. A victory over Connecticut reverberated nationally in ways no non-conference success could. A road win at Georgetown announced the team's maturity. A tight contest at Louisville, even in defeat, signaled that Marquette could withstand the chaos of a program that played with perpetual urgency. In this league, the calendar felt heavier than in previous eras. Each game carried a different emotional temperature. Each matchup contained layers of meaning, some inherited, some newly formed.

Behind the scenes, Crean understood the symbolic stakes of these games and addressed them without sentimentality. He reminded his players that history did not confer immunity on their opponents. It only informed their habits. If Marquette learned to recognize these habits—to disrupt them, exploit them, or simply endure them—then the program could move beyond the status of a welcomed newcomer. It could force the league to re-map itself around Marquette's presence. He told them that the Big East did not reward those who admired its architecture. It rewarded those who refused to be defined by it.

This mindset began to influence how Marquette prepared for games that carried historical significance. Film study became archaeological. The staff pored over years of footage to understand how Syracuse disguised the weak point in its 2–3 zone, or how Georgetown's Princeton-influenced offense used backdoor movement to lure defenders into overcommitment, or how Pittsburgh's physical interior play created foul trouble for teams unwilling to adjust early. These details mattered not as trivia but as markers of respect. To enter the Big East without studying its cultural codes was to enter unarmed.

The players responded with a seriousness that mirrored the league's own character. Practices took on an academic tone. Film sessions produced quiet intensity rather than passive observation. The team learned to speak the league's language —the language of adjustments, counters, and the slow accumulation of advantage. They recognized that talent alone could not overcome the Big East's structural rhythms. Survival required literacy. Advancement required fluency.

Meanwhile, the city of Milwaukee absorbed the league's presence with a mixture of fascination and pride. Local papers began printing analysis of games against Seton Hall or Providence with the same attention once reserved for matchups against regional rivals. Bars on Water Street filled earlier on game nights, televisions tuned to Big East broadcasts from New York, Philadelphia, or Cincinnati. Fans tracked the league standings with heightened urgency, not because the math of the season had changed, but because the emotional architecture of belonging had. Marquette was no longer playing for recognition; it was playing for position in a landscape where identity was measured not only by victories but by the ability to withstand the league's constant friction.

On campus, the shift manifested in student behavior. They followed late-night games from the East Coast, learning the tendencies of opponents and forming opinions about referees who had long histories with the league's older members. They debated matchups with the confidence of insiders. The Big East transformed casual attention into analytic engagement. Students did not simply attend games; they inhabited them.

As the seasons progressed, Marquette encountered something subtler and more revealing: the psychological weight carried by teams born into the league. Programs like Syracuse or

Georgetown played with an unmistakable sense of entitlement —not arrogance, but a certainty born from the knowledge that they had been shaped within this crucible since the league's inception. Their players understood instinctively when momentum was turning, how to manipulate pace, how to draw fouls in moments of vulnerability, how to lean into a home crowd's energy at precisely the right moment. These instincts were not coached in isolation; they were inherited across generations of players who had lived within the league's cadence.

Marquette's challenge was different. It had to acquire these instincts through deliberate effort. It had to learn the league's timing—the way February games carried a different emotional gravity, the way teams played differently after suffering consecutive losses, the way officiating tightened or loosened depending on the arena, the way a midseason injury could alter the competitive balance. These lessons were absorbed incrementally, through experience rather than lineage.

Yet in this process, something important happened. Marquette began to develop its own internal memory of the league. Players who stayed for multiple seasons passed down knowledge to newcomers. They spoke of hostile arenas not as threats but as rites of passage. They explained how Pittsburgh defended the post differently in the final five minutes, how Villanova closed out on shooters from particular angles, how Providence's guards used hesitation dribbles to draw help defenders out of position. These details formed the foundation of an institutional memory that would sustain the program long after the first generation of Big East players had left.

This accumulation of knowledge allowed Marquette to confront another challenge: the emotional weight of the league's history. The Big East's identity was not only competitive; it was narrative. Games unfolded within stories that stretched back decades. Rivalries were fed by memory more than proximity. Success carried symbolic meaning.

Failure carried a certain sting. Marquette learned that to thrive in this environment required more than toughness. It required an ability to withstand the psychological complexity of facing opponents who carried their past into every possession.

By the middle of its Big East tenure, Marquette had internalized this complexity. The team no longer looked surprised by the league's pressure. It no longer entered arenas with the posture of a guest. It moved with a grounded confidence born not of dominance but of adaptation.

The league had tested Marquette in every way—physically, tactically, psychologically. And in the slow, often invisible process of accepting these tests, Marquette discovered that the weight of history was not a burden to be feared. It was a weight to be carried, sharpened by, and eventually used.

What distinguished the middle years of Marquette's Big East experience was not any single victory or dramatic turning point, but a gradual realization that the league's greatest challenge was its density. Every team sat close enough in quality to threaten the standings, yet far enough apart in style to demand constant reinvention. A week could begin with the methodical pace of Notre Dame, pivot abruptly into the open-floor aggression of Providence, and end in the half-court trench battles against Pittsburgh or West Virginia. In most conferences, teams adapted to one or two dominant styles. In the Big East, adaptation became a permanent condition.

This constant recalibration reshaped Marquette's internal rhythm. Mondays no longer felt like resets; they felt like continuations of a single, unbroken march. Practices grew more situational, preparing players for tactical contrasts rather than season-long themes. Crean and his staff emphasized the ability to shift gears—to press against one opponent, to retreat into disciplined half-court play against another, to survive endurance tests against a third. The players learned that emotional flexibility mattered as much as physical preparation. The legal pads in team meetings filled with diagrams not of singular plays but of decision trees: if Louisville traps here, pivot to this action; if Georgetown switches, run this counter; if Notre Dame refuses to guard the ball handler tightly, initiate a different rhythm.

This perpetual adaptation created a deeper kind of resilience. The players no longer viewed discomfort as a signal of failure; they understood it as the baseline condition of Big East life. The league forced them to reach beyond instinct and into intention. A closeout could not be lazy, because Seton Hall's perimeter shooters punished hesitation. A box-out could not be casual, because St. John's lived on put-back points. A pass thrown half a second late against Syracuse's zone risked turning into a run-out dunk at the other end. The league rewarded precision and punished anything less. Over time, this pressure forged a sturdier program identity—not flamboyant, not rooted in any singular style, but anchored in adaptability.

Amid this grind, moments arose when Marquette glimpsed its emerging place in the league. These recognitions often came not from wins but from the tenor of games. A tight contest in Hartford suggested that UConn had begun to take Marquette seriously. A defensive slugfest in Pittsburgh indicated that the Panthers recognized Marquette's toughness. A win in Washington signaled that Georgetown no longer viewed Marquette as a new arrival but as a legitimate threat. These shifts in perception traveled quietly through the league, communicated through changes in scouting emphases, in the physicality of matchups, in the tone of postgame comments from opposing coaches. Respect, in the Big East, was rarely given with words. It revealed itself through how hard teams played against you.

Milwaukee recognized these shifts with an almost visceral sense of pride. The city understood the meaning of being tested by established powers. It also understood the significance of proving capable of standing among them. Local fans spoke about Big East games with a new vocabulary —terms like "identity win," "possession game," "tournament résumé"—phrases that belonged to programs playing for more than local relevance. Bars filled earlier on Saturdays. Alumni gatherings across the Midwest synchronized with television schedules. The league transformed Marquette from a regional story into a national conversation, and the city embraced that expansion.

The campus absorbed this elevation in subtler ways. Student attendance rose not only for marquee opponents but for midseason games where implications exceeded glamour. Season-ticket lines formed earlier. Pre-game classroom chatter shifted from general hopefulness to analytical anticipation. Students debated matchups with Georgetown's frontcourt, the difficulty of guarding Villanova's ball screens, or the challenge of deciphering West Virginia's pressure. Basketball became not only entertainment but a shared academic language, a way of understanding the world through strategy and adaptation.

Within the program, the physical toll of Big East life deepened the bonds among players. They experienced the league's grind together—bruises from Cincinnati, exhaustion from long stretches in Syracuse's zone, fatigue from back-to-back road trips that blurred days into one another. These strains cultivated a camaraderie not formed through ease but forged through endurance. Players became caretakers of one another's confidence. Veterans reassured newcomers during rough stretches. Younger players lifted older ones during late-season fatigue. The culture thickened, built not on slogans but on the shared knowledge of what it meant to survive January and February in this league.

These internal dynamics shaped how Marquette approached adversity. In earlier eras, a two-game losing streak might have threatened destabilization. In the Big East, such stretches became expected. What mattered was not avoiding them but responding to them. The team learned to study losses without panic, to diagnose problems without melodrama, to trust that effort and clarity could restore momentum. This attitude represented a meaningful maturation. It allowed the program to inhabit the competitive weight of the league without being crushed by it.

One of the strongest measures of this maturation came in the way Marquette executed during tight games. The Big East produced fewer blowouts than other conferences because its members shared a cultural stubbornness. Games often remained undecided until the final minute. Marquette learned to embrace these moments. Timeout huddles grew calmer. Players communicated more clearly. They understood how to seek mismatches, how to adjust defensive schemes, how to guard without fouling, how to manufacture a good shot when play designs broke down. These late-game executions signaled something central: the program no longer panicked under pressure. It belonged in these moments because it had been shaped by them.

Yet the Big East tested Marquette in ways that extended beyond the court. It challenged the institution's sense of itself. It demanded investment—not only financial, but emotional and cultural. Administrators recognized that the stakes of membership reached far beyond athletics. Games broadcast from Madison Square Garden or the Carrier Dome became moments of national visibility for the university. Victories carried institutional pride. Losses exposed areas where growth was still required. The Big East was not simply a stage; it was a mirror, reflecting back the university's ambitions, vulnerabilities, and evolving identity.

It also revealed something about Milwaukee's relationship to the program. The city, often protective of its own history and character, embraced the idea that Marquette could compete on a stage that stretched beyond regional boundaries. The bond between team and city tightened as each recognized itself in the other: resilient, overlooked, underestimated, and capable of rising when the moment required it.

By the midpoint of its Big East life, Marquette no longer entered arenas as an outsider. The players walked onto the court with an awareness that the league respected their presence, that opponents prepared differently for them, that every game carried the expectation of difficulty. This shift did not happen quickly or dramatically; it unfolded through months of friction, adaptation, and sustained effort. But it happened.

The identity Marquette had carried into the Big East—one shaped by ambition and uncertainty—began to transform into something sturdier. The program had endured the weight of history, absorbed the league's complexity, and emerged with a deeper understanding of itself. It had not yet reached its apex, but it had acquired the foundation that any true ascent requires: belonging not by invitation, but by proof.

What became clearest in the later years of Marquette's early Big East tenure was that the league did not simply test teams through competition; it tested their sense of continuity. Programs that rose too quickly without establishing internal stability were swallowed by the relentlessness of the schedule. Programs that relied too heavily on individual brilliance without developing an institutional backbone found themselves exposed when styles shifted or personnel changed. The Big East, in its unyielding structure, required endurance not just within seasons but across them. It demanded that a program know why it existed—and that it act on that knowledge even when circumstances wavered.

Marquette discovered this truth gradually, through the friction of the league's cyclical pressures. Each season unfolded with a mixture of promise and strain, revealing where the program's foundation had hardened and where it still needed reinforcement. Early successes hinted at upward mobility, but each subsequent year brought new challenges: graduated seniors whose leadership could not easily be replaced; opponents who had adjusted to Marquette's tendencies; subtle shifts in league tempos that required tactical adaptation. These changes formed a kind of annual recalibration, a reminder that past progress offered no protection from the present.

Within the program, this reality reshaped how coaches and players understood the experience of belonging to a major conference. Instead of viewing each season as a separate pursuit, they began to see themselves as participants in a longer arc, one that required patience, persistence, and a willingness to inhabit complexity. The staff approached recruiting with an eye toward coherence—seeking players whose mental and emotional dispositions matched the league's demands. They understood that Big East basketball favored those who could endure contact, absorb pressure, and play through noise rather than around it. The players who arrived during this period entered a culture already defined by these expectations, and their development reflected a program that now taught not only skill but temperament.

This emphasis on temperament revealed itself most clearly during stretches of the season when external narratives intensified. A ranking in the national polls brought increased scrutiny. A difficult road trip generated doubt. A midseason losing streak stirred anxiety. Yet the team learned to navigate these fluctuations with a steadying rhythm. Film sessions emphasized detail rather than drama. Practices refocused on habits rather than correction. The coaches maintained a tone that resisted both triumph and despair, grounding the players in the belief that identity, not circumstance, determined trajectory.

The fans, too, began to sense this internal maturation. At the Bradley Center, reactions to adversity grew more measured. Where earlier crowds might have groaned audibly in tense moments, the newer fan response shifted toward encouragement, a recognition that the team had earned patience. This change reflected something deeper: Milwaukee no longer viewed Marquette as a program struggling to rejoin the national conversation. It saw a team fully embedded within one of the sport's defining leagues, a team whose challenges were not signs of decline but markers of belonging to an environment where stability was hard-won and always provisional.

The broader Big East landscape during this period added another layer of complexity. The league was shifting beneath the surface—programs rising and falling, coaching philosophies evolving, institutional identities adjusting to the accelerating commercialization of college basketball. The arrival of new coaches at traditional powers introduced fresh styles; the emergence of new stars across the league tilted competitive balance in unexpected directions. Even the culture of the conference, long anchored by its rugged physicality and territorial rivalries, began to feel the early tremors of a sport preparing to change. Marquette had to adapt not only to the league it had joined, but to the league as it was becoming.

This dynamic placed Marquette in a unique position. The program's recent reinvention meant it was still flexible, still building, still capable of adjusting without the burden of an entrenched identity. At the same time, its growing success created expectations of consistency. Balancing these forces required a degree of institutional introspection not always visible to the public. The athletic department assessed facilities, resources, and long-term strategies. The coaching staff examined its developmental pipeline. The university recognized that membership in the Big East demanded a sustained commitment to being competitive at the highest level—not just occasionally, but habitually.

The players absorbed this environment in ways that shaped

their understanding of what it meant to represent Marquette. Younger athletes arrived with a clearer sense of the program's place: not as an independent brand, not as a nostalgically remembered force, but as a contemporary member of a league that demanded clarity of purpose. They learned to move through arenas with a posture that reflected both respect and confidence. They learned that effort alone was insufficient; precision mattered, discipline mattered, and the ability to execute under duress mattered most of all.

Across seasons, the accumulation of these habits created a kind of internal architecture. Marquette was no longer simply responding to the league; it was learning how to anticipate it. The program had begun to understand the rhythms of conference play—the early-season jockeying for identity, the midseason collisions when standings tightened, the late-season battles that defined tournament seeding. This understanding transformed how Marquette approached preparation, how it interpreted setbacks, and how it absorbed success.

In time, the league's weight—its history, its expectations, its competitive rigor—ceased to feel foreign. It became something closer to familiar terrain. The players walked into games not as visitors to a storied environment but as contributors to its ongoing narrative. Their experiences, once shaped by intimidation or novelty, grew more grounded, more assured. They understood that the Big East did not confer status; it revealed it.

By the end of this era, the program's transformation was unmistakable. Marquette had gained more than wins, more than national relevance, more than a schedule filled with high-stakes contests. It had gained a deeper sense of who it was within the landscape of college basketball. The league had not altered Marquette's identity so much as clarified it, stripping away illusions and strengthening the parts capable of enduring.

The Big East had tested Marquette with pressure, complexity, and expectation—and in that process, it had prepared the program for the next stage of its evolution.

The Big East revealed itself most fully not in the loud moments, but in the quiet ones that followed. Long after the fans had emptied into the Milwaukee night, after the coaches had retreated into their offices with stacks of film and the arena lights had dimmed to a faint blue glow across the hardwood, something lingered in the building—an echo of the league's unspoken demands. It was in these late hours that Marquette most clearly felt the weight of its new home. The Big East was not merely a schedule or a set of opponents; it was a climate, an atmosphere, a way of being tested. And the stillness after each game revealed how deeply the program had learned to live within that test.

On nights when the snow fell thickly across Wisconsin Avenue, muffling the city's usual sounds, the walk from the Bradley Center to campus carried a particular gravity. Students moved in clusters, their breath visible in the cold, talking about possessions that had swung the game or missed chances that lingered in the mind. Some nights the conversations held excitement; on others, frustration. But the tone had changed. The league's presence had reoriented their sense of context. A win no longer felt like an isolated triumph; it felt like a step in a longer ascent. A loss did not signify collapse; it revealed where the program still needed to harden. The Big East had introduced a different scale of measurement—one that stretched beyond the horizon of a single season.

In apartments and dorm rooms, the night continued in the glow of television replays and message-board discussions. Highlights played on ESPN, narratives condensed into soundbites, commentators debated implications. Yet the reality beneath these conversations was quieter, more persistent: Marquette had become part of a world where meaning gathered with each possession, each February game, each late-season surge. The league's history had folded into the program's daily life, and with it came a deeper awareness of what it meant to compete at that level.

Inside the locker room, after the showers had cooled and the last players drifted out, the room often sat in a kind of reflective calm. Jerseys hung motionless. Towels lay abandoned near benches. The air carried the faint mix of sweat, resin, and adrenaline dispersing. In this emptiness, the lessons of the league settled more clearly. The players understood that the Big East would not remember them for easy wins or lopsided losses; it would remember the accumulation of effort, the steadiness of identity, the character revealed in the weeks when fatigue pressed hardest. They lived that reality daily, finding purpose in the grind itself.

Milwaukee, for its part, absorbed the transformation with a sense of recognition. The city had always understood work, friction, and endurance—traits carved into its industrial past. Now it watched a basketball program live out those same values on a national stage. In taverns along State Street, in living rooms across the metro area, in the quiet corners of third-shift break rooms, the league's narrative intertwined with the city's own sense of itself. Marquette's games became more than entertainment. They became moments when Milwaukee could see its own resilience reflected and affirmed.

The Big East had challenged Marquette to grow into its history, to stand beside programs that had shaped the sport's identity for decades. And in responding to that challenge, Marquette discovered that the league's weight was not something to fear. It was something to carry, something that clarified purpose and revealed character. The pressure did not diminish the program; it sharpened it. The complexity did not confuse it; it disciplined it. The history did not overwhelm it; it invited Marquette to contribute to a longer, more demanding story.

On certain nights, when the arena was empty and the court

lights had been reduced to a faint glow for the cleaning staff, the building seemed to hold its breath. The lines on the floor appeared almost translucent. The baskets stood in a quiet symmetry. This was the hour when the next game was already taking shape in the minds of coaches and players alike. The Big East offered no rest; it offered continuity. And Marquette, shaped by years of adaptation, had learned to find meaning in that continuity.

Nothing about this league was gentle, but everything about it was clarifying. It revealed what mattered, what endured, what required rebuilding. And in that slow, cumulative revelation, Marquette found its footing, its voice, and its place within a landscape defined by weight, rivalry, and the unrelenting demand to prove, again and again, that belonging is an act rather than an inheritance.

CHAPTER NINE – BUZZ WILLIAMS, SHAKA SMART, AND THE MODERN REAWAKENING

"Culture eats game plans for breakfast."
— Buzz Williams

The first thing people noticed about Buzz Williams was motion. He paced the sideline as if tethered to an invisible current, leaning forward, pulling back, cutting angles around assistant coaches, his body a restless extension of the game's unfolding tension. Yet beneath that kinetic exterior lived something far more deliberate: a philosophy shaped around the belief that culture—real culture, not the slogans or veneers programs sometimes paste over their vulnerabilities—was the force that sustained winning long after schemes were scouted and talent cycled out. When he arrived at Marquette in 2008, the Big East was reaching its densest, most pressurized form. Every night presented a new challenge, not only of execution but of identity. Williams embraced this environment with an intensity that seemed to match the league's own pulse.

His early teams reflected that urgency. Practices ran with a tempo that resembled controlled chaos, players chasing loose balls as though each one contained a fragment of future possibility. Williams talked about details as if they were moral obligations. Footwork, positioning, eye level on closeouts—everything mattered because nothing in the Big

East came easily. He recruited players who mirrored this ethic: undersized forwards who rebounded like heavyweights, guards with shoulders scarred from years of driving into bodies stronger than their own, wings who understood that toughness was not simply a physical trait but a way of interpreting the world.

The city responded instantly. Milwaukee, long attuned to the value of labor, recognized in Williams's teams a kind of industrial ferocity. Fans watched players dive across the hardwood for deflections, trap ball-handlers in corners with suffocating angles, and chase rebounds that seemed mathematically unreachable. These acts registered not as theatrics but as affirmations of a cultural truth: basketball in Milwaukee could be beautiful, but only after it was hard. In taverns across the city, people noted that Williams did not merely coach effort; he demanded conversion—turning fatigue into resolve, pressure into clarity, discomfort into cohesion.

Within the locker room, Williams constructed a vocabulary of honesty. Players learned quickly that there was no sanctuary for half-truths. Film sessions cut with precision, revealing not only tactical lapses but emotional ones. A missed rotation was problematic, but a lack of communication was unacceptable. Williams taught his players that the game exposed character more reliably than any personality test. In these moments, he was not simply coaching basketball; he was shaping an interpretive framework through which his players understood themselves. The intensity was exhausting, but it also produced alignment. Over time, that alignment became the foundation for teams that outperformed their projections, that won games they seemed too small or too undermanned to claim.

Those early years built toward something larger. By the time Marquette reached its string of Sweet Sixteen appearances between 2011 and 2013, the program carried itself with a confidence that reached beyond the box scores. The team's identity—tough, unselfish, relentless—had hardened into something opponents respected even when they couldn't fully explain it. The aesthetics of victory mattered less than the evidence of cohesion. Williams's teams rarely coasted. They accumulated advantages through persistence, eroding opponents with the sheer consistency of their effort.

But the intensity that fueled success also carried weight. The Big East realignment years introduced a new uncertainty across the league, unsettling traditions and altering the landscape Williams had mastered. Marquette continued to compete, but the foundations underfoot shifted. The volatility of conference identity, the widening pressures of modern college basketball, and the cumulative strain of years spent coaching at emotional full pitch began to shape the atmosphere around the program. When Williams left in 2014, the departure felt abrupt yet strangely inevitable, as though the tension that had held the era together had stretched beyond its natural limits.

The period that followed revealed how delicate continuity can be. The program did not collapse, but the emotional architecture Williams had constructed loosened. Players and coaches worked earnestly, yet something in the atmosphere no longer held with the same clarity. The fault lay not in effort but in coherence. A program that had spent years thriving on intensity had to learn how to breathe differently, how to rebuild identity not from pressure but from reflection. Milwaukee watched with a mixture of patience and concern. The team still worked, still competed, still represented the university with integrity—but the unmistakable sharpness of purpose that defined the Williams era had dispersed into the air like steam on a winter night.

In those transitional years, Marquette lived in a kind of suspended state, as though waiting for a narrative to form. The Big East itself had changed, its membership reconstituted, its rivalries realigned, its character subtly shifted. Yet the league remained demanding, its identity still rooted in pressure and proximity. Marquette needed not a restoration of the past but a reawakening of purpose, a leader capable of reading both the city's temperament and the program's deeper rhythms. The search was not simply for a coach but for someone who could translate institutional memory into modern coherence.

That figure arrived, unexpectedly and yet unmistakably, in the form of Shaka Smart.

His return to Wisconsin in 2021 carried an emotional resonance that stretched beyond biography. Born and raised in Madison, Smart understood the landscape intuitively—the humility, the quiet confidence, the belief in work done without spectacle. He arrived at Marquette not as a savior but as someone who recognized what had been lost and what could be rebuilt. His early remarks hinted at an ethos grounded in connection: joy, toughness, unity. Words that might elsewhere betray sentimentality felt in Milwaukee like a return to elemental truths.

Where Williams had electrified the air with intensity, Smart grounded it with clarity. His teams pressed defensively not as an act of desperation but as an expression of freedom. His practices emphasized communication, rhythm, and the emotional intelligence needed to read a possession as though it were a line of music. He brought analytics into the program not as a foreign language but as a way of illuminating instinct. And he asked his players to root themselves in something deeper than performance: an understanding that identity grows from within before it manifests outward.

The city heard this change long before it fully saw it. Fans noticed a new ease in how players moved, a looseness that did not diminish effort but reoriented it. They saw a coaching staff that approached development with patience, teaching players not simply how to act under pressure but how to interpret it. Over time, the team's style reflected this philosophy—fluid, unselfish, defensively suffocating, joyful without being naive. The reawakening did not arrive with spectacle. It grew quietly, like clarity emerging after a long spell of noise.

And slowly, unmistakably, Marquette rediscovered its center. The program found its rhythm not by replicating past eras but by reconciling them—joining the grit of Williams's years with the emotional intelligence of Smart's. It learned that toughness could coexist with joy, that discipline could coexist with freedom, that history could coexist with reinvention.

The modern reawakening was not a moment. It was an understanding.

The return of clarity at Marquette did not arrive all at once. It emerged gradually, in the layered work of reshaping a program that had drifted between structures, voices, and ambitions. When Shaka Smart accepted the job in 2021, he stepped into an environment that held both promise and fragility. The roster had talent, but not yet coherence. The fan base carried hope, but also fatigue from seasons that lacked an identifiable rhythm. The university sought stability, yet understood that stability without identity meant little in a sport defined by pressure. Smart recognized these conditions not as impediments but as opportunities. He knew that programs do not awaken through tactics alone; they awaken through meaning.

His first task, then, was not to implement schemes. It was to establish tone. Smart believed that a team's emotional architecture determined its ceiling far more than any set of plays could. He introduced concepts that sounded almost deceptively simple—joy, toughness, unity—yet carried weight in their application. Joy was not frivolity; it was presence, engagement, and the ability to love the work. Toughness was not machismo; it was endurance, communication, and the willingness to sustain intensity without fracturing. Unity was not uniformity; it was alignment, the agreement that each possession belonged to all five players, not merely the one holding the ball. These principles became less slogans than disciplines.

In early practices, their impact was visible in small gestures. Players huddled more quickly. They communicated more frequently. They closed out more responsively, talking through switches with a cohesion that suggested trust forming in real time. Smart's staff, many of whom had followed him through earlier coaching journeys, moved with ease and familiarity, modeling the interpersonal clarity they wanted from their players. The gym radiated a sense of renewal—not a loud, dramatic resurgence, but the quiet steadiness that precedes transformation.

Milwaukee sensed the shift. The city has always responded instinctively to teams that recognize its temperament, and Smart's approach aligned seamlessly with its sensibilities. He respected detail, valued humility, and embraced work that happened out of view. His press conferences avoided spectacle. His presence in the community felt natural rather than obligatory. When he spoke about the program, he invoked both history and possibility without promising shortcuts. The city recognized itself in him: measured, grounded, attentive to the long arc rather than the isolated moment.

The players responded in similar fashion. They found in Smart a coach who demanded effort but also explained its purpose. Film sessions became collaborative rather than punitive. Practices emphasized problem-solving, teaching players to read defensive cues, anticipate movement, and understand the emotional momentum of a possession. Smart reinforced that basketball was not merely a contest of athleticism but an expression of character—and that identity, once established, guided decision-making under pressure.

The transformation became most visible on the defensive end. Smart's teams pressed not for spectacle but for structure. They used ball pressure to shrink passing lanes, to disrupt timing, to force opponents into haste. Rotations became sharper. Angles became cleaner. Defenders communicated as though interpreting a shared language. This cohesion created what Smart often referred to as "connected stops"—moments when all five players acted with synchronized intention, generating a defensive possession that felt less like an isolated action and more like a collective declaration of identity. The city loved these moments. They mirrored Milwaukee's own ethic of interdependence.

Offensively, the changes unfolded with equal intentionality. Smart emphasized spacing, pace, and decision-making. He encouraged players to see passing not as a sacrifice but as vision—to notice openings before they appeared, to trust teammates to occupy the right spaces, to understand that the best shots emerged not from individual skill but from collective rhythm. Gradually, the ball began to move more freely. Shooters received cleaner looks. Drivers found clearer lanes. The team's style took on a kind of looseness that remained disciplined beneath the surface. Even when possessions broke down, the players moved with a sense of purpose that suggested they understood what they were trying to build.

The arena reflected these changes. The crowd noise became warmer, more connected to the cadence of the game. Students arrived earlier, responding not only to wins but to a feeling —an impression that the team was building something authentic. Older fans, whose memories stretched back to McGuire, Raymonds, Deane, Williams, and beyond, recognized the reemergence of a certain intangible: the sense that Marquette basketball carried a pulse again, that it mattered not only for its results but for how it expressed itself.

This reawakening did not erase the structures Buzz Williams had built years earlier. In fact, Smart's identity fused seamlessly with elements of the Williams era. Both coaches believed in intensity, in physical commitment, in the value of undersized players who refused to interpret size as destiny. Both understood that Milwaukee embraced workers more readily than prodigies. Both believed that culture was not a decorative phrase but a discipline. Yet Smart introduced a new emotional dimension—one that emphasized joy alongside toughness, reflection alongside urgency, and connection alongside pressure.

Behind the scenes, Smart also addressed the infrastructure of long-term success. He elevated player development as a central pillar, working individually with athletes to refine their footwork, improve decision-making, and elevate their psychological resilience. He deepened Marquette's engagement with Milwaukee high schools, not through token gestures but through sincere involvement. He strengthened relationships with alumni, many of whom felt newly invited into the program's evolving identity. In every direction, he reinforced the idea that Marquette's future depended on the coherence of its community as much as its on-court execution.

Recruiting followed naturally from this foundation. Prospects visited campus and encountered not simply a basketball program but a cultural environment—one that spoke to emotional intelligence, intentional living, and the joy of collective pursuit. They saw a coach who did not merely instruct but connected. They met players who owned the program's values not because they had memorized them but because they lived them. And they saw a city that supported its team not with conditional enthusiasm but with a steady, grounded pride.

As results improved, national attention returned. Analysts who had once spoken of Marquette in terms of potential now began to describe it in terms of identity. The team's style was unmistakable: ferocious defense, intuitive passing, pace elevated but never uncontrolled, a willingness to embrace the unglamorous parts of the game with visible passion.

Smart's presence on the sideline—measured, expressive without volatility—contrasted with the restless energy that had defined the Williams era. He coached as though guiding a conversation rather than conducting a storm, and in doing so he allowed his players to inhabit clarity rather than chaos.

In time, the program's atmosphere shifted from hope to belief. Players walked onto the court carrying themselves with a confidence rooted not in bravado but in understanding. Practices became less about learning systems and more about refining instincts. The team began to impose its rhythm on opponents rather than reacting to theirs. The reawakening had taken hold.

And through it all, Milwaukee recognized something essential: Marquette basketball had entered a new phase—not a return to past eras, not a replication of old identities, but a synthesis of toughness and joy that felt uniquely suited to the modern game and to the city that sustained it.

The deeper Smart settled into the rhythms of Marquette, the more his program revealed an architectural quality—an understanding that culture was not a mood but a structure, built deliberately, reinforced daily, and sustained through the invisible habits that outlast individual seasons. What distinguished this era from the volatility that preceded it was not merely the return to winning but the coherence of the environment from which those wins emerged. Smart did not chase momentum; he cultivated it. And as his approach took root, the program began to exhibit a rare quality in modern college basketball: emotional stability.

This stability expressed itself first in how players related to one another. Smart emphasized communication so deeply that it became the texture of practice. Teammates called out screens with timing so consistent it resembled music. They congratulated one another not with empty enthusiasm but with specific language—naming a well-executed rotation, a sharp cut, a difficult rebound. These exchanges created a running conversation that sustained the team's internal rhythm. The gym no longer echoed with isolated voices; it pulsed with a collective intelligence.

Such habits produced on-court consequences. Defensive sequences unfolded with a clarity that suggested anticipation rather than reaction. When opponents sent the ball into the post, help arrived from angles rehearsed hundreds of times. When guards fought over ball screens, the coverage felt less like a struggle and more like choreography. Even breakdowns had a distinct quality, as though players understood how to contain chaos before it spilled into disaster. Smart's defensive system did not rely on length or brute force; it relied on cooperation, trust, and the understanding that pressure —applied deliberately and collectively—could unsettle even superior talent.

Offensively, the program developed an identity built on motion and generosity. Players moved without expecting the ball, trusting that opportunities would arise not through assertion but through syncopation. Smart encouraged decisions made at game speed, insisting that hesitation turned good ideas into bad outcomes. Over time, the team learned to read micro-moments: a defender leaning too heavily on one hip, a help-side rotation arriving a half-step late, a cutter emerging into space just as a passer elevated the ball. These were not improvisations; they were expressions of shared understanding. The ball moved with a freedom that suggested joy, yet the discipline beneath that joy was unmistakable.

This marriage of toughness and looseness, of pressure and delight, began to shape the atmosphere around the program. The Bradley Center—once defined by the grind of Big East battles—felt newly alive with the distinctive cadence of Smart's teams. Fans recognized not only the effort but the expressiveness of the style. They saw players smiling between whistles, celebrating one another without theatricality, embracing the physical and emotional demands of the game without bitterness. The city responded deeply to this ethos. Milwaukee, a place where pride often expresses itself through modesty, recognized the authenticity of a team playing with both humility and conviction.

Yet what truly distinguished the modern reawakening was Smart's attention to the inner life of his players. He spoke frequently about relationships being the engine of performance, and he devoted as much time to understanding the emotional architecture of his athletes as he did to refining their footwork. Individual meetings became spaces for reflection, where players articulated their aspirations, frustrations, and fears. Smart approached these conversations not as a mentor dispensing wisdom but as a listener guiding discovery. His players began to carry themselves differently— not with arrogance but with a clarity born from feeling seen.

This emotional grounding allowed the team to navigate adversity with a steadiness that contrasted sharply with the volatility of earlier years. Losses did not fracture morale; they clarified it. Slumps did not trigger panic; they invited recalibration. When the team confronted challenges— whether injuries, difficult road stretches, or the ever-shifting pressures of the Big East—it responded not with tension but with cohesion. The program had developed a center of gravity strong enough to withstand external disruption.

Marquette's national reputation evolved accordingly. Analysts who had once described the program through the lens of post-Williams inconsistency now began to speak of its intentionality. They noted the precision of its offensive spacing, the relentlessness of its defensive rotations, the emotional balance on its bench. They recognized that Marquette had become one of the few programs whose identity remained visible even when personnel changed. This was the hallmark of a stable architecture: the system shaped the players, and the players breathed life into the system without distorting its foundation.

Recruiting benefited from this clarity. Prospects visited campus and discovered a program where the values articulated in conversations matched the behaviors observed in practice. They saw a coaching staff that demonstrated as much patience as intensity. They saw a team whose cohesion extended beyond the court—shared meals, communal rituals, an evident closeness that did not seem performative. Many prospects remarked on the authenticity of the environment. Marquette offered not only playing time or exposure but belonging.

This sense of belonging extended into the city as well. Smart understood Milwaukee's history intimately—its racial complexities, its economic disparities, its proud working-class roots, its narrative of quiet perseverance. He built relationships with youth programs and community leaders, not through ceremonial appearances but through genuine engagement. When he spoke about representing the city, he did so with a familiarity that carried weight. The community responded with increasing trust, sensing in Smart a steward rather than an outsider.

In these years, the university itself began to move with more confidence. Administrators recognized that the program now projected a coherence aligned with Marquette's broader values: intellectual curiosity, Jesuit humanism, social responsibility, and resilience. Smart's presence brought these elements into athletic expression, offering a modern interpretation of what it meant for a university to compete with integrity in a high-stakes sport. The program's internal alignment, which had frayed in earlier years, began to tighten once more.

By the time the reawakening became widely recognized, its character was unmistakable. Marquette had become a program capable of imposing its identity rather than borrowing one. It had rediscovered how to play with urgency without frenzy, with joy without frivolity, with toughness without despair. And in this rediscovery, it had forged a model for modern college basketball that felt both contemporary and deeply rooted in the city's sensibilities.

The transformation was not a flashpoint. It was the cumulative work of seasons spent learning, adjusting, clarifying, and reconnecting. Smart had not rebuilt the program in the image of its past; he had allowed the program to see itself again, to inhabit its history without being overshadowed by it, and to imagine a future grounded in coherence rather than nostalgia.

What emerged was a team that played with both freedom and responsibility, both urgency and joy—a team that reflected the best of what Milwaukee had always hoped to see when it looked toward the court.

What gave the modern reawakening its particular depth was the way it reconciled two seemingly opposing truths about Marquette basketball: that the program had always thrived on intensity, and that it needed emotional spaciousness to grow. Buzz Williams embodied the first truth. Shaka Smart articulated the second. Their eras, though separated by years and by differing temperaments, now appeared less contradictory than complementary—two movements in the same long composition, each carving out conditions the other could not. Understanding this relationship required stepping back from the game-by-game pulse of seasons and noticing how institutions evolve across decades, absorbing fragments of identity from one era and refining them in the next.

Williams's tenure had injected the program with a fierce clarity. Under him, Marquette rediscovered the power of edge: the ability to outwork, outlast, and outwill opponents regardless of ranking or pedigree. He restored the belief that toughness could compensate for limitations and that collective resolve could create competitive advantage. His best teams, especially those that advanced deep into March, played as though animated by a shared defiance. They were not always graceful, but they were never passive. They reminded Milwaukee of something essential: that success in basketball, as in the city itself, rarely arrived clean or comfortable. It had to be wrestled from the world.

But that intensity came at a cost. The emotional atmosphere around the program became compressed, leaving little room for reflection. Pressure accumulated season after season. When Williams departed, the program possessed strength but lacked breath. The interim years reflected this imbalance. Coaches and players worked earnestly, yet the environment felt taut, lacking the connective tissue required to sustain identity through turbulence. The team sometimes played well, sometimes faltered, but continuity eluded it. Without a clear emotional center, intensity frayed into inconsistency.

This was the environment Smart inherited, and it was precisely where his unique expertise mattered. He did not try to replicate Williams. He did not attempt to recreate the past's intensity. Instead, he introduced something the program had not experienced in years: psychological space. His practices demanded effort, but not frenzy. His film sessions encouraged accountability, but not fear. His conversations with players emphasized growth rather than judgment. The effect was subtle at first, then unmistakable. Marquette began to exhale.

This exhalation transformed the way players interpreted competition. They fought just as hard, defended just as aggressively, and dove for loose balls with the same tenacity that had defined earlier eras. But they did so from a place of centeredness rather than urgency. Smart taught them that calm was not the absence of intensity but the foundation from which intensity could be applied deliberately. His players learned to press without panic, to space the floor without hesitating, to rebound with both technique and determination. They became competitors whose aggression carried precision.

Smart also reoriented the program's emotional currents toward connection. He asked players to know one another's stories, to recognize that trust was not simply the product of shared practice time but of shared humanity. Team meetings often began with personal reflections rather than tactical diagrams. Players discussed their families, their fears, their aspirations. This practice—quiet, consistent, and deeply Jesuit in spirit—strengthened the empathy that undergirded their on-court cohesion. When they defended together, it was not because they had been drilled into compliance. It was because they understood the stakes for one another.

Milwaukee sensed this shift. The city, long attuned to detecting sincerity, recognized the authenticity of Smart's approach. Fans saw players who celebrated one another's success with unguarded joy, who embraced adversity with poise, who played with an affect that felt neither forced nor theatrical. This emotional transparency resonated with the city's cultural ethos. Milwaukee admired hard work, but it also valued humility, grace, and collective purpose. Under Smart, Marquette began to embody these values in ways no other era had fully captured.

The Big East responded, too. Opponents noticed that Marquette played with a different tempo—not faster or slower, but clearer. They recognized that the team's defensive pressure came from coordination rather than desperation. They saw that players understood their roles not as limitations but as contributions to a coherent whole. Even in losses, Marquette's identity remained intact. That consistency earned respect across the league, where volatility often undermined talented teams.

Recruiting reflected this earned reputation. Smart targeted athletes who fit the program's ethos more than its positional needs. He looked for players with emotional intelligence, self-awareness, and the capacity to thrive within a relational environment. These recruits arrived on campus ready to absorb the culture rather than resist it. They embraced the principles of joy, toughness, and unity not because they were told to, but because they experienced them daily. Over time, these values became self-sustaining.

As the program matured under Smart, its style began to crystallize into something distinctly modern yet unmistakably Marquette. Offensively, the team played with a controlled freedom—a willingness to attack early, to pass with instinct, to read the game as a fluid narrative rather than a fixed script. Defensively, it pressed with a philosophy that blended aggression with anticipation, forcing opponents into quick decisions while remaining disciplined against overextension. The team did not rely on one star or one system; its strength came from the sum of its parts. This balance made Marquette difficult to prepare for and even harder to disrupt.

But the true measure of the reawakening lay not in stylistic effectiveness but in the emotional tone sustained across seasons. The program no longer lurched between extremes. It did not oscillate between tension and release, identity and confusion. It moved with a steadiness that allowed players to grow without fear of collapse. This stability, rare in modern college basketball, created a sense of inevitability around the program's progress. The city began to anticipate not only strong seasons but meaningful ones. The university saw in its team a reflection of its own values—disciplined, compassionate, responsive to challenges.

In this era, the past and present seemed to converge. Williams had restored Marquette's sense of edge. Smart restored its sense of breath. Together, these legacies shaped a program capable of carrying its history without being weighted down by it, capable of competing with national ambition without losing its local soul.

The reawakening was not loud. It did not declare itself with dramatic gestures. It grew steadily, quietly, until the truth became unmistakable: Marquette basketball had rediscovered its internal alignment. It had reentered the national conversation not as a revival but as a continuation of something that had always lived within the program—the belief that identity, once clarified, becomes a form of power.

By the time the modern era reached its full stride, the cumulative effect of these transformations revealed itself in ways that extended beyond records, rankings, or tournament placements. The reawakening under Smart's leadership—built atop the foundation Buzz Williams had laid—did not simply restore Marquette's competitive relevance. It illuminated something deeper about how a basketball program becomes inseparable from the civic imagination of the place that sustains it. What distinguished this period was not only the level of play but the way the city and the university began to see themselves reflected in the team's habits, values, and emotional tone. The program had become a kind of cultural interlocutor, translating Milwaukee's temperament into athletic form.

You could sense this in the rituals that developed around game nights. Fans arrived earlier, not out of obligation but out of anticipation. Students filled sections with a kind of orchestral energy, responding to the rhythms of the team rather than forcing their own. Even long-time season-ticket holders, many of whom had lived through eras of turbulence, seemed steadier in their expectations—not because they assumed victory, but because they trusted the coherence of what they were watching. The crowd was no longer bracing itself for extremes. Instead, it occupied a shared emotional middle, confident that the team would express itself consistently even in the face of formidable opponents.

At practice, that same steadiness expressed itself in the culture Smart crafted. It was a space governed not by hierarchy

THE CITY OF GOLD AND BLUE

but by reciprocity. Coaches communicated laterally with players, players with one another, and the entire environment hummed with a collective attentiveness that suggested something more like a workshop than a proving ground. When mistakes occurred—and they did, because mistakes are integral to any evolving system—the response was instructive rather than punitive. Teammates stepped forward, not to criticize but to clarify. Coaches intervened with questions rather than corrections. Over time, this produced athletes who played with unusual poise: they understood that error was not catastrophe but information.

The clarity of this environment manifested most vividly in late-game situations. Whereas earlier Marquette teams occasionally struggled with composure when pressure tightened, Smart's teams learned to experience tension as a familiar landscape. They executed inbound plays with precision. They navigated traps with patience. They defended without fouling even as the clock drained toward single digits. These moments carried the unmistakable signature of a program that understood itself. Fans noticed. Broadcasters noticed. Opponents certainly noticed. Marquette no longer reacted to pressure; it digested it.

Recruiting during this era also revealed a program that had sharpened its lens. The staff sought players who understood the difference between individuality and isolation—athletes who could bring their distinctiveness into a collective framework without fracturing it. They valued players who communicated on defense, shared the ball instinctively, and understood that body language is part of performance. Prospects who visited campus encountered not a sales pitch but an environment. They saw coaches who moved with purpose, players who trusted one another, and a city that treated the team not as entertainment but as part of its civic memory. Many recruits later spoke of a feeling of recognition —"I knew right away this was for me." That instinct was not accidental; it was structural.

The Big East era sharpened these dynamics. Night after night, Marquette faced programs with decades of tradition, entrenched fan bases, and national expectations. Competing in this environment required more than talent; it required internal cohesion. Smart's teams responded to these challenges not as interlopers but as rightful participants in the league's emotional and historical fabric. They embraced the physicality of conference play, the tactical complexity, the psychological demands of competing against elite coaches in hostile arenas. The Big East did not intimidate them; it clarified them.

Milwaukee saw this, and something shifted in the civic imagination. The program no longer felt like it existed slightly outside the national spotlight, hoping to catch its glow. It felt anchored, defined, articulate. The city recognized that Marquette no longer relied on nostalgia to sustain relevance. It had built a modern identity from the ground up—an identity agile enough to meet contemporary basketball's demands without abandoning the sensibilities that had always made Marquette distinct.

This identity echoed in small gestures. After home wins, Smart often walked slowly toward the student section, not celebrating but acknowledging. His raised hand lasted only a moment, but it conveyed partnership. Players lingered on the court, speaking with fans, thanking ushers, greeting alumni. The gym lights seemed less harsh in those moments, as if the space itself understood that the evening's work belonged to more than the scoreboard. These scenes did not feel choreographed; they felt earned.

Even in defeat, the atmosphere carried integrity. Losses prompted reflection rather than recrimination. Postgame interviews maintained the same tone of clarity and calm that victories did. Smart never deflected blame. Players never sought excuses. The program behaved as though every result was part of a longer arc—an arc defined by coherence more than by volatility. Milwaukee respected this immensely. A city shaped by endurance, by labor, by slow, cumulative progress understood the value of a team that responded to adversity without fracturing.

As the modern reawakening matured, it became clear that what Marquette was building extended beyond tactical style or seasonal success. The program had begun to articulate a philosophy: that basketball, at its highest level, is an expression of intellect, relationality, and emotional steadiness. It is a conversation between five players whose shared understanding can either falter under pressure or expand in it. Smart's teams pursued the latter. They played with a kind of intentional joy that reflected both Milwaukee's pride and Marquette's Jesuit ethos—a belief that excellence is not accidental but cultivated through reflection, discipline, and compassion.

The city embraced this ethos. Bars near campus filled not with restless anxiety but with anticipatory warmth. Alumni who had once drifted away returned to the fold. National commentators remarked on the distinctiveness of Marquette's culture—a word once used vaguely but now employed with precision. The program had, through years of careful construction, become one of the most coherent basketball environments in the country.

And through it all, the connection to history remained not burdensome but clarifying. Marquette had known eras of fire, eras of strain, eras of drift. It had experienced moments of triumph so bright they cast long shadows. But the modern reawakening did not define itself against those pasts. Instead, it gathered from them—drawing Williams's intensity, Smart's emotional architecture, Milwaukee's temperament, Jesuit clarity—and formed something new. Something balanced. Something sustainable.

By the end of this period, the truth had become unmistakable: Marquette basketball had rediscovered not only how to win but how to inhabit its identity fully. It had become a program that understood its own soul.

What lingers from this long arc is not a single season, nor a defining win, nor even the contrast between the eras that shaped it. What remains is the recognition that a basketball program becomes whole only when its internal rhythm aligns with the deeper temperament of the place that carries it. For Marquette, that rhythm has always lived somewhere between intensity and quiet, between the grit that once defined its golden years and the reflective steadiness that characterizes its modern rise. The city has passed through cycles of aspiration and austerity; so has the team. Yet in these most recent years, the dialogue between program and place has felt newly fluent, almost as though each has learned to recognize itself in the other with uncommon clarity.

Walk through the city on a winter night after a home game, and the feeling becomes unmistakable. The streets near campus glow faintly in the lamplight, still carrying the residual warmth of the arena even as the air bites at ungloved hands. Groups of students, bundled against the wind, recount particular possessions as though revisiting shared memories rather than isolated plays. Older fans move more slowly but with a similar lightness, sensing that they have witnessed something more coherent than spectacle. The high windows of the practice facility stand dark, yet the building feels inhabited by a kind of stillness that suggests preparation rather than emptiness. Even the lake wind seems to pause before resuming its movement eastward.

In that quiet, the contours of the reawakening become visible. Buzz Williams's years now register as the period that taught the program how to fight again, how to reclaim its edge, how to believe that identity could be forged rather than inherited. Shaka Smart's tenure reveals itself as the period that taught the program how to breathe again, how to convert intensity into insight, how to build trust deep enough to sustain ambition. Their contributions do not compete; they interlock. Taken together, they form the foundation of a program that has ceased looking backward for definition or outward for validation. It has begun to move with the assurance of something that understands its purpose.

For the city, too, this reawakening has meant something. Milwaukee has always housed contradictions—industry and artistry, austerity and beauty, endurance and reinvention. The team now reflects those tensions with an honesty that feels earned. It plays with sharpness but without denial of vulnerability. It celebrates joy without performing it. It competes with urgency but not with fear. In doing so, it embodies a civic imagination that has taken decades to articulate: the belief that excellence arises not from dominance but from coherence, not from spectacle but from the steady accumulation of clarity.

And so the meaning of Marquette basketball in this era resides not in coronations or collapses but in the fullness of its self-understanding. The program no longer searches for a voice. It speaks in one that is unmistakably its own—formed through the pressures of the Big East, refined through seasons of transition, strengthened by the return of a coach who understood the city's tones long before he led its team. What has emerged is a program that plays as though carrying an inheritance, yet refuses to treat that inheritance as weight.

When the gym finally empties and the echoes fade into the rafters, what remains is the sensation of a program that has learned to meet its history without flinching. The court rests in darkness, waiting for drills that will begin again in the morning. Beyond the windows, the city exhales. The season continues, the work resumes, the identity endures. And in that endurance lies the quiet truth of the modern reawakening: Marquette basketball has become not a search for what was lost, nor a chase for what might be gained, but a practice of recognizing what it already is.

CHAPTER TEN – THE AFTERLIFE OF AL MCGUIRE

"Al never really left. He just moved somewhere we couldn't follow."
— Rick Majerus

The afterlife of Al McGuire begins in places where his name is never spoken, yet his logic continues to shape the atmosphere: in late-night gyms where the echo of a ball against hardwood feels older than the players using it, in the corner bars where Milwaukeeans recount games as if they were scenes from family history, in the wind-lashed walkways that link the university to Wisconsin Avenue, and in the quiet moments before tipoff when the arena lights dim just enough to suggest that something long past is preparing to inhabit the present. McGuire's presence lies in these textures, the subtle weave of emotion and expectation that has threaded itself into Marquette's bloodstream for nearly half a century. He was too intuitive to be easily categorized, too theatrical to be ignored, too authentic to fade. When he stepped away from coaching in 1977, leaving behind a championship banner and a city transformed by its own improbable triumph, he did not remove himself from the program's future. He simply moved into its undercurrent.

That undercurrent pulses in the tension he cultivated between structure and improvisation. McGuire's teams were both carefully disciplined and joyfully unpredictable. They trained with rigorous precision, yet they carried themselves with the looseness of playground players who believed instinct was its own kind of intelligence. He taught his athletes to trust the world as it unfolded, to improvise at the edges of structure, to find advantage not through rigid conformity but through emotional acuity. That paradox—order balanced by intuition —has become so deeply embedded in Marquette's identity that it surfaces even in eras with no direct connection to him. When modern teams push the pace, when they exploit mismatches with an opportunistic clarity, when they play with a mix of grit and swagger that seems to arise from nowhere, they are drawing from an inheritance that never required articulation. It is simply there, like a coefficient in the program's DNA.

His afterlife persists as well in the way Marquette evaluates personality. McGuire never believed in the bland uniformity of mid-century coaching culture. He recruited players whose uniqueness felt like an advantage, men whose rough edges and unpredictable instincts could disrupt opponents more effectively than sanitized order ever could. He believed that the emotional life of a team mattered more than its statistical profile and that a roster gained its strength not from symmetry but from the friction of distinct characters learning to coexist. This conviction did not fade when he retired. It shaped how Marquette came to understand itself. Even now, when coaches speak of the "right fit" or fans describe a player as a "Marquette guy," they are speaking a language McGuire taught them, one grounded not in measurable attributes but in the temperament he believed made basketball—and life— worth watching.

And then there is Milwaukee itself, a city whose affection for McGuire borders on folkloric. His afterlife survives in the tone with which older fans speak his name, in the way their eyes brighten with mischief and reverence at once, as if remembering a man who embodied the city's contradictions better than anyone else ever had. They revisit the walk down Wisconsin Avenue after the 1977 championship, recounting how he embraced strangers with the exuberance of someone who understood the emotional hunger of a place long waiting for its moment. These stories are not simply nostalgia. They are civic memory, the inheritance of a community that learned through McGuire to see basketball as more than entertainment. He gave Milwaukee a narrative of joy in a city accustomed to measuring itself through endurance.

Even the city's physical spaces carry faint traces of him. The old MECCA Arena, reimagined over the decades, still holds a residue of the nights when his teams performed under its peculiar yellow lights. Its idiosyncratic court—the later pop-art design that became iconic—echoes McGuire's belief that basketball could be theatrical without losing its soul. To walk through the building when it is empty, the lights low and the shadows long, is to sense an atmosphere shaped by something more durable than memory. It feels inhabited by an emotional presence that has outlasted eras, conferences, and architectural renovations.

McGuire's afterlife also persists in the university's quieter traditions. His conversations with administrators—half remembered, half mythologized—emphasized the fragility of athletic glory and the moral weight of institutional identity. He believed deeply that a university's athletic program must reflect its intellectual and ethical commitments, that success meant little if not joined to purpose. This conviction shaped decisions long after he departed. Marquette learned, partly through him, that victory without soul was hollow and that soul without ambition risked disappearance. The balance he struck became a compass that later eras followed even when they believed themselves to be innovating.

But the most enduring part of McGuire's afterlife is the emotional logic he left behind: the belief that basketball functions as a vessel for memory, that a city's hope can crystallize around a coach who understands its temperament, that the meaning of sport often reveals itself only in retrospect. When Marquette fans speak of McGuire, they do not emphasize strategy or trophies. They speak of how he made them feel—proud, unpredictable, alive in a way that transcended the boundaries of the game. He gave them permission to believe in joy as a civic principle.

This emotional architecture outlived him. It informs the way fans interpret comebacks, how they endure slumps, how they evaluate talent, how they describe intangibles that statistics cannot contain. It shapes the way players carry themselves when they pull on a Marquette jersey. It influences how coaches talk about belonging, how administrators speak about vision, how the city responds to the team's triumphs and disappointments. McGuire's afterlife does not assert itself loudly. It hums beneath everything.

In this sense, McGuire did not leave behind an era. He left behind a worldview. It is present in the way fans lean forward in tight games, in the way players celebrate one another after a loose-ball scramble, in the way Milwaukee embraces humility even in victory, and in the way every coach who arrives on campus eventually discovers that the program's soul predates them. His afterlife has become the quiet grammar through which Marquette expresses itself. Not nostalgia. Inheritance.

The afterlife of Al McGuire deepened as the decades unfolded, not through deliberate preservation but through the way his sensibilities quietly infiltrated the habits and self-perceptions of the program. What persisted was less the memory of particular games than the enduring intuition that Marquette was supposed to look and feel a certain way, even when the people enforcing that intuition had never known him personally. This diffusion of influence is what separates legacy from myth. McGuire did not become a statue on a pedestal or a name invoked ceremonially at alumni dinners; he became a reference point for coherence, a barometer by which the city and university unconsciously judged whether the program remained true to itself.

You saw this most clearly during eras when Marquette temporarily drifted from its center. When teams played without personality, fans sensed it immediately. When the offense grew mechanical or the defense tentative, when the roster felt assembled rather than cultivated, when the coach's emotional temperature seemed mismatched with Milwaukee's instincts, there was a particular tone to the disappointment —an almost bodily recognition that something essential had gone missing. The critique rarely invoked McGuire explicitly, yet it drew its power from his shadow. Even in anonymity, he supplied the standard.

This standard was not stylistic; it was emotional. McGuire believed teams should play with the kind of humanity that makes sports meaningful: unapologetic joy, visible resilience, and a willingness to embrace the game's strangeness. He believed players should be allowed to inhabit their personalities fully and that conformity was a form of dishonesty. He believed Milwaukee needed a team that reflected its contradictions—gritty but playful, modest but proud, provincial but unafraid to attempt the improbable. These convictions did not fade after he left. They lingered, subtly pressurizing the air of the program, reminding each new generation that Marquette at its best was never a team of perfect parts but a mosaic of unlikely harmonies.

During coaching transitions, the city often sorted new leaders unconsciously through this lens. Hank Raymonds— a quiet man steeped in the technical language of the game— earned early trust because he understood McGuire's emotional architecture from the inside. Though temperamentally opposite, he preserved the essential tenderness and eccentricity that kept players both grounded and imaginative. Rick Majerus, who served as an assistant before his own ascent into national prominence, internalized McGuire's skepticism of orthodoxy and his belief that basketball rewarded those brave enough to interpret its patterns differently. Even in his later years at Utah and Saint Louis, Majerus spoke of McGuire not with nostalgia but with a sense of apprenticeship, as though he had inherited a grammar of coaching that extended beyond tactics.

The decades that followed carried both continuity and rupture. As conferences shifted, arenas changed, recruiting landscapes evolved, the memory of McGuire became a kind of touchstone for recalibration. When the program entered the Big East, fans wondered whether its identity would be swallowed by the enormity of the league. Yet games at Madison Square Garden, the crucible where McGuire once thrived as a broadcaster, often felt like reunions with his ghost. The league's theatricality—the din, the spotlight, the collision of personalities—summoned the very energies he understood intuitively. In those early Big East years, when Marquette repeatedly punched above its weight, there was a sense that the program was tapping into something elemental, something McGuire had named long before: that basketball in Milwaukee thrived on adversity, embraced the peculiar, and found a strange freedom in being underestimated.

When losses arrived, or when internal discord surfaced, the critique sharpened in the voice of the city. Fans did not merely want wins; they wanted coherence. They wanted to recognize themselves in the team's courage, creativity, and spirit. They wanted the fragments of McGuire's worldview—his warmth, his mischief, his belief in improvisation—to reappear in new forms. Even state newspapers, conscious of the emotional stakes, wrote about the program in tones that hinted at deeper anxieties: whether the soul of Marquette basketball had dimmed, whether the program still possessed the spark that once animated the 1977 champions.

But the clearest evidence of McGuire's enduring presence came in the players themselves. Long after his passing, former athletes who never met him would speak of the "Marquette way" as though inheriting a tradition older than any playbook.

They described a culture that demanded individuality but prized selflessness, that rewarded toughness but insisted on joy, that valued precision yet welcomed improvisation. Some spoke of an unspoken expectation that games should contain moments of flair—not for spectacle's sake, but because basketball, when played honestly, reveals the personality of those who love it. McGuire believed this deeply. His players, decades removed, seemed to breathe that belief without needing to know where it originated.

This inheritance was not always easy to bear. Coaches who failed to grasp the emotional complexity of the program often struggled, not because they were tactically deficient but because they misread the psychic landscape. Milwaukee is a city of layered identities—Catholic, industrial, Midwestern, immigrant—and McGuire had somehow fused those identities into a coherent basketball language. Coaches who treated Marquette as merely a job or a stepping stone found themselves out of step with expectations that were never fully articulated yet deeply felt. The city did not demand championships every year; it demanded a certain way of walking toward the court, a recognizability of soul.

During the modern reawakening under Shaka Smart, this inheritance re-emerged with new clarity. Smart never coached a game under McGuire's gaze, yet his teams played as if conversing with the older man's sensibilities. They moved with freedom but defended with grit. They expressed joy without arrogance. They embraced their individuality without losing cohesion. Fans did not have to speak McGuire's name to feel his presence in the coaching philosophy, in the way players celebrated one another, in the way the team treated basketball not merely as competition but as communal meaning. Smart's program felt less like a return to the past and more like an affirmation that the past had never left.

What McGuire left behind, then, was neither doctrine nor nostalgia. It was a psychological architecture—a way of interpreting pressure, community, and possibility. It shaped the program's response to triumph and adversity alike. It taught the city to look at its basketball team not as an escape but as a mirror. And it offered Marquette something rare in college athletics: continuity of spirit across eras of radical change.

His afterlife is not defined by statues, although they exist; nor by stories, though they proliferate; nor by the 1977 banner, though it remains a shrine. It is defined by a feeling that courses through the program's history like an underground stream, surfacing whenever the team plays with recognizable courage or humor or imperfection redeemed by effort. It is defined by a belief—quiet, stubborn, and distinctly Milwaukeean—that joy is a form of toughness and that basketball, at its highest level, is less about dominance than about the capacity to express who you are under pressure.

And so McGuire's afterlife endures not because people invoke him, but because the program cannot stop speaking in his emotional cadence. His grammar of the game—the pauses, the bursts, the contradictions—remains the uncredited author of Marquette's most honest moments.

If the afterlife of Al McGuire shaped the emotional grammar of Marquette basketball, it also shaped the way the program confronts time—how it remembers, how it forgets, and how it navigates the tension between honoring its past and reinventing its future. Few programs in the country face this tension as acutely as Marquette. Some schools are built on long chains of continuity, with eras flowing seamlessly into one another; others refresh themselves so regularly that memory accumulates shallowly, without pressure. Marquette belongs to neither category. Its history is punctuated by leaps, ruptures, renaissances, and near-extinctions. Through all of that instability, McGuire's shadow has served as both anchor and challenge. His presence lingers not to preserve a fixed version of the program but to test each new generation against

271 THE CITY OF GOLD AND BLUE

a set of expectations that cannot be reduced to trophies or systems.

What complicates this inheritance is that McGuire's influence does not operate as a straightforward template. He did not leave behind a tactical manual or a culture expressed in neat aphorisms. Instead, he left behind a temperament— one that resists reduction, defies replication, and yet insists on being recognized when it appears. His afterlife demands not imitation but interpretation. Each era must decide what, precisely, it means to carry forward the spirit of a man whose genius lay in refusing to approach the game predictably. As a result, his legacy functions less like a monument and more like a weather pattern. It shifts, resurfaces, recedes, then returns unexpectedly, shaping the psychological climate even for those who do not consciously invoke his name.

This climate became particularly evident during the years when Marquette moved from the independent days of the MECCA into the Big East, a transition that forced the program to confront the possibility of being overshadowed by institutional giants. For many fan bases, such a transition would have invited a sense of inferiority. Yet in Milwaukee, the response was different. There was an instinctive refusal to be intimidated, a willingness to walk into Madison Square Garden or the Carrier Dome or Cincinnati's old Shoemaker Center with the defiant humor of a city accustomed to being underestimated. That posture, conscious or not, belonged to McGuire. He had taught Marquette that identity is not granted by conference affiliation, market size, or past reputation but earned through the willingness to treat every opponent as equal in the only category that matters: vulnerability under pressure.

This attitude endured into the twenty-first century, particularly during seasons when analysts underestimated the team or dismissed it as a middle-tier program in a top-heavy league. Fans grew accustomed to hearing that Marquette lacked the depth or size or pedigree to sustain success against the powers of the Big East. And yet, year after year, the team reasserted itself through the very qualities McGuire had prized: improvisation, resilience, emotional sharpness, and the capacity to win games that seemed unwinnable through sheer willingness to read the moment differently. This was not coincidence. It was cultural memory expressing itself through action.

Nor was this afterlife limited to style of play. It extended into the way the program approached talent. McGuire's eye for players was notoriously unconventional. He valued instincts, fearlessness, and raw creativity as much as traditional measurables. He recruited men who had lived real lives before arriving at Marquette, men whose toughness came from circumstances rather than self-promotion. This philosophy shaped how the program evaluated talent long after his departure. Even in modern recruiting landscapes saturated with metrics, highlight tapes, and evaluative algorithms, Marquette has consistently found space for players who do not fit standard molds—wings with unusual angles, guards who thrive in chaos, big men who compensate for size with intellect, and athletes who grow into their potential not through polish but through hunger.

This profile echoes across generations: Butch Lee, Doc Rivers, Tony Smith, Travis Diener, Dwyane Wade, Jae Crowder, Jimmy Butler, and countless others who arrived without the coronation of five-star status yet left having carved unforgettable chapters in the program's story. It is not that McGuire discovered this blueprint for all time. Rather, he revealed something about Marquette's natural alignment: the program thrives when it invests in players who see the world with an edge, who carry a chip, who view the court as a place where improvisation and will can overcome what more structured programs take for granted. This outlook did not disappear after 1977; it remained embedded in the program's recruiting instincts, resurfacing whenever the team rediscovered its identity.

The afterlife also shaped the program's relationship to the city itself. Milwaukee is a place of paradoxes—deeply Catholic yet deeply secular, industrial yet creative, modest yet ferociously proud. McGuire managed to hold all these contradictions together because he embodied them. His unique personality —equal parts philosopher, street poet, psychologist, and comedic provocateur—mirrored the city's temperament. He treated Milwaukee not as a backdrop for basketball but as the emotional geography required for the game to make sense. And because he saw the city so clearly, the city saw itself in him. This mutual recognition forged a bond that endured long after he left. It left the program with an obligation: to honor not only its own history but the psyche of the place that sustains it.

This obligation became especially clear during periods of internal strain. When the program drifted—whether through losing seasons, misaligned leadership, or stylistic dissonance —the discontent among fans was never about wins and losses alone. It was about the feeling that the team was no longer expressing something true about Milwaukee. That sense of dislocation was always temporary, however, because the underlying emotional architecture remained intact. The afterlife of McGuire functioned like a compass, tugging the program back toward its essential instincts. Coaches came and went, systems were rebuilt or discarded, but the gravitational pull endured.

You felt this gravitational pull most profoundly in the modern era, when Shaka Smart's arrival seemed less like a hire and more like a return. Smart did not set out to emulate McGuire; that would have been both impossible and insincere. Yet the alignment was immediate and unmistakable. His emphasis on joy, toughness, and unity spoke to the same emotional frequencies McGuire once tuned. His belief in relationships mirrored McGuire's conviction that basketball was first a human endeavor. His willingness to let players express their individuality felt like a contemporary translation of McGuire's own instincts. And the city responded with a recognition deeper than nostalgia: a sense that something lost had been found again not by replication but by resonance.

Thus the afterlife of Al McGuire is not a relic. It is a living force, shaping decisions made by people too young to have watched him coach, influencing players whose grandparents were children in 1977, informing a city navigating its own modern complexities. The afterlife does not assert itself loudly; it murmurs. Yet its murmuring is unmistakable. It is present in the way Marquette regards pressure not as a threat but as a stage. It is present in the way the program values creativity alongside discipline. It is present in the way the university and city both insist that basketball means more here than it does elsewhere—not because it is a grander spectacle, but because it has always been a form of collective self-understanding.

The afterlife of Al McGuire reveals itself most vividly in the spaces where memory and invention converge—places where the program reshapes itself while remaining tethered to an emotional lineage it never formally codified. Nowhere is this convergence clearer than in the distinct cadence of Marquette's most resonant seasons, those years when the team's performance seems to gather the city's pulse into a single, coherent rhythm. These periods are not identical, nor do they rely on the same tactics or personalities. But they share a sensibility that feels unmistakably McGuirean: a willingness to turn chaos into advantage, a flair for transforming constraint into creativity, and a quiet pride in defying expectations that were never written for Milwaukee in the first place.

This sensibility emerged forcefully in the early 2000s, when a wiry sophomore guard from Chicago elevated Marquette into the national consciousness with an improvisational brilliance that seemed to channel the city's longing for resurgence.

Dwyane Wade's ascent did not mirror McGuire's style; it echoed his belief that greatness often appears in unscripted form. Wade's footwork, mid-air contortions, and instinctive timing belonged not to standard basketball pedagogy but to the kind of cultivated unpredictability McGuire once celebrated in players who saw angles others could not. When Wade led Marquette to the 2003 Final Four, Milwaukee recognized something familiar: a team that thrived not by imitating powerhouses but by disrupting them through temperament. The echoes of McGuire vibrated beneath the hardwood—not because Wade played like the teams of the 1970s, but because he embodied a conviction that style is never ornamental; it is a form of intelligence.

Yet the afterlife does not operate solely through moments of triumph. Its presence is equally visible in the times when the program faltered, especially when the faltering revealed a misalignment between the team's internal tone and the city's expectations. During stretches of disjointed play—seasons when leadership seemed tentative or the roster felt assembled without emotional coherence—fans reacted not merely with sadness but with a kind of existential unease. They felt the absence of something, a dimming of the spark that made Marquette recognizable to itself. These reactions were never only about wins and losses; they were responses to the erosion of a worldview. It was as though the city knew, even when coaches and players did not, that the program had drifted from McGuire's foundational sensibility: the belief that the team must reflect a specific psychological clarity, a specific way of seeing.

This tension between drift and realignment intensified during the years of conference realignment, when Marquette's place within the shifting geography of college basketball seemed uncertain. Amid these changes, the afterlife operated as a stabilizing force. Even as the Big East fractured and reconstituted itself, the program's sense of self endured, buoyed by the memory of McGuire's insistence that Marquette's identity was never dependent on external validation. He had once told reporters that Milwaukee was the "perfect place" for him because the city "understood his kind of basketball." That remark, humble on its surface, revealed a profound truth about his worldview: the relationship between coach, team, and locale must be symbiotic. The city shaped the program's courage. The program shaped the city's sense of possibility. Neither existed independently of the other. This reciprocity survived realignment.

It also helped shape the way fans embraced the arrival of new voices, especially those who intuitively grasped the city's temperament. Buzz Williams, with his kinetic energy and ferocious emphasis on effort, tapped into the harder edges of McGuire's inheritance: the belief that Milwaukee thrives when underestimated, that toughness must precede elegance, and that victories earned through sheer grit are victories that carry the city's fingerprint. His personality, contrasting sharply with McGuire's humor and theatricality, nonetheless echoed a deeper continuity. Williams coached as though haunted by the same moral imperative: that effort is a form of truth-telling.

But it was Shaka Smart who revealed the breadth of McGuire's afterlife most clearly, not by mirroring him but by translating his sensibility into a modern dialect. Smart's emphasis on joy, connection, and emotional intelligence did not revive the past; it reinterpreted it. His program resurrected the belief that basketball is made meaningful by relationships, by the interplay of individuality and unity, by the capacity to play with freedom within structure. These lessons, foundational to McGuire's philosophy, returned not as nostalgia but as renewed relevance. Smart's teams played with a kind of buoyancy—alive to possibility, unburdened by fear—that felt like the twenty-first-century embodiment of McGuire's most enduring instincts.

This continuity across eras suggests that the afterlife behaves not like a haunting but like a grammar. It does not demand replication. It demands fluency. Coaches who speak its language succeed not because they mimic the past, but because they understand the emotional truth that underlies Marquette basketball: that the sport becomes an art form when lived rather than performed, when players move with intention rather than compliance, when the court becomes a space where creativity is not only permitted but required.

This grammar shapes the way players relate to one another. The connective tissue of the modern program—the unselfish passing, the anticipation on defense, the eagerness to celebrate a teammate's success—resembles the camaraderie McGuire cultivated in ways that transcend eras. He believed the team must feel like a neighborhood. He believed basketball was a medium through which young men learned to trust, argue, forgive, and ultimately bind themselves to a shared purpose. That ethos persists in the way contemporary Marquette teams treat one another not as interchangeable parts but as personalities whose full humanity matters.

It also shapes the way Milwaukee responds to those teams. The city, grounded in humility yet ferociously loyal, recognizes authenticity instinctively. When a Marquette team plays with the emotional clarity that McGuire championed—toughness without bitterness, flair without arrogance, joy without artifice—Milwaukee welcomes them as their own. When the program strays from that clarity, the city withdraws not out of spite but out of disorientation. McGuire gave Milwaukee a way to recognize itself in basketball, and when that recognition falters, the bond frays. Not permanently. But perceptibly.

And so the afterlife of Al McGuire continues to shape Marquette not by freezing the program in amber but by offering a living standard of authenticity. It continues to suggest that success is not merely a matter of victories but of coherence—coherence with the city's temperament, with the university's ethos, with the restless yet hopeful soul of

Milwaukee. It continues to whisper that basketball, at its highest level, is a conversation between past and present, between memory and invention, between the improbable victories of 1977 and the unfolding ambitions of the present.

The afterlife of Al McGuire settles most deeply into the moments when the program encounters uncertainty—the seasons defined not by triumph or crisis but by the subtler drift that accompanies transition. It is in these liminal spaces, when identity is neither affirmed nor abandoned, that McGuire's presence reveals itself as a stabilizing force. Not as nostalgia. Not as myth-making. But as a reminder of how Marquette learned to see itself, long before the lexicon of modern college basketball evolved to describe identity-building as a strategic objective. His influence endures because it provides a vocabulary for navigating doubt.

This influence becomes especially visible in years when the roster changes abruptly, when a lead scorer departs or a promising season unravels under the weight of injuries, or when the program meets the familiar turbulence that accompanies shifting conferences, shifting staffs, shifting expectations. In these years, fans turn instinctively to a set of emotional cues inherited from the McGuire era: Do the players understand who they're playing with? Is the team's energy alive or merely loud? Does the coach recognize the soul of Milwaukee basketball, or does he treat the city as a place he must endure rather than a place he must understand? These questions are not asked explicitly, yet they shape every conversation in the bars on Wells Street, in the unhurried talk between alumni after a disappointing loss, in the subtle murmurs that ripple across Fiserv Forum when a possession goes sideways.

Marquette fans do not demand perfection. They demand coherence. And they learned this from McGuire, who never promised dominance but insisted on emotional truthfulness. His teams were imperfect on paper but unmistakable in presence. They played with personality, grit, humor, and the refusal to capitulate to whatever shape the game—or the opponent—tried to impose. That sensibility has become the baseline against which every Marquette team is measured. Not whether they win the NCAA Tournament, but whether they embody a worldview.

The worldview persists because it was never merely tactical; it was existential. McGuire understood that basketball in a Midwestern Catholic city like Milwaukee required more than execution. It required the ability to interpret atmosphere. He read the room, the arena, the city's working-class stoicism, its joy-in-disguise, its instinct for skepticism and its quiet hunger for belief. He understood that Milwaukee did not want to be dazzled; it wanted to be recognized. And so he built teams that played in a way that allowed the city to recognize itself—hardworking, inventive, unpretentious, a little unruly, a little poetic. Over time, that recognition became a form of belonging.

This belonging grew even more important as the college basketball landscape accelerated into the era of transfers, NIL negotiations, and the increasingly transactional nature of program-building. In the midst of such flux, Marquette's connection to McGuire functions as a cultural ballast. It reminds the program that identity cannot be outsourced. While other institutions chase star power or branding initiatives, Marquette continues to emphasize feel: the instinctive understanding of whether a player fits not simply into a scheme but into the emotional logic of the team. And when the program gets this right, the results surpass what the raw materials predict.

Consider the way recent teams, particularly under Smart, have been built: players who thrive in connection rather than isolation, who read the floor with improvisational intelligence rather than brute athleticism, who express joy not as celebration but as a way of staying attuned to one another.

None of this is explicitly McGuire's doing. Yet all of it feels like a continuation of the emotional architecture he left behind. Smart did not study McGuire in order to replicate him. He simply arrived at a worldview that happened to rhyme with McGuire's instincts. It is why the city embraced him with such immediacy—not because he resurrected the past, but because he unknowingly stepped into its echo.

This echo is not always benevolent. McGuire's afterlife also generates pressure—pressure on coaches who misunderstand the program's expectations, pressure on players who assume the city wants only results rather than resonance, pressure on administrators who occasionally forget that Marquette's basketball identity is not a brand but a relationship. When the program loses this relationship, even briefly, the afterlife asserts itself as reproach. Fans feel it before anyone else. Something has gone colorless. Something has gone flat. The team is no longer speaking in its native emotional register.

But the critique is never mean-spirited, because the afterlife is not possessive; it is protective. It exists to ensure that the team remains recognizable to its own community. It reminds the program that victories achieved without personality feel hollow and that losses endured with coherence can strengthen identity rather than weaken it. This is not a sentimental belief; it is historical observation. Marquette's proudest seasons were not its most statistically dominant but the ones in which personality, grit, and city found one another in the same emotional frequency.

That frequency still animates the present. It is why Milwaukee leans forward during closing minutes, sensing not merely the stakes of the scoreboard but the stakes of continuity. It is why alumni speak passionately about the "Marquette way," despite struggling to define it. It is why players from different eras, when asked what connects them, often answer with stories rather than statistics: stories of camaraderie, humor, improbable victories, unlikely heroes. These stories are the syntax of McGuire's afterlife. They teach each generation how to interpret the program's soul.

And so the afterlife persists—not as a frozen era, not as a shrine to the past, but as a dynamic inheritance that continues to shape how Marquette interprets itself in moments of triumph and uncertainty alike. It reminds the city that basketball at Marquette is not merely an athletic pursuit but a cultural expression. It reminds the university that success must be human before it can be strategic. It reminds the players that the program's greatness lies not in perfection but in authenticity. And it reminds the coaches that they are entering not a job but a conversation—one that began before them and will continue after them, guided by the grammar of a man who believed that basketball, like life, was most beautiful when lived honestly.

On certain winter nights, when the lake wind cuts hard across Wisconsin Avenue and the sky hangs low in its familiar gray weight, the campus feels momentarily suspended between past and present. The lights inside Fiserv Forum dim after a home game, the crowd disperses into the cold, and the echo of the final buzzer lingers in the rafters like a memory reluctant to dissolve. It is in this interval—after the noise, before the city fully resumes its nightly rhythms—that the afterlife of Al McGuire reveals its clearest form. Not as a ghost, not as a sentimental projection, but as a presence woven into the way people breathe on their walk back toward campus, into the way players replay moments quietly in their minds, into the way Milwaukee receives the silence as something meaningful rather than empty.

In the muted hum of departing conversations, you can sense how deeply the program has learned to interpret itself through a tone McGuire once set without ever naming. His afterlife is not located in the old film clips or the stories retold in taverns; it lives in the unspoken expectation that Marquette basketball must carry both humor and grit, that it must respond to tension with invention, that it must move with authenticity even when the path is unclear. These expectations are not burdens. They are forms of recognition. They bind the present to a lineage that does not constrain but steadies, like a hand resting lightly on the shoulder.

The players who linger on the court after a game—stretching, speaking softly with teammates, nodding to fans still gathering their coats—do so with no awareness that they are participating in a ritual older than themselves. Yet this quiet gives shape to the continuity that McGuire left behind. It reflects his conviction that the game's meaning resides not solely in victory but in the way it gathers people into a shared emotional space. The arena, emptying slowly around them, becomes a place where the past does not impose itself but listens. And the city, watching from outside, senses in these gestures the persistence of a worldview that has outlived its originator.

For the coaches, too, the afterlife operates without announcement. They inherit a program whose cultural architecture predates them, whose emotional resonance they must learn the way one learns the acoustics of a room. When they speak about joy or toughness or unity, when they emphasize relationship over rigidity, when they encourage players to trust their instincts, they are entering into the long conversation McGuire began—one that insists the game's truths are human before they are tactical. Whether they know it or not, they are responding to the echoes of a man who believed that basketball was not merely strategy but expression.

And for Milwaukee, the afterlife remains a companion. The city walks beside the program, carrying its history like a story it has told so many times that the telling has become indistinguishable from lived memory. The people who file into the arena on cold nights do not come simply to watch a team. They come to participate in a lineage—to feel themselves inside the continuity that stretches from the MECCA to the modern era, from the improvisational brilliance of the 1977 champions to the clarity and connection of the present. That lineage gives shape to belonging, reminding the city that it has always been capable of joy, even in its sternest seasons.

In this sense, McGuire's afterlife endures not in statues or banners or ceremonial tributes but in the simple, recurring moments when the lights dim, the noise softens, and the night collects the residue of a game just played. His legacy is carried in the pause between one heartbeat of the program and the next—in the quiet understanding that Marquette basketball continues because it remembers how to feel, how to improvise, how to reflect the city that holds it.

The afterlife lives in the silence. And from that silence, the program rises again.

EPILOGUE — GOLD LIGHT THROUGH THE WINTER

"You see Milwaukee's soul in winter. That's when the gold really shows."
— Al McGuire

The winter night settles over Milwaukee with a calm that is never quite still, as if the city carries its own quiet pulse beneath the snowpack. After a game, when the crowd disperses and the last echoes fade from the arena rafters, the streets absorb a softened glow, a gold that seems to rise from the pavement rather than fall from the lamps above. The wind moves in low, deliberate currents off Lake Michigan, brushing against the facades of old brick buildings that have held generations of memory. In this hour, walking westward or southward toward campus, the world feels pared down to essentials—cold air, warm breath, the muffled cadence of boots on salted concrete—and something in that simplicity allows the city's soul to show itself with unusual clarity.

This clarity is not dramatic. It does not announce itself in shouts or declarations. It murmurs through the familiar shapes of the winter streets: the steam that curls from manhole gratings, the faint glow of tavern windows where postgame conversations drift between disappointment and hope, the slow procession of bundled figures tracing paths they have walked for years. These gestures form a kind of quiet liturgy, a civic ritual that replays itself across decades. Marquette fans know these streets intimately. Some walked them during the roaring ascent of the 1970s, others during the restless years that followed, others still during the modern awakenings under Crean, Williams, and Smart. The snow absorbs all those footfalls without distinguishing between eras, as if memory itself were a single, continuous surface.

On certain nights, when the temperature drops quickly and the lake wind sharpens its edge, the air carries a trace of something older—an echo of the MECCA's bright interior, of games played beneath low ceilings that trapped sound like a heartbeat, of the distinct cadence that once belonged to McGuire's teams alone. The modern arena is grander, more polished, anchored in its own architectural logic, but the emotional geometry remains traceable. Fans file out with the same mixture of joy and weariness that marked earlier generations, and the gold light spilling outward seems to remember how to behave, how to settle into the creases of the city without losing its warmth.

Milwaukee in winter is a place of honest edges. The cold does not flatter; it exposes. It sharpens silhouettes and quiets distractions. And in that sharpening, the relationship between the city and the program becomes unmistakable. The university rises from the surrounding blocks with a kind of understated dignity, its old limestone and brick warmed by interior lights, its steeples and towers catching what little glow the night permits. Students moving between the buildings carry the rituals of campus life in their movements, but their presence after a game carries something more: the sense of belonging to a story larger than their own semester or their own team. They walk through winter not as spectators but as inheritors.

This inheritance is not simply athletic. It is emotional and historical, shaped by the way generations have used basketball as a way of interpreting the city around them. Milwaukee's winters have always held a sense of mutual recognition: the people endure the cold with a stubborn grace, and the city rewards them with moments of unexpected beauty. Marquette basketball mirrors that exchange. A season rarely unfolds without difficulty, without a stretch of missed shots or injuries or doubt, yet the gold—the way the team coheres, the way a player emerges at the right moment, the way the arena lifts its voice in unison—shows most clearly when the conditions are harshest.

And so the winter walk home becomes part of the architecture of the program's meaning. Each step carries the residue of the game just played, its triumphs or frustrations still shifting in the mind. The cold heightens the memory. A defensive stand seems sharper. A late turnover feels heavier. A moment of brilliance from a player—an angled pass, a contested rebound, a midrange jumper at the horn—glows against the night's muted palette. Memory in winter is both precise and generous. It enlarges what matters and lets the rest fade into steam rising through street grates.

There is always a moment, usually halfway between arena and campus, when silence takes hold. It is not the silence of emptiness, but the silence of reflection—the kind that allows a city and a university to breathe together. The hum of the freeway dims, the lake wind steadies, and the snow-covered rooftops reflect what little light remains, creating a faint shimmer across the Old World facades. This shimmering is the gold McGuire spoke of: not the color of triumph or banners, but the color of clarity. It signals the city's recognition of itself in its team, the team's recognition of itself in its city.

In this quiet shimmer, history feels present but not heavy. The past does not crowd the moment; it accompanies it. The 1977 coronation, the turbulence of the years that followed, the reawakenings of the modern era—all move alongside the night like familiar companions who know when to offer a word and when to remain silent. The city understands that its bond with Marquette is not anchored in any single season or coach or victory. It is anchored in this winter rhythm, in the shared endurance that makes beauty sharper when it arrives.

The gold light fades slowly as you approach campus, but the feeling remains. It lingers in the breath forming small clouds before the face, in the sound of boots against snow, in the narrow glow of residence hall windows where students discuss plays long after midnight. It lingers in the quiet certainty that the program's identity is not simply an accumulation of games or names but a way of moving through the world, shaped by cold nights and warm interiors, by a city that has learned to glow precisely where winter threatens to dim it.

Winter presses itself against Milwaukee with a patience that feels almost architectural, shaping the city not through sudden storms but through the slow, deliberate accumulation of cold. By January, the landscape has settled into its familiar austerity: the skeletal outlines of trees along State Street, the grain elevators rising like frozen monuments at the lakefront, the narrow lanes of shoveled sidewalk threading through the city's older neighborhoods. Yet inside this starkness, a surprising intimacy emerges. People greet one another more warmly. Conversations linger in doorways. Light, filtered through overcast skies, softens the rough edges of brick and limestone. It is within this seasonal contrast— harsh wind, gentle light—that the deeper story of Marquette basketball becomes legible, because the program has always drawn its meaning from the interplay between difficulty and illumination.

This interplay has shaped the program across generations. Through the decades, Marquette teams have found their identity not by bypassing adversity but by moving straight through it, learning to locate coherence in the spaces where the game resists resolution. When the offense sputters or the roster reshapes itself unexpectedly, when the conference grows formidable or the season's early optimism gives way to the grind of February, the team's character is revealed not in the clarity of its successes but in the way it adapts to uncertainty. This capacity for adaptation is not a modern discovery. It is woven into the history of Marquette basketball, a thread that can be traced from McGuire's intuitive boldness through the disciplined structures of later eras and into the improvisational confidence of the present.

Even the city feels different during these stretches of uncertainty. The lake wind tightens its grip, yet the streets near campus pulse with the same mixture of anticipation and reflection that has marked winter nights for generations. Students cluster in small groups, shoulders hunched against the cold, talking through the nuances of a defensive rotation or the urgency of an upcoming stretch of games. Alumni return to familiar taverns, their conversations threaded with a memory that grants perspective without overshadowing the present. The city absorbs these rhythms the way it absorbs the winter itself: steadily, with an unspoken willingness to endure.

What distinguishes Marquette, especially in winter, is the way the program's emotional language aligns with the emotional language of the city. Milwaukee has always been a place that values perseverance over spectacle, substance over self-display. The factories that once lined the Menomonee Valley, the breweries that scented the air with malt sweetness, the shipyards and foundries that shaped the economy— these industries taught the city to prize endurance and workmanship. Even today, as the landscape has shifted and new forms of labor have taken root, the temperament remains. Effort is a form of respect here. Humility is understood as strength. And whenever a Marquette team steps onto the court, the city watches not only to see whether the team will win but to see whether it will honor those deeper values.

This connection becomes particularly evocative in seasons when the roster includes players whose paths to Marquette were shaped by difficulty—injuries, under-recruitment, overlooked talent, or the subtle misalignments that kept them from flourishing elsewhere. Milwaukee recognizes these players immediately. Their stories resemble the city's own: resilience without bitterness, ambition tempered by modesty, the capacity to turn limitations into angles of approach. When these players succeed, the applause carries a different timbre. It is not simply celebration; it is recognition. The city sees in them a reflection of its own persistence through long winters, its own refusal to let harsh conditions dictate the boundaries of possibility.

And yet, winter does not exist solely to illustrate adversity. It also reveals beauty by narrowing one's focus. The lines of the court appear sharper under arena lights. The sound of the ball striking the hardwood carries further. A sequence of passes, perfectly timed, can feel almost luminous against the contrast of the season. In these moments, Marquette basketball becomes a study in how clarity emerges from restraint. The players move with deliberate intention, each cut and rotation shaped by the training that precedes instinct. The team's coherence—the way its members read one another, the way they respond to the staccato rhythms of the game—becomes a kind of winter light: pure, steady, compelling.

This light spills outward from the arena in ways that are difficult to measure but impossible to miss. After victories, its glow seems to warm the sidewalks themselves, as if the city's cold were merely a backdrop for something enduring. After losses, the light softens rather than recedes, leaving space for introspection rather than resignation. In either case, the walk home becomes a continuation of the game, a time when the mind replays possessions not out of anxiety but out of affection. Even the frustrations—missed free throws, defensive lapses, late turnovers—become part of a ritual that binds fans to the team with more intimacy than triumph alone could provide.

This intimacy extends beyond the season's arc. Years later,

alumni recall winter games not only for their outcomes but for the texture of the nights that surrounded them: the heavy boots, the wind off the lake, the glow of campus buildings against the dark sky. These details persist because they are part of how memory organizes itself. For Marquette fans, basketball is seldom detached from place. It is spatial, atmospheric, sensorial. One remembers the warmth of entering the arena after the cold, the sudden brightness of the court, the collective rising of the crowd during a late run. One remembers how the gold uniforms caught the light, how the team carried itself with a quiet confidence that felt native to the city's character.

In this way, winter becomes not merely a season but an interpretive frame. It reveals what summer or autumn often conceal—that the heart of the program lies in its capacity to generate warmth where cold would otherwise prevail. This warmth is communal rather than individual, arising from the shared experience of fans who endure the city's harshest months together, bound not by perfection but by presence. The gold that shows in winter, as McGuire once said, is not metaphorical alone. It is visible in the light reflecting off snowbanks, in the glow of streetlamps on ice, in the quiet pride that fans carry with them long after the season's final game.

And so the winter remains the city's truest companion. It narrows distractions, intensifies emotion, reveals character. It reminds Milwaukee that beauty often arrives through perseverance rather than ease. And in doing so, it allows Marquette basketball to speak with unusual clarity, offering the city not escapism but recognition—a reminder that gold shines brightest when framed by cold.

Winter deepens in Milwaukee not by announcement but by accumulation. The cold settles into the city's architecture— into the seams of old brick apartments, into the narrow alleys behind Wisconsin Avenue, into the ironwork of the bridges spanning the Menomonee Valley. By February, the landscape has acquired a peculiar stillness, a kind of muted persistence in which the smallest gestures take on heightened meaning. A passerby pulling a scarf tighter, a bus exhaling warm air at a stoplight, a cluster of students huddled near a crosswalk— all appear framed against a backdrop that strips the world to its essential elements. This seasonal austerity shapes the way the city experiences basketball. When daylight dwindles and temperatures plunge, each game becomes a source of warmth, each possession a spark in a world otherwise defined by monochrome.

Inside this sharpened atmosphere, the identity of Marquette basketball reveals its depth. The winter months of a season, often the most difficult stretch of the schedule, become a proving ground not only for skill but for temperament. It is during these weeks—when the conference race is unforgiving, when bodies tire and scouting reports grow thicker—that the program's defining characteristics become unmistakable. Teams that thrive in this period do so not through novelty but through a kind of emotional coherence. They learn to endure the grind without losing clarity, to absorb setbacks without surrendering rhythm, to find in the season's coldest span a strange kind of momentum.

This coherence is a product of culture more than talent. It comes from the ways players look at one another during timeouts, from the shared resilience that emerges when a deficit begins to shrink or a hostile arena quiets under defensive pressure. The city senses this. Milwaukee has always understood perseverance, having survived economic shifts, industrial decline, and the long winters that test both patience and spirit. When Marquette plays with unity, when its movements on the court suggest mutual understanding rather than individual improvisation, the city recognizes its own reflection. This recognition is not tied to winning streaks or rankings; it arises from the alignment between the team's posture and the city's character.

That character sharpens during road games. Watching Marquette compete far from home—whether in packed Big East arenas or neutral-site tournaments—elicits a unique form of solidarity. Fans gather in bars across Milwaukee, their voices braided into a single communal register. The glow of televisions reflects off windows fogged by breath and cold. For a moment, the distance between the team and its city seems irrelevant; the connection remains intact, carried by memory and anticipation. When the team responds to pressure with discipline or flair, when a key defensive stop triggers a surge of momentum, the energy in these bars lifts as if the city itself were exhaling frost and drawing in warmth.

The winter road game has a paradoxical effect: it makes the team's absence feel like presence. The city becomes aware of its dependence on the program not as entertainment but as companion. In the quiet between possessions, the rhythmic bounce of the ball and the sharp squeal of sneakers feel like messages transmitted across distance—a reminder that Marquette is still out there, still carrying the weight of its history and the hope of its supporters. And when a victory arrives at the end of a hard-fought away game, it warms the city in ways the weather cannot. The joy is modest but enduring, the kind that slips into conversations the next morning in coffee shops and classrooms, into nods exchanged by strangers who share an unspoken allegiance.

Yet winter also brings moments of tension. The schedule tightens. Shots fall short. Injuries linger. A promising season can tilt toward uncertainty without warning. These stretches test the program's emotional foundations. The crowd inside the arena grows more attentive, leaning forward during defensive possessions, exhaling collectively during free throws. The city listens to these games with the same seriousness it applies to its own hardships: not with despair but with a sober acceptance that struggle is part of the landscape. In these moments, the gold light that

McGuire spoke of does not shine brightly; it glows more subtly, flickering in small acts of persistence—a chase-down block, a well-timed screen, a quiet word exchanged between teammates.

The players feel the weight of these nights. They emerge from the locker room after a loss with a certain gravity, their breath mixing with the cold as they step into the night. Yet even here, winter provides context. The city does not turn away. Fans walking the same sidewalks offer simple gestures— a nod, a brief encouragement, a remark about the next game —that reaffirm the bond between program and community. Milwaukee understands the rhythm of seasons too well to demand perpetual ascent. What it asks instead is steadiness, the willingness to respond to difficulty with integrity.

This steadiness becomes most visible in the spaces between games—the early morning practices, the film sessions illuminated by the blue glow of projectors, the quiet repetitions in the Al McGuire Center where players refine footwork or adjust angles long after the rest of campus has gone to sleep. These unseen hours form the winter heart of the program. They reflect the ethos of a city that has always valued work done without spectacle, preparation undertaken without applause. Marquette's players carry the city's temperament into these sessions, learning that excellence in February is constructed in the half-lit mornings of January.

And then, occasionally, winter offers moments of grace. A struggling player finds his rhythm. A team previously marked by inconsistency discovers balance. A game that threatens to drift away is reclaimed through a burst of energy that electrifies the arena. These moments feel larger than the plays themselves. They signal the emergence of coherence, the alignment of effort and identity. The crowd rises, the gold uniforms shimmer under the lights, and for a few seconds the cold outside seems unable to penetrate the walls of the arena. This feeling—brief, bright, unmistakable—becomes part of the program's memory, resurfacing in later seasons whenever the city needs to recall what it is capable of.

In this way, winter becomes the proving ground and the sanctuary, the season that reveals both vulnerability and strength. It shapes how Marquette sees itself and how Milwaukee sees Marquette. The gold light that shows in winter is not triumphal; it is resilient, reflective, earned. It arises not from ease but from the city's long practice of finding warmth where cold would otherwise dominate. And though each season unfolds differently, the pattern remains: winter reveals what endures.

By late winter, Milwaukee enters a phase that feels suspended between exhaustion and anticipation. The snow no longer falls with ceremony; it arrives in small, steady increments, coating the city in a familiar palette of gray and gold. The days begin to stretch, but the stretch is modest, almost reluctant, as if the season is unwilling to relinquish its hold. It is during this hinge between deep winter and the first hints of thaw that Marquette basketball acquires a different resonance. The season is no longer new, no longer governed by the optimism of November or the steady grind of January. Instead, every game carries the accumulated weight of what came before and the promise of what might still emerge.

This is the moment when a team either becomes itself or drifts into ambiguity. The months of repetition—the early practices, the long flights, the adjustments and missteps— have carved patterns into the team's habits, and those patterns reveal themselves most clearly now. A well-timed rotation on defense, a cut made instinctively rather than debated, a willingness to trust a teammate in a crowded lane—these are the signs of a team that has found its coherence. And Milwaukee recognizes that coherence with the same instinct it applies to weather: not by measuring conditions, but by feeling the air shift. In February, a single sequence—a blocked shot igniting a fast break, a corner three after a series of crisp passes—can alter not only the game but the mood of a city.

Inside the arena, this mood becomes palpable. The crowd, wrapped in layers against the cold outside, sheds its winter reserve the moment the ball is tipped. The clapping begins sooner. The exhortations come louder. An arena in late February carries the tension and exhilaration of a season distilled to its essence. Fans are no longer evaluating possibilities; they are living inside them. The sightlines feel sharper. The sound seems to reverberate more deeply through the rafters. Even the players appear more attuned to one another's presence, as if the snow and cold have compressed time and sharpened their sense of collective urgency.

For the players, the late-winter stretch offers an emotional architecture different from the earlier months. Freshmen begin to carry themselves not as newcomers but as contributors. Veterans shift into a kind of leadership that is less verbal than spatial—they occupy the floor with assurance, directing traffic with gestures rather than speeches. The coaching staff, too, adopts a quieter intensity. Early-season instruction gives way to refinement; the goal is not transformation but clarity. Small adjustments—changing the tempo of a possession, shading a defender differently, altering the rhythm of a ball screen—take on disproportionate significance. These are the margins in which games are won or lost. These are the margins in which a season secures its place in memory.

Outside the arena, winter's hold shapes the psychology of the city. The cold encourages reflection. The long nights foster a sense of introspection that deepens the emotional bond between Milwaukee and the team. People follow the season with greater intimacy, reading not just articles but atmospheres, not just box scores but body language. A player's resilience after a missed shot, a bench's energy during a comeback, a coach's composure during a tense possession—these details take on meaning beyond the immediate narrative of wins and losses. They become part of a shared lexicon, teaching the city how to interpret both the team and itself.

This interpretive instinct becomes especially vivid when the team confronts adversity. A mid-season slump, a key injury, a game lost at the buzzer—these moments do not break the bond; they deepen it. Milwaukee is a city that understands the intricacies of endurance. The steel mills and factories of past decades taught residents to keep moving through adversity without theatrics or complaint. When Marquette stumbles, the city reacts not with despair but with a kind of calibrated concern. Conversations shift toward possibility rather than blame. What adjustments can be made? Who might emerge? What latent strength has yet to announce itself? These questions animate discussions in living rooms, in grocery store aisles, in the quiet murmur of people leaving mass on Sunday mornings.

And then, often when least expected, the season produces a moment that seems to gather all these tensions into a single burst of recognition. A late steal that turns into a game-winning layup. A role player hitting a crucial shot. A defensive possession so disciplined it feels choreographed. These moments do not simply win games; they recalibrate the season, offering a glimpse of what coherence looks like under pressure. The gold light of winter sharpens around them, illuminating the team's identity with a clarity that feels earned rather than bestowed.

As the season edges toward March, the city's anticipation becomes almost palpable. The sidewalks remain slick, the air remains sharp, but an undercurrent of possibility begins to move through Milwaukee. People speak with a mixture of caution and hope, aware that the season has entered a phase where every game carries the potential for transcendence. This cautious hope is itself a hallmark of the Marquette identity: faith without presumption, optimism without forgetting the lessons of winter. It is the emotional stance of a city that has learned to cherish what is hardest won.

This final stretch of winter, then, becomes a threshold. It is the moment when the season's story clarifies itself, when identity crystallizes, when the gold that has flickered through the dark months begins to glow with steady confidence. And as Milwaukee gathers itself for the transition into March, the city carries with it not only the memory of what the team has endured but the quiet conviction that endurance has meaning. The gold light that showed itself through the cold now prepares to follow the team into whatever lies ahead, not as spectacle but as accompaniment.

As winter nears its end, Milwaukee enters a stretch of days when light and cold coexist in uneasy equilibrium. The sun lingers a little longer in the sky, but its presence does not yet warm the streets; instead, it casts long, pale reflections along the frozen sidewalks, illuminating the remnants of snowbanks like small altars to endurance. In this transitional moment, the city feels neither entirely winterbound nor entirely free. It is a threshold season—one marked by uncertainty, by the quiet anticipation of change, by the sense that something long prepared for is now gathering just beyond immediate perception. For Marquette basketball, this is the terrain where a season reveals its final meaning.

March approaches not with fanfare but with a subtle tightening of the air. The games grow consequential in a way that defies casual observation; even the warm-ups feel charged. Coaches move with heightened focus, players listen with sharper attention, and the crowd senses that the familiar rhythms of winter basketball are giving way to something more exacting. It is as though the season itself has spent months in apprenticeship to the cold and is now stepping into a space where clarity matters as much as resolve.

The university campus reflects this shift. Students, who only weeks earlier hurried across icy sidewalks with heads bowed against the wind, now linger outside buildings, discussing bracket projections or debating matchups with an immediacy that bridges academic life to the emotional pulse of the season. Posters appear on residence hall doors, chalk messages scatter across the quads, and in the cafeteria the conversation tilts toward the possibilities unfolding in real time. Marquette's campus does not treat March as a conclusion but as a revelation—an unveiling of all the subtle work done in earlier months, the countless repetitions in practice, the quiet internal adjustments players made in the shadows of winter.

Inside the Al McGuire Center, the atmosphere shifts in equally perceptible ways. Practices take on a different tone—not more intense, but more distilled. Gone are the sprawling sequences of early-season instruction. In their place emerges a series of focused, purposeful movements: a defensive rotation repeated until it becomes muscle memory; a late-game sideline out-of-bounds play rehearsed with monastic concentration; a series of free throws taken in silence, without commentary, as players internalize the gravity of moments not yet encountered. Coaches speak less, but when they do, the room stills. The team has become its own teacher.

And yet, the pressure of late winter is not solely internal. It pulses outward, absorbing the emotional geography of the city. Milwaukee reads the season with an acuity sharpened by decades of winters. The people understand how to recognize a team that is emerging from its crucible and a team merely enduring it. They detect cohesion not only in victories but in how the team carries itself after setbacks—the unhurried poise following a loss, the way players interact when the cameras are off, the steadiness that reveals itself in posture rather than speech. Milwaukee trusts teams that show unity in the gray weeks of February because it knows that unity forged in winter has a different quality than unity found in easier months.

This trust transforms the city. A victory on a cold weeknight radiates outward into taverns and living rooms, into late-night bus rides where bundled passengers share smiles with strangers, into grocery store aisles where people pause beside shelves of cereal to discuss the team's defensive rebounding. Milwaukee is not a city that performs its fandom; it inhabits it. The emotions of a season are absorbed into daily life, woven into conversations that appear mundane but carry the weight of belief. When Marquette plays well, the city moves just slightly differently—more buoyantly, more attuned to the small sparks of joy that winter had momentarily dimmed.

But March also carries an edge, a reminder that seasons can turn abruptly. A misstep in a conference tournament. A cold shooting night. A team whose identity seemed firm suddenly must confront the fragility of momentum. These moments do not erase what came before; they heighten it. They reveal whether a team has simply survived winter or truly been shaped by it. For Marquette, the best seasons have always carried the sense that adversity has been not merely endured but absorbed, transformed into an internal vocabulary the players speak without needing to articulate.

This vocabulary reveals itself most dramatically in tournament play. The stakes intensify. Neutral courts erase the familiar acoustics of home, replacing them with a different sensory field: brighter lights, tighter timeouts, crowds divided into conflicting allegiances. Yet even here, the influence of winter lingers. A team that has learned to generate its own warmth carries an advantage. It does not depend on environment for energy. It does not require the affirmation of familiarity to perform with conviction. Winter has taught it to find coherence in stillness, in cold, in the discipline required to pursue clarity in conditions that refuse to soften.

When the team succeeds on these stages, the moment returns to Milwaukee with amplified resonance. Fans gather for watch parties in living rooms and taverns, the glow of televisions cutting through the dimness. Outside, the last remnants of snow catch the light spilling through windows as if gathering fragments of the game and storing them in icy relief. Even the familiar gusts of wind off the lake feel different—less punitive, more purposeful, as though the city is leaning into the tension rather than bracing against it.

But the true meaning of late-winter basketball lies not in outcomes but in the emotional continuity it creates. Wins and losses are recorded in newspapers and bracket histories, but the deeper truth resides in the way the city feels itself renewed through the team's effort. The players, now moving with an ease earned through months of cold practices and late-night study sessions, embody the city's belief in endurance as a form of artistry. Their movements on the court echo the city's rhythms: persistent, grounded, unwilling to surrender the smallest advantage. Each possession becomes a distillation of months of quiet labor.

And then, as the season edges toward its final days, Milwaukee experiences a phenomenon that occurs every year but never quite the same way. The cold loosens. The light deepens. The sidewalks, long buried beneath snow, begin to show their texture. People walk with lighter steps, the burden of winter lifting even as the unpredictability of March intensifies. The gold light that accompanied the darkest days now blends with the first hints of spring, creating a palette that matches the emotional spectrum of the program—resilient, luminous, open to possibility.

In this convergence of seasons, Marquette basketball reveals its truest meaning. It is not simply a winter companion or a spring hope. It is a bridge between the two, a way the city interprets itself across time. In the games played during these final weeks, one sees not only the culmination of a season but the expression of a long relationship between program and place, built through cold nights, warm interiors, and the intricate dance between endurance and aspiration.

When the season's final horn fades and the arena empties

for the last time, Milwaukee stands at the edge of winter and spring, held momentarily in a kind of luminous pause. The snowbanks that once bordered every sidewalk have thinned into uneven rivulets, their outlines softened by days of tentative sunlight. The cold remains, but it no longer dominates; instead, it lingers like a habit the city cannot quite shake. In this between-season quiet, the gold light that carried the city through the harshest months reveals its deepest resonance. It no longer reflects off the ice with sharp brilliance; it settles into the air as a gentler hue, illuminating the textures of old brick, narrow streets, and the faces of people who have spent months leaning forward inside arenas, taverns, and living rooms.

This is the moment when memory gathers itself. The season stretches out behind you—not as a sequence of scores or standings, but as a pattern of scenes, each one colored by winter's particular light. A late steal that turned a game. A player who found confidence when the year seemed to waver. A crowd rising as one during a run that felt like defiance made visible. These images settle into the mind the way snow once settled onto the city: quietly, steadily, without insisting on their permanence. They become part of the internal landscape, shaping how Milwaukee remembers not only the season but itself.

What lingers most strongly is not triumph or disappointment but continuity. The realization that another chapter has joined a lineage stretching back through decades of winters and the people who walked through them. The great teams, the middling seasons, the unexpected upsets, the bitter losses—all become part of a single conversation between the city and the program, a conversation renewed each year with the first drop in temperature and carried through until the final shred of snow melts. Marquette basketball does not conclude with the season's end; it disperses into the daily life of the city, absorbed into its rhythms like breath into cold air.

Even in the quiet after the final game, the echoes remain. A father and daughter replay a pivotal possession on their walk home. Two alumni passing one another downtown exchange a knowing nod. Students on campus discuss next year's prospects with the urgency of people who understand that belief must be practiced if it is to endure. Inside a darkened arena, the last bits of tape are swept from the floor, and the lights dim in long, deliberate stages. The building empties, but something of the season holds on, suspended in the air as though unwilling to depart entirely.

That unwillingness is part of the program's essence. Marquette's story has never belonged solely to the months when games are played. It persists through the off-season, carried by memory and expectation, by the work done behind closed doors, by the city's habit of looking toward winter even in the height of summer. The gold light that once glowed against the snow now finds other surfaces: an afternoon thunderstorm, a late-autumn sunset, the polished floor of a practice gym where next year's team begins its long preparation. It becomes a companion rather than a spectacle, a reminder rather than a command.

Milwaukee embraces this transition without ceremony. The city moves forward the way it always has—quietly, steadily, aware that endurance is not a task but a temperament. And in that movement, the afterlife of the season persists. Not as a weight, but as a warmth. Not as nostalgia, but as continuity. The program carries its history the same way the city carries winter: with respect for its trials, gratitude for its clarity, and an understanding that the light it revealed will return when needed.

As spring finally takes hold, the last patches of snow recede into the earth, and the sidewalks clear. Students walk with unburdened strides. Families open windows long kept shut. The lake sheds its winter austerity and begins to shimmer again. And in these signs, subtle yet unmistakable, lies the enduring truth that Al McGuire once recognized: winter sharpens the soul of Milwaukee, and in that sharpening, the gold becomes visible. Even when the season ends, the light remains—quiet, steady, waiting for its moment to return.

BIBLIOGRAPHIC ESSAY

The history of Marquette basketball lives at the intersection of Midwestern labor culture, Catholic educational mission, and the evolving architecture of the college game. Writing its story requires attention not only to the obvious historical markers —coaches, players, championships—but also to the broader textures of place and time. Milwaukee's industrial past, its winterbound temperament, its immigrant neighborhoods, and the city's long-standing devotion to craft and community give the program a sensibility distinct from other Catholic basketball powers. The sources that illuminate this sensibility span archival records, newspaper reporting, oral histories, institutional documents, and the reflections of coaches and players whose voices shaped the narrative of an era.

The earliest chapters of the program's history are best understood through the archives of the *Milwaukee Journal* (later *Journal Sentinel*), which chronicled Marquette's early modern teams with striking intimacy. Long before basketball became a national spectacle, local beat reporters captured the sport's rhythms in the language of a city still finding its cultural footing. These accounts, written as much for neighborhood readers as for sports enthusiasts, show the emergence of basketball as a communal ritual, tied to the winter months when indoor spaces became sanctuaries of warmth and spectacle. Game recaps from the 1920s through the 1950s reveal details that rarely appear in later histories: the texture of small gymnasiums, the improvisational nature of early coaching, and the ways Catholic schools in industrial cities used basketball to build both discipline and identity.

A foundational source for Marquette's transformation under Al McGuire comes from the reporting of local columnists and national writers who recognized that McGuire's genius was not merely strategic but theatrical, psychological, and cultural. *Sports Illustrated*, in particular, played a significant role in capturing his contradictions—his streetwise persona, his philosophical digressions, his instinct for turning pressure into performance art. But Milwaukee's papers and smaller regional outlets provided the more revealing details: McGuire holding court in local taverns, his rapport with working-class fans, his intuitive grasp of the city's humor and anxieties. These accounts help explain why McGuire's teams felt inseparable from Milwaukee itself. They also serve as essential counterpoints to later hagiographic treatments, grounding the legend in the realities of a coach who was restless, emotional, improvisational, and profoundly attuned to the psychological fabric of the communities he served.

The 1977 championship, often retold in broad strokes, comes into sharper focus through contemporary game coverage, tournament broadcasts, and the retrospective interviews conducted in the decades that followed. The national reporting from that year—particularly coverage in *The New York Times*, *The Washington Post*, and *Chicago Tribune*—shed light on how improbable Marquette's run appeared to outside observers. These papers offer clear portraits of the dynasties Marquette had to navigate: Dean Smith's North Carolina, Jerry Tarkanian's UNLV, Gene Bartow's emerging power at UCLA. These reports also capture the star power of the era —individual performances that shaped national perception before analytics refined the vocabulary of the game. Meanwhile, Milwaukee's own journalists preserved the local emotional arc: the anxieties, the late-night celebrations, the sense of civic validation that came from defeating programs whose institutional prestige seemed unassailable.

The decades after McGuire's departure introduce a different

historiographical challenge. The years of transition—from the coaching tenures of Hank Raymonds and Rick Majerus to Kevin O'Neill, Mike Deane, and the eventual arrival of Tom Crean—often lack the dramatic narrative coherence of the 1970s. Yet the sources for this period are rich with atmospheric detail. Press conferences, regional sports commentary, and university publications document the struggle to maintain identity in the wake of a transformative figure. What these sources reveal is not decline, but recalibration. They show a program renegotiating its place within changing conference structures, adapting to shifts in recruiting geography, and redefining its relationship to a city undergoing both industrial contraction and cultural renewal.

The modern era—shaped by the tenures of Crean, Buzz Williams, and Shaka Smart—benefits from a more extensive digital archive. Game broadcasts, advanced analytics, player interviews, and long-form reporting offer layered perspectives on how Marquette adapted to the contemporary college game. Williams's teams, with their defensive ferocity and overachieving rosters, are documented not only through traditional journalism but through emerging statistical frameworks that illuminate the structure beneath the chaos. Smart's return to Wisconsin adds another layer: commentary from regional and national outlets that frame his arrival as a fusion of personal history, cultural alignment, and strategic reinvention. Throughout these years, the university's own media—podcasts, student journalism, documentary segments—provides a textured account of how the program's identity is perceived internally.

To understand Marquette beyond wins and losses, sociological and urban history sources also prove critical. Studies of Catholic higher education in the Midwest, analyses of Milwaukee's demographic shifts, and oral histories of working-class neighborhoods all serve as scaffolding for interpreting why Marquette basketball feels inseparable from its city. The program cannot be disentangled from the winter landscape in which it plays, nor from the generational familiarity that binds fans to a team that has long served as a public expression of Milwaukee's endurance.

Together, these sources—journalistic, archival, analytical, atmospheric—form a mosaic rather than a linear record. They reveal a program shaped by improbable triumphs and quiet reawakenings, by winter clarity and generational memory, by coaches who understood that basketball at Marquette was never merely a sport but a medium through which the city reaffirmed its belief in resilience, connection, and the enduring promise of gold light through the coldest months of the year.

Selected References

Milwaukee Journal and Milwaukee Journal Sentinel archives, 1920–present.

Sports Illustrated feature reporting on Al McGuire, Marquette's 1977 season, and subsequent retrospectives.

NCAA Tournament game broadcasts and commentary archives, 1977–present.

The New York Times sports coverage of major Marquette tournament runs, including the 1977 and 2003 Final Four appearances.

The Washington Post and *Chicago Tribune* reporting on Marquette's national profile across eras.

Marquette University publications, including alumni magazines, press releases, and historical retrospectives on coaches and players.

Oral histories and interviews with former Marquette players and coaches, published across regional media outlets.

Urban histories of Milwaukee, including works on industrial labor, demographic change, and Catholic education in the Midwest.

BILL JOHNS

Analytical resources from KenPom, ESPN, and other modern statistical frameworks documenting strategic evolution in the contemporary game.

SELECTED TITLES BY
THE AUTHOR

Dynasties on the Hardwood: College Basketball and the Architecture of Greatness
From Wooden to Krzyzewski, Summitt to Auriemma, the story of dynasties reveals how memory, loyalty, and identity shaped college basketball's soul.

College Basketball Rivalries: Regional Identity, Competitive Memory, and the Battles That Built the American Game
A journey through the arenas, regions, and clashes that shaped the sport, where identity is forged in conflict and every rivalry becomes a story of place, pressure, and memory.

Brackets and Madness: The Science, Stories, and Culture of NCAA Tournament Predictions
Every pick is a gamble, every upset a story—this book unpacks how bracketology became a national obsession and a metaphor for American life.

Dancing Beyond Midnight: March Madness Cinderella Teams and the Making of NCAA Tournament History
From UMBC to George Mason, relive the improbable runs that turned March Madness into America's greatest stage for belief, hope, and basketball miracles.

Melo: Carmelo Anthony—From Baltimore to Syracuse, the Knicks, and Olympic Glory
From Baltimore's blacktops to Olympic gold, Carmelo Anthony's story is one of artistry, resilience, and a layered legacy beyond rings.

Len Bias: The American Ghost — The Celtics, the NBA, and the Costs of Lost
The life that promised greatness, the death that changed a nation—Len Bias remains basketball's brightest ghost and America's lasting reckoning.

Bluegrass Dynasty: Kentucky Basketball and the Making of a Nation's Game
Kentucky basketball is not only history but survival, its permanence carried by memory, devotion, and blue that refuses to fade.

UNC Basketball: The Tar Heels, March Madness, and the Carolina Way
Carolina Basketball is more than a game—it's memory, ritual, and tradition, stitched in blue and carried from Chapel Hill into the nation's story.

Husky Nation: UConn Basketball and the Making of a Modern Dynasty
Husky Nation rose from obscurity to empire, carving a legacy in both men's and women's basketball that no other school can claim.

Rock Chalk: Kansas Basketball and the Making of a Tradition
Kansas is the origin, the cathedral, the sound—basketball's first home and its lasting voice, where Rock Chalk binds past and future as one.

Westwood Glory: UCLA Basketball and the Making of a Dynasty
Ten titles in twelve years, an eighty-eight-game streak, and lessons that outlasted the scoreboard—UCLA remains the game's eternal benchmark.

The Brotherhood: Duke Basketball and the Making of a Modern Dynasty
Five titles, twelve Final Fours, and a brotherhood that remade Durham into the epicenter of the game's greatest drama.

Hoosier Hysteria: Indiana Basketball and the Soul of a State

In Indiana, basketball is not pastime but destiny. From high school gyms to crimson banners, the game shapes faith, memory, and community.

Wildcats and Classics: Villanova Basketball and the Spirit of Philadelphia
Villanova's story is Philadelphia's story: Catholic roots, working-class grit, and basketball as creed and community.

Fear the Turtle: The Rise, Fall, and Redemption of Maryland Basketball
Discover the legacy of Maryland basketball, from Len Bias to Juan Dixon, from ACC rivalries to Big Ten battles—a century of grit, loss, and renewal.

Florida Gators Basketball: From the Swamp to Back-to-Back Champions
Witness the improbable rise of Florida basketball—titles, stars, and a culture that reshaped the South and left a national imprint.

Cardinal Faith: The Rise, Fall, and Redemption of Louisville Basketball
In Louisville, the ball still bounces—faith, failure, and forgiveness carried in every echo from the court to the river's edge.

Red Storm Rising: The Faith, Fire, and Legacy of St. John's Basketball
From Lou Carnesecca to Rick Pitino, this is basketball as devotion—a story of patience, rhythm, and faith that endures long after the final buzzer.

Houston Basketball: Cougars, NCAA Final Fours, and Phi Slama Jama Legacy
Clyde Drexler, Hakeem Olajuwon, and the Cougars rewrote basketball—where flight, flair, and heartbreak became Houston's lasting legend.

Purdue Basketball: Boilermakers, Big Ten Battles, and March

Madness Heartbreaks
Purdue basketball endures as a symbol of resilience, where hope returns each season and March Madness heartbreak becomes part of the legacy.

Crimson Ascent: Alabama Basketball, Southern Velocity, and the Making of a Modern Power
Southern speed, bold ambition, and a program reshaping its identity through pace, pressure, and an unrestrained belief that modern power can be forged far from basketball's traditional capitals.

Michigan State - Green Fire and the Long March: Spartan Basketball, Toughness, and the Midwestern Will to Endure
A program defined by steel-edged resolve and the harsh clarity of Midwestern winters, built on repetition, discipline, and a belief that greatness emerges only through sustained endurance.

The Edge of the Inland Empire: Gonzaga Basketball and the Small-School Rebellion That Reshaped the West
A boundary-breaking rise from regional obscurity to national force, driven by precision, defiance, and the conviction that the edges of the map can become basketball's new center of gravity.

Orange Noise in the Snow Belt: Syracuse Basketball, Carrier Dome Legends, and the Identity of a Northeastern Kingdom
A dome, a city, and a climate intertwined, where long winters, legendary names, and the echo of orange-clad crowds shape a region's deepest sense of basketball identity.

Arizona - Desert Run: Wildcat Basketball, Tucson Nights, and the Rise of a Western Power
A program forged in desert heat and midnight energy, built on fearless guards, rhythmic offense, and the belief that Western basketball thrives through motion, daring, and relentless pace.

Storm on Figueroa: USC Basketball, Grit, Glamour, and the Battle

for Los Angeles
A cinematic journey through USC basketball's grit, glamour, and Los Angeles fire—where rivalry, ambition, and city pressure forge a program fighting for its place in the spotlight.

Heat on the Plains: Auburn Basketball, Southern Ferocity, and the Art of an Unlikely Ascent
A sudden blaze of Southern energy transforming a once-quiet program, fueled by audacity, passion, and a team discovering how belief can outpace tradition and expectation.

Ohio State - Scarlet Court: Buckeye Basketball, Midwestern Order, and the Struggle for Greatness
Midwestern steadiness, winter light, and the pressure of potential define a program fighting to convert deep resources and restless ambition into a lasting claim on greatness.

Hoya Blood and the Capital City Blues: Georgetown Basketball, Big East Violence, and the Washington Identity Crisis
Power, elegance, and urban fracture collide in a program whose intimidating past mirrors a capital city wrestling with ambition, influence, and the burden of its own mythology.

Arkansas - The Hill of Noise: Razorback Basketball, Forty Minutes of Hell, and the Furnace of Ozarks Identity
A soundscape of pressure and chaos forged in Ozarks heat, where relentlessness becomes culture and every possession carries the unmistakable volume of Arkansas identity.

House of Orange and Blue: Illinois Basketball, Midwest Cities, and the Long Pursuit of a Restless Ideal
Chicago streets, prairie towns, and generations of near-arrivals shape a program defined by swagger, resilience, and the enduring belief that an elusive ideal is still within reach.

Wisconsin - Cold Rhythm: Badger Basketball, Winter Patience, and the Geometry of Discipline
A northern program built on spatial clarity, deliberate tempo, and cold resolve, where precision replaces spectacle and

winning emerges from the geometry of disciplined play.

Texas Tech: The Red Line: Texas Tech Basketball, West Texas Grit, and the Architecture of a Modern Contender
Harsh landscape, defensive ferocity, and a culture of grit bind a rising program whose modern blueprint blends toughness, innovation, and the uncompromising character of West Texas.

Irish Light on Hardwood: Notre Dame Basketball, Faith, Independence, and the Echoes of a National Program
Tradition, faith, and independent identity shape a program defined by elegance and stubborn resolve, carrying the echoes of a national following across decades of shifting fortune.

Oklahoma State: The Stillwater Code: Cowboy Basketball, Iba's Shadow, and the Birthplace of Defense
A defensive ethos born on prairie soil, shaped by Iba's meticulous vision and generations of players who embraced structure, pride, and the quiet rigor of Stillwater's basketball code.

The City of Gold and Blue: Marquette Basketball, Milwaukee Identity, and the Afterlife of Al McGuire
Urban grit, Catholic tradition, and the enduring shadow of McGuire form a program where style merges with identity, and where Milwaukee's restless pulse drives every season's ambition.

The Wasatch Rise: BYU Basketball, Mountain Identity, and the Ethics of Ambition
High altitude, disciplined ambition, and a mountain ethos define a program forging its rise through belief, structure, and the tension between independence and national aspiration.

Blue Fire on the Prairie: Creighton Basketball, Midwestern Precision, and the Making of a Modern Rivalry
A portrait of a prairie program forged in precision, rising from Midwestern quiet into a fierce rivalry culture that reshaped basketball on the Great Plains.

The Red Line of the South: Georgia Basketball, SEC Identity, and the Long Fight for Hardwood Relevance
A Southern struggle for identity and relevance, where basketball ambition meets regional pride and the fight for hardwood legitimacy becomes its own enduring rivalry.

Iowa State — *Cyclone Faith in the Corn Belt*
Hilton Magic, plains grit, and the emotional force of a fan base that built its rivalries from belief, heartbreak, and the restless winds of the Midwest.

Bayou Heat: LSU Basketball, Louisiana Swagger, and the Creation of a Southern Basketball Storm
A Louisiana battleground of swagger, talent, and regional tension, where basketball rises through heat, chaos, and the rivalries that define life along the bayou.

The Wolfpack Signal: NC State Basketball, Tobacco Road Turbulence, and the Rebellions That Defined a Carolina Rivalry
A Carolina chronicle of rebellion and defiance, where NC State battles giants on Tobacco Road and rivalry becomes a declaration of identity and survival.

Red Dirt Ascension: Oklahoma Basketball, Frontier Identity, and the Fierce Rivalries of the Great Plains
A frontier program shaped by grit and rivalry, where ambition rises from the plains and every contest becomes a test of character written in red dirt.

Vanderbilt Basketball: Memorial Gym, Nashville, and the Rise of an SEC Contender
Vanderbilt's raised floor, Nashville's shifting identity, and the SEC battles that forged a singular basketball tradition. A history shaped by geometry, grit, and place.

Rocky Top Ascent: Tennessee Basketball, Appalachian Ferocity, and the Rise of a Borderland Rivalry Culture
A story of Appalachian resolve, where orange-clad crowds and borderland rivalries carve a basketball identity out of mountains, music, and unshakable pride.

Burnt Orange Ascent: Texas Basketball, Lone Star Ambition, and the Rivalries That Forged a Western Power

A portrait of modern ambition in the Lone Star State, where every rivalry carries the weight of scale, swagger, and the drive to redefine Western basketball power.

ABOUT THE AUTHOR

Bill Johns writes about American sport with the discipline of an archivist and the temperament of someone who understands how games become the emotional architecture of a place. His work refuses the shallow boundary between sportswriting and cultural history. He treats athletics as one of the last remaining civic mirrors—a public stage where belief, identity, and ambition reveal themselves without disguise. Across four interlocking series on college football, college basketball, college baseball, and college hockey, he approaches the American athletic landscape as a sprawling atlas of regional codes, generational rituals, and the unspoken values communities pass down through shared seasons.

He grew up in a household where sports were never dismissed as entertainment. They were languages. They offered the family a way to talk about perseverance, fairness, calm under pressure, and the discipline of showing up even when the odds lean hard in the other direction. That sensibility remained with him, shaping his conviction that the games Americans gather around explain as much about the country as any archive, election map, or census record. When he began writing about these landscapes, he wrote with the sense that the ordinary rituals of game days deserved the seriousness of history and the patience of ethnography. Out of that conviction emerged a body of work dedicated to the underlying structures and emotional tensions that define American sport.

His series on college football laid the foundation. There he maps the sport as a civic religion woven through regions: blue-blood dynasties whose stadiums echo with inherited pride; borderland programs that treat survival as accomplishment; cities and rural towns that attach their identity to fall Saturdays with a devotion that borders on mythic. In these books, he captures the sound of marching bands rolling across hardwood bleachers, the communal choreography of tailgates, and the way coaching legacies become a region's secular genealogy. Football, in Johns's writing, is the nation's great ritual of belonging and defiance, a place where states articulate who they believe they are.

From that foundation, his work expanded onto the hardwoods of college basketball. There he found a sport defined not by scale but by the intimacy of its dimensions. A court is compact enough that hesitation becomes visible, strategy becomes personal, and identity becomes unmistakable. Across his basketball series, he studies each program not as a collection of scores but as a moral ecosystem: some overshadowed by football powers, some weighed down by their own history, some thriving on urban electricity, others on rural austerity. He writes about the discipline that lives in practices, the psychology embedded in arena design, the ethic a coach imposes on a team, and the winter logic that defines the Big Ten, the ACC, the Big East, the SEC, and the West Coast in different ways. Basketball, for Johns, is the architecture of character made immediate.

His series on college baseball introduces a different register —one shaped by spring patience, long shadows, and the humid rhythms of Southern and Southwestern nights. He writes about ballparks as secular sanctuaries and about the way families pass down loyalty to programs with the same devotion usually reserved for local churches or community rites. In these books, he explores the distinct flavors of diamond culture: the ferocity of SEC baseball, the quiet resolve of Midwestern programs, the Pacific calm and ambition of West Coast powers. Baseball becomes a meditation on endurance, ritual, and the poetry of repetition.

In college hockey, he enters the landscape where winter itself becomes the defining antagonist. That series explores northern arenas that hum with cold air and defiant energy, programs built on scarcity and steel, and communities whose self-image is inseparable from the brutality and beauty of the season. He captures the clang of puck against boards, the stark geometry of ice under arena lights, and the strange mixture of solitude and allegiance that defines the sport. Hockey, in his writing, becomes a form of moral clarity—a test of identity conducted in a season that forgives nothing.

Across all four series, readers encounter a consistent worldview. Johns does not treat sports as diversions but as structures through which regions understand themselves. He writes with empathy but resists sentimentality, trusting that the complexity of human ambition needs no embellishment. His books are filled with players whose names never reached national broadcasts, with coaches who kept programs alive through seasons of quiet strain, and with fans whose lifelong devotion formed the emotional infrastructure of their communities. He brings attention to the unseen workers who prepare courts, chalk lines, sharpen skates, and maintain locker rooms—people whose labor becomes the stage upon which identity is performed.

Before writing full time, Johns worked in cybersecurity and systems architecture, a career that sharpened his eye for hidden frameworks and the patterns that govern complex networks. That background informs his sports writing in unexpected ways. He approaches teams as systems: coaching philosophies are protocols, locker room cultures are networks, arenas are physical architectures that shape behavior, and traditions are inherited scripts. He is drawn to the way structure shapes performance, to the tension between constraint and imagination, and to the moments when human character breaks through the limits of design.

What distinguishes his body of work is its refusal to simplify. He understands that programs live in contradiction: football dynasties built on the edge of decline, basketball teams both blessed and burdened by their own history, baseball programs chasing the ghost of an almost-season, hockey teams carrying the pride of places most Americans barely see on a map. Johns writes these contradictions with clarity and steadiness, knowing that the truth of a team lies not in its banners but in the seasons when expectations faltered, when character became the only fuel left.

Readers trust him because he writes with a cadence that honors memory. He understands the quietness of empty arenas after a loss, the shifting light in stadium tunnels, the long bus rides through snow or heat, the particular ache of a season ending too early. His sentences carry the weight of lived experience without resorting to nostalgia. He writes for readers who love the games not because they are easy, but because they reveal something real.

Bill Johns writes from Maryland, a region whose blend of ambition, skepticism, and enduring loyalty mirrors the national contradictions he studies. His work continues to map the hidden structures that shape American life, guided by the belief that sport remains one of the last places where communities gather without needing to explain themselves. In those gatherings, he finds a story worth preserving—one program, one season, one ritual at a time.

Made in the USA
Coppell, TX
19 March 2026